HITLER'S
HANGMEN

HITLER'S HANGMEN

The Secret German Plot to Kill Churchill

December 1944

Brian Lett

Greenhill Books

Hitler's Hangmen
First published in 2019 by
Greenhill Books,
c/o Pen & Sword Books Ltd,
47 Church Street, Barnsley,
S. Yorkshire, S70 2AS

www.greenhillbooks.com
contact@greenhillbooks.com

ISBN: 978–1–78438–529–3

CIP data records for this title are available from the British Library

Designed and typeset by Donald Sommerville

Printed and bound in the UK by TJ International Ltd, Padstow

Typeset in 10.5/15.3pt Kuenstler 480 BT

For my granddaughters Zoe and Maggie
in the hope that the world you grow up in
is much, much better than the one
that I describe in this book.

Contents

Plates

Sir Oswald Mosley's British Union of Fascists paper, February 1933.
  Courtesy of the National Archives, Kew (TNA)
Newspaper article on Captain Ramsay's release. *Author's collection*
Arnold Leese. *TNA*
Oliver Gilbert. *TNA*
Arnold Leese's account of his trial. *TNA*
Anti-Semitic pamphlet by William Joyce. *TNA*
The murdered body of Werner Dreschler. *US National Archives*
The hut where Werner Dreschler's body was displayed.
  US National Archives
Views of Camp 23 by Hermann Gensler. *All courtesy of the*
  Wiltshire Museum, Devizes
The former armoury of Le Marchant barracks and the keep. *Author*
Sketch of Camp 21, Chieti, Italy, by Jack Hodgson Shepherd.
  Courtesy of Mrs Barbara Shepherd
Drawings of the Polish guards and the Camp 21 site by an
  unknown German artist. *By kind permission of the Comrie*
  Development Trust
Compound C at Camp 21 today. *Author*
Hut 4, where Wolfgang Rosterg was beaten and tortured.
  By kind permission of the Comrie Development Trust
Camp 17 at Lodge Moor, by Heinz Georg Lutz, prisoner of war.
  Courtesy of www.picturesheffield.com
All that remains of Camp 17 today. *Author*

Introduction

Vehmic Justice
The Hanging Courts

The title of this book describes the men who made it possible for Adolf Hitler to maintain a large, disciplined, and well-trained body of soldiers, sailors and airmen within Great Britain during the closing years of World War Two. They were the Vehmic police and executioners, the hangmen who maintained a brutal Nazi discipline over German prisoners of war in British camps, and who ensured that the prisoners did not view the war as finished. The Nazi creed was that they were German troops, temporarily in captivity, simply awaiting Hitler's further orders. Those who denied the creed were beaten and murdered, and their bodies hung ritualistically by the neck on display for all to see. The Vehmic tradition was to hang the body of their victim from a tree, but since these were seldom available in a prisoner of war camp compound, any public space would do. Vehmic 'justice', meted out by Vehmic courts, was the key to maintaining the iron discipline that made it possible for Hitler to regard the prisoners of war in Britain as an army in waiting.

The Holy Veme, or Vehmic Court, was a punishment court administered by citizens of the German province of Westphalia in medieval times. It nominally drew its jurisdiction and power from the Holy Roman Emperor, but was in fact a home-made, ritualistic vigilante court, designed to deal with local criminals in an area which Imperial justice did not reach. Anyone who was 'a freeman of pure-bred German stock and of good character' could be initiated into the court, whose symbols were a rope and a sword. Once sentenced to death, a victim of the Vehmic court would be killed, and his body then exhibited by hanging in a public place. Sometimes, once the victim had been sentenced, he would be allowed to leave court, but would then be hunted down and killed by the mob. His corpse would be hung from a tree as an advertisement of the court's work, and as a deterrent to others.

The Vehmic Court fell out of use in the late Middle Ages, but was resurrected in twentieth-century Europe by right-wing groups in order to justify acts of violence against political opponents, and those that they viewed as traitors to their cause. It was adopted by Adolf Hitler, the 'Führer of the Third Reich', to empower his followers in faraway prisoner of war camps. It was the duty of Hitler's most ardent followers, the SS, to ensure that after capture Nazi ethics and Nazi discipline were continuously observed and enforced everywhere German prisoners were held, whatever the individual views of the prisoners might be. For a German prisoner in a Nazi-run camp, the war was not over, it continued every day. To express doubts about Hitler's policies, or to suggest that Germany might lose the war, invited punishment by the Vehmic Court, and death by beating. Hitler's hangmen were the executives of that system, carrying out the brutal murders which were an essential part of it.

Echoing the Nazi Vehmic system, Hitler's supporters in Great Britain intended, when their day came, to hang the bodies of Winston Churchill and the members of his government from lampposts, their modern equivalent of the Vehmic tree. The would-be hangmen were the British Fascists.

It is said that Vehmic courts may still exist in the underworld of Europe. Hopefully, that is untrue, but wherever an 'empire' of any sort is created by unprincipled men or women, the medieval system of Vehmic justice is an attractive one to deal with dissenters – historically the only penalty that a Vehmic Court was empowered to pass was one of death.

Long before December 1944, the month with which this book principally deals, the rule of Vehmic law had been established in many Nazi prisoner of war camps. The SS were the fanatical administrators of Vehmic justice. Paratroop Oberstleutnant

Friedrich August von der Heydte described the mystic bonds that bound the SS together:

> 'At SS meetings, all SS men stand, their arms crossed, and sing "*Wenn alle untreu werden* [Even if all others betray their faith]" – that's quite enough. The lights are extinguished and candles are lit – it's most effective. Certain bonds are established which from an initial mystical ritual sphere transcend into ethics . . . their ethics are false, that "faithful unto death" complex which those people have, that idea of sacrificing one's life, of devoting one's life, which they have developed to nearly as incredible a degree as the Japanese.'[1]

In the United States, which had entered the war after the Japanese attack on Pearl Harbor in December 1941, and to which about half of German prisoners were subsequently sent, there were three Vehmic executions, each in a different camp.

Johannes Kunze, aged thirty-nine, was murdered on 4 November 1943 in Camp Tonkawa, Oklahoma. He was suspected of acting as an informant against his fellow Nazis. He was beaten to death. There is no evidence as to whether his body was then hung on display. Five of his fellow prisoners were charged with his murder; all five were convicted, and they were executed by hanging on 10 July 1945.[2]

Werner Drechsler, a U-boat (submarine) crewman aged twenty-one, was murdered on 12 March 1944 in the Papago prisoner of war camp, Arizona. Once taken prisoner and transported to the United States of America, Drechsler had changed sides and had worked as an informant for US Intelligence, acting as a stool pigeon to extract intelligence from fellow prisoners. When he had ceased to be useful, he was sent to a camp mainly for German naval personnel containing many Nazis and U-boat crewmen.[3] On arrival there, Drechsler was almost immediately recognised, and survived only a few hours. He was 'tried' during the night of 11/12 March 1944, attacked and beaten into unconsciousness, had a noose placed around his neck, and was dragged to a shower block where he was hanged. His body was left on display, with the windows to the shower block open, and it is said that between one and two hundred men filed past the window and viewed the body. The authorities found Drechsler's body the next morning. Seven German U-boat men were later tried for and convicted of his murder, and all seven were executed by hanging on 28 August 1945.

Drechsler should never, of course, have been sent to Papago camp by the US authorities. It was a U-boat crewmen's camp, where Nazi Vehmic law was enforced, and where Drechsler was highly likely to be recognised. A memorandum from the Office of the US Provost Marshal dated 16 July 1944 reads: 'Responsible officers transferring such prisoners . . . are bringing about their deaths more rapidly and efficiently than our Courts Martial are trying their murderers.'[4]

Horst Günther, aged twenty-three, was murdered on 6 April 1944 at Camp Aiken, South Carolina. He was suspected of being a traitor. His body was found hanging from a tree in the camp, in classic Vehmic style. Two fellow prisoners were convicted of his murder – Erich Gauss and Rudolf Staub. They were executed on 14 July 1945. It was suggested that Gauss and Staub had strangled Günther before they strung him up in the tree. Staub is said to have protested: 'All I did was done as a German soldier under orders. If I had not done so, I would have been punished when I returned to Germany.'[5]

It could, of course, be argued that these killings were simply mob violence meted out to traitors by enraged fellow prisoners of war, but the use of 'courts' and the ritualistic hanging of a body on display suggests a more structured approach. The Vehmic model of a court made up of men of 'pure-bred German stock of good character' appealed to the Nazis, and there is clear evidence that the Nazis referred to this revenge court system as the modern version of the Vehmic Court (and on occasion so did the British).

This Vehmic system of justice meant that the Nazis could retain absolute control of what their soldiers, sailors and airmen did whilst held in British or American prison camps. The iron discipline imposed, and the threats that backed it up, directed not just at the servicemen but also at their families at home in Germany, meant that Hitler could order his captured troops to do whatever he wanted them to do – including to rise up en masse, seize arms and break out of their camps. Covert communication between prisoner of war camps, and with Germany, which always existed, ensured that all German prisoners knew what their orders were, and what would happen if they disobeyed them.

There is no doubt that the system of Vehmic justice was in use in the camps in the United Kingdom as well as in the United States. A report in mid-December 1944 concerning Camp 21 at Comrie, in Scotland, confirms how the Vehmic courts were working in the United Kingdom. The report begins:

'In the Officers' sections B and C at Comrie, the SS and para-troopers had organised a regular system of spying on the other Officers. In Camp [Compound] B, which was the worst, there was a sort of Vehmic organisation, i.e. a secret police with executive powers. If, for instance, they recognised a man who had ever made an anti-Nazi remark, they maltreated him under cover of darkness. They were careful to note for punishment those who did not give the Nazi salute. Their activities became those of organised terrorism. They had spies in all the huts and compiled lists of anti-Nazis which were to be smuggled into Germany by means of exchanged prisoners of war. There is a regulation in Germany that, if a prisoner of war does anything against the Government or opposes it, the Government has the right to take steps against both his private property and against the lives of members of his immediate family. A copy of the list of Officers selected for the anti-Nazi Camp 13 [to which prisoners could ask to be transferred if they were anti-Nazi] is said to have been made by a supposed Unteroffizier working in the Interpreter's Office in Camp B at Comrie, and to have come into the possession either of the spies or of the out-and-out Nazis, who openly threatened those included in the list that, if they went to Camp 13, they would see to it that the German Government and the Security

Service in Germany heard that they had moved to an anti-Nazi camp and the members of their families in Germany and their property treated accordingly. If this list could not be smuggled into Germany, it was intended that some Prisoner of War who was going to be exchanged should inform the SD [the Security Service] in Germany that everyone in Camp 13 was suspect, was friendly to England and was anti-National [anti-Nazi].'

Camp 13 was a 'White' camp, and was meant to be a safe haven for anti-Nazis. However, the Nazis sought to deter their fellow Germans from going to Camp 13 on the basis of these threats. The report continues:

'A number of ardent Nazis wormed their way into Camp 13 and immediately started to stir up political trouble as before. When the War Office turned out these spies, they threatened those remaining that if they did not get turned out quickly too [for pro-Nazi activities], they would make it public that they were in Camp 13.'[6]

The ringleader of the Vehmic organisation at Comrie at that time was said to be SS Obersturmbannführer Jaeckel. Although there is no mention in this report of Vehmic executions, the first death by hanging in Camp 21 occurred on 29 November 1944. Major Willi Thormann was found hanging in the shower block. No satisfactory explanation was ever provided for his death, and the evidence is sparse. However, it was a feature of Vehmic justice that the victim's body should be hung on display in a public place. A shower block was such a public place, where a body might hang for a while without the camp guards being aware of it, and yet many of the prisoners in the camp would see it.

A report of 17 February 1945 reads:

'At Oxford there are about 5000 German Prisoners of War, among which are 500 Austrian anti-Nazis. All the Camp Leaders and leading posts are in the control of rabid Nazis who make use of their authority to victimise the anti-Nazis and to keep the National-Socialist [Nazi] spirit alive. The consequence is that, through fear, many anti-Nazis are being reconverted to National-Socialism . . . Camp Leaders destroy at once all British newspapers . . . given to them for distribution. They prohibit the switching on of the radio to any stations other than a German one. The Hitler salute is made compulsory, as well as attendance at a weekly National-Socialist lecture.'[7]

A report on the interrogation of a prisoner apparently called Erich Gille from Camp 199 says:

'Almost all prisoners in the Camp were paratroopers or SS men [1,450 in all], and they openly said that if the British did not let them have their own way they would burn down their huts. One hut had already been burnt down . . . A posse of SS-men were detailed as the cage police . . . Gille and Schneefus were threatened by the police . . . just before Christmas [1944], Gille and Schneefus were taken by the SS police who accused them of being "stool pigeons" and of spreading anti-Nazi propaganda, and threatened to hang them if they had any further evidence of such activities.'[8]

The Nazis came for Gille in due course. The report describes an attack on Gille on 17 January 1945 at 2030 hours. He was attacked by ten men armed with iron bars as he left his hut, was badly beaten and kicked. Happily the noise of the attack attracted attention, the attackers ran off, and the prisoner's life was saved. Otherwise no doubt Hitler's hangmen would have executed Gille, and hung his body on display, to be found the next day. A search of the camp for weapons took place in the morning, but news of the search had leaked out, and many weapons had been successfully buried or hidden. Nonetheless, four wheelbarrows-full of weapons were found.

Diary entries by paratrooper Feldwebel Walter Madel explain how the vehement Nazis would control any anti-Nazi dissent in a camp. Following his arrival in a camp at Bury, Madel wrote:

'I am together with several parachutists in Room 3. There is also Navy. A whole submarine crew. Got in touch with those boys, also with the paratroopers, and have arranged a *"Rollkommando"* [a beatings squad] with them. With those boys I have openly beaten up each man who openly showed himself to be against Germany and National Socialism to such an extent that he did not dare to open his mouth any more. The German *Lagerleitung* [camp leadership] supports this in that they do not take action against us. The German Staff itself is not racially pure . . . An Obergefreiter of Room 6 said he would not fight for his Fatherland, he also got his beating up. Obergefreiter Stier, also an anti-Nazi, got a beating and had to be taken into protective custody. These are all sad stories of which a good German can only be ashamed.'[9]

At Glen Mill Camp, Oldham, the rule of fear was enhanced by a unit calling itself the Black Hand Society.[9] The Black Hand would leave threatening notes to frighten its victims. Unteroffizier Helmut Stenzel received one written on lavatory paper, adorned with a skull and crossbones and a black hand. The message read [when translated]: 'Opponents of National Socialism and "sky pilots" [priests] have forfeited their lives here with us and will be exterminated.' Stenzel's sin was that he had been in correspondence with a Protestant clergy-man about religious matters. When one of these letters was found by a Nazi called Hengst, Stenzel was subjected increasingly to threats, until he eventually sought refuge with the British authorities. Stenzel told the authorities that the Nazis were supported by the *Lagerführer* [the camp's Senior German Officer] and his deputy. The Black Hand Society was based in a barrack room occupied solely by SS men and paratroopers. It was clear from investigations, however, that violence and threats did not come only from this group, but from all the Nazis in the camp, who would turn on a prisoner upon the slightest of suspicion and beat him up.

There can be no doubt, therefore, that what can be fairly described as Vehmic law was being applied in camps throughout Britain, and that Nazi discipline was being maintained thereby. By December 1944, Hitler had more than 250,000 troops in prison camps in the British Isles. They were an army waiting for his orders.

Chapter 1

Plans for the Ardennes and Serchio Offensives

In the autumn of 1944, Adolf Hitler was simply not prepared to contemplate Germany's total defeat. Despite the fact that August and the first half of September brought heavy defeats on both Western and Eastern Fronts, Hitler planned for a counter-offensive of such strength and speed that he believed that it could split the Allied forces in Europe in half. He aimed to drive a huge blitzkrieg force of men and armour through the Allied front line in the Ardennes forest. Using vastly superior force, speed and total surprise, Hitler planned to divide the US armies from the British armies, and to recapture the vital port of Antwerp and the southern bank of the Scheldt estuary. Having reduced the Allied forces to confusion, Hitler hoped to negotiate at the very least a favourable peace with his Western opponents, excluding the Soviet Union from the peace treaty. That would gain him some time to develop various improved weapons, and he could then concentrate on the Soviet forces in the east.

The central part of Hitler's plan as it developed was for the most powerful force that he could muster at this stage of the war to break out from their defensive line between Monschau and Wasserbill in the Ardennes, and to thrust through the US front line. He would get his armour through the Ardennes forest by the end of Day 2, reach the Meuse between Liége and Dinant by the end of Day 3, and seize Antwerp on Day 4. The strike would be so powerful and so unexpected that the Allies would not have time to move their superior numbers to the Ardennes sector. Hitler was counting on disagreements between the US and British commanders to confuse the Allied response. It was no secret that Bradley and Montgomery (respectively the principal American and British ground commanders) were often in dispute as to tactics. At this stage of the war, the Allies had total superiority in the air, but Hitler would wait for winter weather that was bad enough to prevent effective combat flying.

At about the same time, together with some of Mussolini's Fascist Italian troops, there would be a German break-out from the Gothic Line in Italy. The Germans had fought a long and bitter defensive campaign in Italy since the Italian Armistice in September 1943, when the Italians, having disposed (so they thought) of Mussolini, changed sides. The Germans were now pinned behind a line of fortifications which stretched from coast to coast across northern Italy, known as the Gothic Line. Their counter-attack here would be named Operation Winter Storm. The site for it would be the Serchio valley, which (like the Ardennes Forest) was lightly defended by the Allied troops. There would be problems with an Italian offensive, because troops and equipment were in short supply, the Allies had total air superiority, and the mountainous terrain of the Gothic Line, whilst perfect for defence, was difficult for attack. However, in the Serchio Valley the defending troops were the US 92nd 'Buffalo' Division, black troops under the command of white officers, an unhappy combination since many of the white officers would have preferred to be in command of white troops, and the black soldiers felt that they did not have the respect or confidence of their leaders. The Buffalo Division also lacked battle experience, and was thought to be a soft target. Whatever the eventual result of it might be, Operation Winter Storm would be a worrying distraction for the Allies as they struggled to stop the Ardennes offensive.

Hitler had little trust in his Army generals. In July 1944, a group of senior military officers had tried to assassinate him with a bomb. Hitler survived, and his vengeance against the conspirators was ruthless. However, the effect of the bomb plot was that the number of his generals whom Hitler genuinely trusted was substantially reduced. From July onwards he preferred to operate through the SS, whose soldiers were loyal Nazis.

It is not the purpose of this book to analyse the 'Battle of the Bulge', as the Ardennes offensive is often known. That has already been done by a number of fine historians.[1] Hitler had been planning for some time what historians describe as a desperate, final throw of the dice, a last offensive, which would save Germany from defeat by the Western Allies and then bring him victory over the Soviets. In order to carry it out, he would have to use all the available reserves that Germany had. As his troops had been forced back towards Germany by the Allied successes of the summer and autumn of 1944, his lines of supply had shortened (as those of the Allies lengthened), but Germany was increasingly short of resources, and constant heavy bombing by Allied planes was causing significant damage to roads and railways.

Hitler hatched his plan for the Ardennes offensive at the *Wolfsschanze*, his lair in East Prussia, and on 16 September he summoned a meeting of senior officers, including Generaloberst Alfred Jodl, General der Flieger Kreipe, Generaloberst Guderian (the Army Chief of Staff, responsible for the Eastern Front) and Hermann Göring. It was a significant moment, if only because on 11 September Allied troops had arrived on German soil for the first time. In effect, as Commander-in-Chief of the armed forces of the Third Reich, Hitler simply announced to these officers what his plan for the Ardennes offensive was – a blitzkrieg attack through the Ardennes forest to the coast to divide Allied forces, and seize back the vital port of Antwerp. All this was to be achieved in four days. German formations would then be able to sweep round behind the severed parts of the Anglo-American armies and force their surrender. Having defeated the Western Allies, Hitler assured his generals that they would be free to concentrate on the Soviets in the east and would mount a winter offensive against them. Despite the strong views of some of his generals that his plan would not work, Hitler refused to be moved from it.

Because the Allies had superiority in the air, Hitler ordered that

1,500 fighter planes be available to support the offensive, most of which would have to be built from scratch. He ordered that they be available by 1 November 1944, but there was no real possibility that they could be. Perhaps because he knew he was asking for the impossible, at the same time Hitler said that the offensive would be launched during a period of bad weather, so the Allied aircraft could not fly. Hitler emphasised the absolute need for secrecy. If the Allies found out what he was planning to do, they would simply move a strong force to the Ardennes forest to defend it.

Hitler's initial intention was that the attack would be launched on 27 November 1944, a date which has some significance to this book, but practical considerations finally forced him to delay until 16 December. He appointed Generalfeldmarschall Gerd von Rundstedt to command the offensive, even though he had sacked Rundstedt as his Commander-in-Chief in Western Europe in July. Hitler swore all those whom he had told about his plan to total secrecy, and that secrecy endured remarkably well until the offensive began. Preparations got under way immediately after the 15 September meeting. Hitler believed that two panzer divisions would be enough to force their way through the Ardennes region and split the Allied armies, but even though the Ardennes was thinly held by American troops, the speed of the attack would be all important. German forces must reach Antwerp in four days – before the Allies had time to move enough troops to defend the area. Surprise was vital – thus complete secrecy must be maintained. Secrecy would not be easy, of course, during the massive build-up of German forces that was necessary, but Hitler was helped by the fact that since the July assassination attempt, the SS security forces had strengthened their control over everything – including the German Army. The SS ruled through threats and terror, and no German soldier, sailor or airman was exempt. It is a compliment, perhaps, to the SS that the secret was kept. Hitler was aware, too, that the forces arrayed against him were those of two separate commands, British and American, and however good or bad relations were between them, some time would be needed for them to consult, thus delaying their response.

The delay which caused the switch of dates was brought about by a combination of factors: continued Allied attacks, particularly on lines of communication; the gathering of the necessary troops and armour; the stockpiling of fuel; and the training (which was minimal because of lack of time) of new recruits. The Waffen-SS received the bulk of the new equipment that arrived, and had the pick of the new recruits, since the SS were very much in favour with Hitler for the reasons stated. He was confident that he could trust them. However, the new recruits were mainly youngsters transferred from the Luftwaffe (German Air Force) and Kriegsmarine (German Navy). The Sixth Panzer Army which was to spearhead the attack was made up mainly of Waffen-SS troops.

In the interests of secrecy, no troops were to be briefed until the evening before the attack. Regimental commanders would only be briefed the day before. The men and vehicles moved by night, and lay up out of sight in the villages during the day, their vehicles hidden in barns and other buildings. No fires were to be lit, and cooking would be done with charcoal, as it provided little smoke. Surprisingly, no Allied aircraft spotted any unusual movement of troops suggesting a heavy build-up of German forces. Total radio silence was observed, and maps were only distributed at the very last moment. A fake headquarters was set up north of Aachen, transmitting instructions that suggested the Sixth Panzer Army was in position there, and a fake Twenty-Fifth Army was created to further mislead the Allies. A rumour was deliberately started that the Germans were going to counter-attack in the Saar area, a good distance south of the Ardennes, in the hope and expectation that the story would reach the Allies and distract them.

As a late decision, in December 1944, Hitler also approved the use of paratroopers. Oberst von der Heydte was appointed to command them. Von der Heydte was ordered to assemble 1,200 paratroopers, and to drop an hour before the advance began in the area of Eupen, to seize vital crossroads, and to prevent American reinforcements advancing south from the Aachen sector to the Ardennes. Von der Heydte's difficulty was that the paratroopers under his command had little if any airborne experience, since there had been no significant paratroop drops since the seizure of Crete in 1941. First notified on 8 December of his duties, von der Heydte had little time to train his men properly. He was also frustrated by his superiors' lack of understanding of the importance of the right weather conditions for parachuting. Despite his concerns, the date of the offensive was finally confirmed for the early morning of 16 December.

The weather forecast was favourable to the Germans, and it was thought that it would prevent any effective use of Allied air power for a week. By that time, if all went well, the German forces would have reached and recaptured Antwerp, and the Allied armies would be split and close to defeat.

There was another element to the attack. Hitler had decided to use all the underhand tricks that he could. On 21 October 1944, before Rundstedt knew anything of the planned offensive, Hitler summoned SS-Obersturmbannführer Otto Skorzeny to a private meeting. Aachen had been under attack, and on 21 October it fell to the Allies. Perhaps its fall persuaded Hitler to use the ultimate military deception, as had already been done both by the Germans and the Allies during World War Two, that of disguising his troops in his enemy's uniforms.

SS man Otto Skorzeny had risen to fame when he had led the team that rescued Mussolini from his mountain prison on the Gran Sasso in September 1943, in order that Hitler might put Mussolini back on the 'throne' of Italy. This operation made Skorzeny's reputation. He had also later kidnapped as a hostage the son of the Hungarian leader, Admiral Miklós Horthy, just before Horthy announced in October 1944 that Hungary was changing sides and joining with the Soviet Union.[2] Germany had learned in advance of this 'treachery', and Horthy was brought back to Germany and a new pro-German Hungarian government established.

Hitler trusted Skorzeny, and recognized him as a ruthless action man. However, Skorzeny was hated by many regular German Army officers. Von der Heydte, referring to the time of the Italian Armistice, and the rescue of Mussolini, described him: 'He had fantastic notions and wanted to use dirty methods. A typical evil Nazi. He planned wearing Italian uniform, using a gun with a silencer, and so on. So he formed a special body of people of the same type as himself.'[3]

Von der Heydte dismissed Skorzeny's rescue of Mussolini as being far from the heroic operation that Skorzeny liked people to think that it had been. The operation had been carefully planned by General Student. Skorzeny, then a captain, was not put in command of the glider-borne paratrooper operation, but was sent along as a representative of the Security Service, to be responsible for Mussolini's safety once he had been rescued. He was to escort Mussolini to Munich after he had been freed.

Instead, according to von der Heydte, Skorzeny bribed an Italian Carabinieri colonel to come with him, since it was assumed that Mussolini was being guarded by the Carabinieri. Skorzeny flew in the tenth glider of the flight. The orders were that the gliders should land together on an appointed landing zone, and if any individual glider broke away and landed individually, according to von der Heydte it would imperil the whole operation. Skorzeny did just that – flying last in the convoy towards the landing zone, he ordered his aircraft to break off and land much closer to the hotel where Mussolini was imprisoned, meaning that he could get there first and claim all the glory. He had no authority to give such an order. When his glider had successfully landed, Skorzeny sent the Carabinieri colonel out of the plane first. The colonel ordered the advancing Carabinieri guards to lay down their arms, and they obeyed him. Skorzeny then descended with his men, and rescued Mussolini without a shot being fired. Von der Heydte asserted that Skorzeny had subsequently lied about the action, claiming that it had been a very dangerous one when it had not.

Whatever did actually happen, the rescue of Mussolini made Skorzeny's reputation and his career, as no doubt he had hoped that it would. Skorzeny was painted as an outstanding commando leader both by his own description of what had happened and by the press. Skorzeny's own account of the action, as reported in Charles Foley's book *Commando Extraordinary*, published in 1954, is very different to von der Heydte's account.

Von der Heydte went on to describe Skorzeny's involvement in the Ardennes operation: 'He collected together people who could speak English for a so-called Skorzeny operation. Those are the people who've now been sent through the lines wearing British and American uniforms.'

On 21 October, Hitler's orders to Skorzeny were to assemble a commando team of English-speakers, who would then be given American uniforms that had been obtained from American prisoners of war, and captured American vehicles. Some of these men would be infiltrated behind the American front lines in American jeeps, and would pretend that they were US troops. They would, Hitler hoped, be able to confuse the enemy, divert them with false orders, carry out acts of sabotage, and cause considerable chaos behind the American lines. There is evidence that the plan also included the assignment of a long-range group of jeeps to drive to Paris, and kill or capture General Eisenhower, the Allied Supreme Commander in Europe.

Skorzeny, supported by orders giving him unlimited powers, signed personally by Hitler,[4] arranged that officers and NCOs from the Waffen-SS, the Army, the Kriegsmarine and the Luftwaffe who spoke English received orders to report to a camp at Schloss Friedenthal for 'interpreter duties'. Once arrived at that camp, they were interrogated in English by SS officers. If their English was good enough, they were told that they were being recruited into a unit called the 150th Panzer Brigade, and were sworn to secrecy. They had to sign a declaration saying that the secrecy surrounding their mission was to be maintained even after the war, and that any breach of secrecy was punishable by death. Those selected were then sent to a training camp at Grafenwöhr.

The Grafenwöhr camp was closely guarded, and what went on there under Skorzeny's command was highly secret. The recruits underwent continuous exposure to the American military culture. They ate US rations, were dressed in US uniforms once these had been obtained, spoke English, watched American movies, and were taught American habits and mannerisms. They were being intensively trained in how to appear to be American. They were also instructed in sabotage, use of American weapons, and close-quarter commando in-fighting.

Skorzeny split his force into the Einheit Steilau commando unit, and the 150th Panzer Brigade. His English-speaking commandos of the Einheit Steilau unit eventually numbered 150. There was difficulty obtaining their American uniforms, despite the powerful authority of the Führer's order, since there were very few to spare in the prisoner of war camps, and it was important that the International Red Cross, who monitored the camps, should not learn what was going on. It is interesting to note that the original 'order' for American uniforms was for a total of 2,400, including clothing and insignia for ten generals, and seventy staff officers. These would have equipped a substantial covert force, and Germans masquerading as US generals would no doubt have caused chaos. Since the initial date for the offensive was 27 November 1944, the uniforms had to be obtained by 21 November. The task proved impossible, and only a far smaller number reached the Grafenwöhr Camp.[5]

The Einheit Steilau commandos were split into demolition sections, tasked with blowing up ammunition, fuel dumps (if not needed by the Germans) and bridges;[6] reconnaissance sections to assess enemy strength and to find good routes of travel; and sections to disrupt American lines of communication by cutting telephone lines, and, in their guise as American troops, giving false orders. Essentially they were to act both as saboteurs and gatherers of intelligence.

The 150th Panzer Brigade was to be under the personal command of Skorzeny. Again, it was intended as a covert force, although it comprised some 2,000 men. There were two tank companies, using a mixture of captured US M4 Sherman tanks (of which there were very few), and crudely disguised German tanks – they were given US markings in the hope of confusing the Americans. The tank companies were supported by a paratroop battalion, panzergrenadier companies, heavy mortars and anti-tank guns. One of the objectives of the 150th Panzer Brigade was to seize bridges across the Meuse, and hold them for the advancing German forces. They would travel only at night, and hide up during the day.

It is clear from Skorzeny's original order for 2,400 American uniforms that his intention had been that all 2,000 men of the 150th Panzer Brigade would wear US uniform. The details of his orders to those he sent to collect the uniforms throw light on what the original plan was. Skorzeny appointed 36–year-old Lieutenant Muntz, a fluent English-speaker with a German father and a British mother,[7] to acquire the uniforms for him. Muntz had responded to the call for volunteers who spoke English. He had passed the test at Friedenthal, and had been sent on to the Grafenwöhr Camp. Muntz survived the war, was taken prisoner in May 1945, and was interrogated about what had happened at Grafenwöhr. Muntz described Grafenwöhr as heavily guarded by a hundred sentries around the perimeter. Once inside, nobody was allowed to leave the camp again (unless on special duties), and there was a great air of secrecy over everything that happened.

Muntz confirmed that he had been instructed to collect in total some 2,400 American uniforms. Muntz and his companion, a Lieutenant Fitze, were also ordered to collect a detailed list of other items – personal belongings, badges, any articles with English writing on them, paybooks and identity cards, all things which could lend credibility to the pretence. They were briefed by Skorzeny, and supplied with papers and passes signed by him, and one pass signed by Adolf Hitler himself, to be used where necessary to ensure complete co-operation.

However, as the team travelled from camp to camp, they enjoyed little success. In particular there was a shortage of the windcheater jackets that US soldiers wore – mainly because there was a shortage of them within the US military. At a camp at Fürstenberg, Muntz demanded that jackets be taken by force from US prisoners of war who were wearing them, even though these bore the black triangular patch of a prisoner of war. The camp commandant resisted the order at first, but was eventually cowed into submission. However, the prisoners managed to tear or set fire to many of the jackets to prevent the Germans from getting them. Out of 800 collected, only a dozen were still wearable.

Muntz's orders had been to collect far more clothing than he was, in the event, able to get, and also to collect it before 21 November. When he returned to Grafenwöhr with far less clothing than ordered, he was told he had completely failed in his mission and taken off the job. However, Muntz told his interrogators, after he was captured in 1945, that a load of one thousand US greatcoats did reach Grafenwöhr later. Muntz was returned to his unit, already sworn to secrecy, and took no further part in the operation. If Muntz had succeeded in getting the clothing and equipment he had been ordered to acquire, Skorzeny's ten generals and seventy staff officers would, if deployed effectively, have caused enormous confusion amongst the US troops, and would have 'opened many doors'.

Skorzeny's disguised panzers and Shermans would, no doubt, have been commanded by a 'general', and his jeep units might also have contained the odd 'general' but why did he want ten? Staff officers obviously also had a value, but why seventy? The numbers needed suggest that Skorzeny was intending, as a number of his men said later, that a part of his force would drive to Paris, and to Allied Headquarters there, with Eisenhower as their target. It was a daring and ambitious plan. Even if they failed to get Eisenhower, they could have caused total confusion. However, because of the difficulties in obtaining such uniforms, Skorzeny did not get all that he wanted when he wanted. The author has been unable to discover how many uniforms were in fact obtained, and of what rank.

The declaration that each man had to sign promising to say nothing of what he had done, to be effective even after the war, shows clearly that Skorzeny and his men knew that what they were planning to do was potentially against the rules of war. If caught in US uniforms by the Americans, they might be shot as spies – and a number of them were.

At 0530 on the morning of 16 December 1944, Hitler's generals launched the Ardennes offensive.

As has already been stated, it was not only in the Ardennes that the Germans counter-attacked. German and Italian Fascist troops in Italy defending the Gothic line (which ran from coast to coast across Northern Italy) planned their break for Christmas time. Preparations for this offensive suffered a blow in late October, because the German Commander-in-Chief in Italy, Field Marshal Kesselring, was involved in a traffic accident on 25 October 1944. As he put it: 'Harassed throughout the day by British aircraft, I was driving along the main road from Bologna to Forli in the late afternoon . . . when my car, passing a column, collided with a long-barrelled gun coming out of a side road. I came off the worst from the encounter, receiving a severe concussion and a nasty gash on the left temple.'[8] In fact, to Hitler's concern, Kesselring was unconscious overnight, and hospitalised for two months. At the beginning of January, he was sent home for a fortnight's convalescent leave, and did not return to duty until mid-January 1945. In his absence, his deputy, General von Vietinghoff, was in overall command. Kesselring claimed in his memoirs that he had had the greatest confidence in Vietinghoff, but within a month of Kesselring's return to duty, Vietinghoff was replaced, at his own request.

Hitler's counter-attack in Italy was on a much smaller scale than the Ardennes offensive – necessarily so because of the lack of men and machinery. Mussolini was the nominal head of state of the new Fascist Republic, the Salo Republic as the post-Armistice Fascist state was known. Although really just Hitler's puppet, Mussolini wanted to flex such military muscles as he had. The Fascist Italians added troops from the *Monterosa* and *San Marco* Divisions to the German forces, but even so the resources for the offensive were far more limited than in the Ardennes. The opposition to the Nazis/Fascists in Italy was a mixture of Allied forces, Royal Italian forces, and partisans.

The area chosen for the offensive, the Serchio valley, was near the western end of the Gothic Line in Tuscany. The objective was to break through the Allied lines and to drive on to the town of Lucca, and then to Livorno (Leghorn) on the west coast. If nothing else, this would relieve Allied pressure on the city of Bologna, still in German hands but threatened by Allied forces. The Germans knew that this sector of the line was held by the American 92nd Infantry Division. They believed that, compared to other parts of the line held by battle-hardened troops, this sector could be breached, providing surprise could be guaranteed. Again, the problem for the Nazis/Fascists was that the Allies held air supremacy, which meant that their observation of the enemy build-up was thorough, and their potential for air attack against any enemy advance significant.

As in the Ardennes offensive, Hitler was prepared to use dirty tricks. The Allies were being assisted by Italian partisans – these were 'resistance' freedom fighters fighting a guerrilla war against the Germans and Fascists behind the lines. As the Allies advanced up Italy, various of these partisan groups were liberated, and some remained in formation fighting alongside the Allied forces and the Royal Italian Army. The partisans had no regular military uniform, and tended to identify their group by badges, or by the coloured scarves that many of the groups wore. In the Ardennes, the plan was for Germans to impersonate American soldiers, wearing American uniforms and using American vehicles. In Italy, where resources were more limited, and with Italians fighting on both sides in what was for them a civil war, the easiest ruse for the Germans and Fascists was to impersonate Italian partisans, and this they did with notable success. They used hundreds of troops disguised as partisans to infiltrate and surprise their enemy, and there are many royalist accounts of the confusion caused.

Hitler therefore was poised in the autumn of 1944 for a major counter-attack in the Ardennes and a significant one in the Serchio Valley. In the event, the two were not entirely simultaneous – the Ardennes offensive was launched on the early morning of 16 December, the Serchio valley attack ten days later. Both attacks had been delayed for logistical reasons. Both campaigns used 'dirty tricks' and breached the rules of war.

Chapter 2

Target Churchill

In the autumn of 1944, Adolf Hitler had another secret weapon. He intended to liberate and activate a German army far to the rear of the Allied positions. Many thousands of Waffen-SS and other specialist Nazi troops were held in prison camps in Britain, guarded by third-rate British and Allied soldiers. In total, there were at least 250,000 German prisoners held in Britain by December 1944. Using the Vehmic court system to enforce discipline, Hitler's hangmen were able to keep most of their fellow German prisoners of war under complete control. Not all of the prisoner of war camps in Britain were under SS control, but enough were to supply Hitler with a murderous potential, spread throughout the country. He ordered a mass break-out from the camps to coincide with the Ardennes offensive. Two large, Nazi-run camps were chosen to lead this: Camp 23, at Le Marchant Barracks in Devizes to the west of London, and Camp 17, Lodge Moor in Sheffield, far to the north, were to form the hard core of the break-out, but orders would go out to all the camps in Britain that could be trusted to keep the plan a secret, that is those where the SS was enforcing Vehmic law and terror.

Hitler also intended to use, at last, the support that he still had in Britain from British Fascists, his enthusiastic Fifth Column who had never been called on to serve, since there had as yet been no invasion of Britain. Over a thousand British Fascists had been interned by Winston Churchill's government from May 1940 onwards. Chamberlain's government had previously arrested very few, and had allowed the others to preach on in freedom against the war. It was only Churchill, in the days before Dunkirk, who saw the real danger of the British Fascists, and cracked down hard. However, by September 1944, the war seemed as good as won to the Allies, and many of the British Fascists were released from prison, on the basis that since the Germans were close to defeat, they were no longer dangerous. In fact, their years of imprisonment had made them all the more bitter against their own, democratic, government.

This book will show how well-placed the British Fascists were to help Hitler at this vital hour. They had long been waiting for the moment when they could call for all British Fascists to rise up in armed rebellion. They held Churchill and his government personally responsible for their loss of liberty, and for allowing 'World Jewry' to thrive, wanted the British government and its leader, Churchill, brought to judgment by the Nazis, and hoped that in the result, Churchill and his ministers would be hung from British lampposts, Vehmic style. That suited Hitler very well.

Until Winston Churchill had taken over as prime minister in May 1940, there had been relatively little interference with the activities of the British Fascists, although MI5 had been monitoring their activities closely. There were many in Parliament who favoured appeasement, and the general view was that freedom of speech remained of the greatest importance in a democracy. Although there was the power to detain those who were believed to be a threat to the state, it was rarely enforced against the British Fascists during the Chamberlain government. There were British Fascists amongst the aristocracy, in the House of Lords, and in the House of Commons. They wished for the war to end, and hoped then to take over the government of Britain.

When Chamberlain resigned on 10 May 1940, the appointment of the 'warmonger' Winston Churchill as prime minister was a serious blow to the British Fascists. Churchill had long been an opponent of appeasement, believing that if the Nazis were allowed to take control of large parts of Europe, Britain would inevitably suffer and eventually fall under the Nazi jackboot. The British Fascists had regularly abused Churchill in their public speeches.

Winston Churchill's term of office began as Hitler unleashed his blitzkrieg in Western Europe. Nazi forces invaded Belgium at dawn on 10 May, and simultaneously thrust through the Ardennes with forty-five divisions. They reached the sea on 21 May, splitting British and Allied forces. This should have been a great day for British Fascists. Had Chamberlain still been prime minister, then they would have expected him to sue for peace, and that a British Fascist government, under Nazi control, would be in power within days. However, from the moment that he took over, Churchill made clear that war was the only option. Using the English language as a weapon, he inspired the British people with his speeches. Whilst Hitler whipped his supporters up into a patriotic frenzy with his populist oratory, Churchill chose his words with great care and delivered them with great eloquence.

On the night of 10/11 May 1940, a German bomb caused heavy damage to the House of Commons and to the Members' Lobby. It was no longer usable as the seat of government. Temporarily, the House of Commons sat in Church House, on Dean's Yard next to Westminster Abbey.

On 13 May 1940, with the battle for mainland Europe raging across the Channel, Churchill told the Commons:

> 'I would say to the House, as I have said to those that have joined this Government: I have nothing to offer but blood, toil, tears and sweat. We have before us an ordeal of the most grievous kind. We have before us many, many long months of struggle and suffering. You ask, what is our policy? I can say: it is to wage war, by sea, land and air, with all our might and with all the strength that God can give us; to wage war against a monstrous tyranny, never surpassed in the dark, lamentable catalogue of human crime. That is our policy. You ask, what is our aim? I can answer in one word: it is victory, victory at all costs, victory in spite of all terror, victory, however long and hard the road may be, for without victory, there is no survival.'

On 4 June 1940, after the disaster of Dunkirk and a degree of salvation due to the evacuation of hundreds of thousands of men by 'the little ships', Churchill told the country:

> 'We shall go on to the end, we shall fight in France, we shall fight on the seas and oceans, we shall fight with growing confidence and growing strength in the air, we shall defend our island, whatever the cost may be, we shall fight on the beaches, we shall fight on the landing grounds, we shall fight in the fields and the streets, we shall fight in the hills, we shall never surrender.'

Churchill was strongly of the view that the British Fascist leaders were dangerous, and should be locked up. He was right. Beginning on 22 May 1940, detention orders were signed by Home Secretary Sir John Anderson, and most of the leading Fascists were taken to Brixton and Holloway prisons. With Churchill as prime minister there was no chance that Great Britain would sue for peace. He had made absolutely clear that, however desperate things might appear, Britain would fight on, and the only objective was victory over the Nazis. As the tide of war changed during the years that followed, and Britain along with its Empire forces and with the United States gained the upper hand, Churchill's position remained constant – he sought victory. A peace favourable to Germany in late 1944 would be highly unlikely if Winston Churchill remained prime minister. He was an inspirational leader and carried the country with him.

Inevitably, Churchill was a target for assassination. In a way, it was fortunate that he even survived to become prime minister in May 1940 – the Germans had a habit of using their Fifth Column in a country that they intended to take over by assassinating before invasion those who were the potential leaders of any resistance. Churchill was publicly and vehemently anti-Nazi. Churchill's personal security, once he had returned to the government after the outbreak of war in 1939, was in the hands of Detective Inspector Walter Thompson of the Metropolitan Police Special Branch, who came out of retirement to organise his protection. Thompson knew

Churchill well – he had worked as his bodyguard when he had previously been in government.[1]

Churchill was a difficult man to guard – he was never frightened of taking risks, loved the prospect of a fight, instinctively wanted to mix with the ordinary British people, and hated air-raid shelters. Thompson described him as having an impetuosity and a love of danger. Churchill was a good shot, and one of Thompson's tasks was to carry Churchill's personal Colt .45 automatic – so that he might hand it to the Prime Minister if they were attacked. Churchill always said that the last bullet would be for him; he would never be captured alive.

Thompson had the very difficult task of keeping Churchill safe. He had a permanent assistant, but the resources at his disposal paled into insignificance when compared, for example, to the heavy security that surrounded US President Roosevelt, whom Churchill met regularly once the United States had entered the war in December 1941, after Pearl Harbor. Churchill travelled extensively throughout the war, and although an assassination attempt upon him was more difficult on the British mainland, when he was flying, travelling by sea, or in foreign lands, there was always opportunity. Much depended on the quality of intelligence that the Nazis had about Churchill's movements. Thompson, who was at the heart of the operation to protect Churchill, recounts two specific occasions when it was known that the Germans planned an attempt on Churchill's life.

In January 1943, Great Britain and the United States held a conference on the future prosecution of the war in Casablanca, Morocco. Churchill and President Roosevelt attended, as did a number of senior Allied commanders including General Eisenhower. Churchill visited Algiers after the Casablanca conference, and was due to fly home from there on 5 February 1943. However, Thompson says: 'There was credible information that a prominent German agent was in Algiers with orders from Hitler to assassinate Churchill.' How the information had reached the Allies is unclear – it may have been the product of Station X, the Allied codebreaking centre at Bletchley Park. The threat was taken very seriously – a decoy B-17 aeroplane was put in the air by General Eisenhower under the pretence that it was carrying Churchill's party, and Churchill's own Liberator aircraft was mysteriously grounded overnight because of a mechanical failure. They flew home to London on the following day. Hitler's plan, if the information was true, had been frustrated.

There was always a danger to Churchill when he was flying. Churchill was in Algiers again on 19 May 1943. The day before he was due to fly back, a commercial civilian flight from neutral Portugal was shot down over the Bay of Biscay, killing its passengers and crew. It was carrying the actor Leslie Howard (of *Gone with the Wind* fame) and his business manager Alfred Chenhalls, who together bore a slight resemblance to Winston Churchill and Inspector Thompson. Churchill was later to write of the stupidity of the German agents in believing that he himself would have flown on a daytime commercial flight – he would always fly by night, and in a wide loop rather than on a commercial flight path. Churchill clearly accepted that the Germans had believed that he was on that flight, and it cost the life of one of Churchill's favourite actors.

Another assassination attempt was avoided at the Teheran conference between Churchill, Stalin and Roosevelt from 28 November to 1 December 1943. The conference was held at the Soviet Embassy in Teheran, Iran. Whilst it was going on, intelligence was received that there was to be an assassination attempt against all three Allied leaders. Sixty German paratroopers were said to have been dropped near Teheran to carry this out. This intelligence was confirmed as true seven years later by General Lahousen, the German Chief of Secret Operations. Hitler had ordered that the assassination attempt be made at the conference, in the hope of taking out all the three major Allied leaders at once. Again, the Allies probably received the intelligence from Enigma intercepts. As a result, security was very substantially increased. At the end of the conference, a diversionary tactic was used – military policemen in civilian clothes were driven to the airport, where, pretending to be VIPs, they boarded a plane and were whisked away into the skies, only in fact to be landed again on an unused airstrip on the other side of Teheran. Roosevelt left from an old military airport near the US Embassy in a different plane, and Churchill left Teheran lying down in the back of a battered army truck (despite his protests), which drove him to a small airfield five miles away at Amirabad. According to Thompson, the route was lined with British Army troops, guns and vehicles, and all side roads were blocked. Hitler's assassination plot was foiled.

Thus it is clear that Adolf Hitler had at least twice ordered the assassination of Churchill, and on the second occasion had included the deaths of Roosevelt and Stalin in his order. Moving forward to the autumn of 1944, Hitler had recently survived an assassination attempt himself, the Allies were advancing successfully across Europe, and Hitler was planning his final counterattack. If he could kill Churchill, Britain's great war leader, and perhaps a number of his ministers at the same time, Hitler's hope of victory for Germany, or at least a favourable peace with the Western Allies, would be greatly enhanced. Britain would be rudderless. If he could kill Eisenhower and perhaps some of his supporting generals, then the same could be true of Allied forces in Europe.

The House of Commons had returned to sit in the House of Lords Chamber of the Houses of Parliament after the bombing of 1940; the Lords gave way and sat in their Robing Room. With the exception only of the months of July and August 1944, when German V-1 flying bombs first began to fall on Britain, the House of Commons sat in the Lords Chamber throughout the remainder of the war. Many of Churchill's most inspiring speeches were therefore made in the Lords Chamber. Although Churchill travelled extensively during the war years, he would always return to London to speak in Parliament. London, and the Prime Minister's Residence at Chequers in Buckinghamshire (when he could get there) remained his home. He preferred to sleep at No. 10 Downing Street, but when the bombing was at its height in 1940–1, he had accommodation elsewhere. Inspector Thompson describes this as:

> '. . . the very powerfully built building at Storey's Gate, two
> blocks south of Downing Street at the park end of the Board of

> Trade building . . . work was being carried out to reinforce the below-ground levels with a fifteen-foot-thick slab of steel and concrete . . . the Annexe, as it became known, provided the Churchills with a flat on the ground floor, above the vast slab that covered the Cabinet War Room, his office and those of his Ministers and Chiefs of Staff, and in a level below this, reached by spiral stairs, a series of low-ceilinged tiny bedrooms.'[2]

Churchill, however, rarely slept below ground in what was, in reality, an air-raid shelter. According to Thompson, he far preferred to go up onto the roof of 'the Annexe', and to watch the bombs falling.

Before D-Day in June 1944, the war was run from London, and even after D-Day, Churchill was most often found in London. As it happened, on both 14 December 1944 and 20 December 1944, Churchill was in the House of Commons (still sitting in the House of Lords). However, there was a crisis brewing in liberated Greece, and on Christmas Eve 1944 Churchill decided to fly out to Athens. He left on Christmas Day.

Churchill, like all effective politicians, liked to be seen. He wanted his people to know that he was sharing their suffering, understood their tragedies, and was doing everything possible to prosecute the war until victory was finally achieved. He could not do this without exposing himself as a target. His personal security was not great, and although he had a permanent bodyguard in Inspector Thompson, a determined assassination squad, if they were able to get close enough, would have been perfectly capable of killing Winston Churchill. The British Fascists wanted Churchill dead, so did Adolf Hitler. As this book will relate, as Britain relaxed into the euphoria of an expected victory over Germany and its Axis allies in December 1944, Hitler and the British Fascists hoped to use their best chance yet to 'take out' Churchill.

Chapter 3

Britain Sleeps

During the nights of November and December 1944, Britain slept as peacefully as it ever would in wartime. British confidence in victory was high, and victory was expected to come soon. Allied forces had landed in Normandy on D-Day in early June 1944. On 20 July, some of Adolf Hitler's own generals tried to assassinate him, and although the attempt failed, Allied euphoria increased, as it seemed that Germany was beginning to fall apart. In mid-August, General George Patton's Third US Army advanced from Normandy to the Seine. At the same time, the Allies successfully invaded the south of France, landing between Cannes and Toulon, in what was known as Operation Dragoon. Thereafter, the Allied forces in northern France pushed forward quickly. US and British troops crossed the border into Belgium, and on 3 September, the British Guards Armoured Division entered Brussels. The next day, 4 September, the British 11th Armoured Division moved into Antwerp, and with the assistance of the Belgian Resistance, seized the port before it could be destroyed by the Germans. This was a highly significant capture, since the Germans had been applying a 'scorched earth' policy as they retreated, destroying installations and ports that might be of use to the Allies. American troops also enjoyed great success. The first American patrol to cross onto German soil did so on 11 September, from north-eastern Luxembourg. The Allies enjoyed almost total air superiority. Meanwhile the Russians were advancing on the Eastern Front, as the Germans suffered enormous casualties there. It was no wonder that the British relaxed and felt that the war was almost over.

In the early autumn, a 'Stand Down' order was issued to the Home Guard. It was believed that its services would no longer be needed. It had been created to resist the threat of a German invasion, by sea or air, or both, but such a threat was now felt to have been finally extinguished. As from 31 December 1944, the Home Guard would not be on any period of notice to return to arms, and in the 'unlikely event' of the Home Guard being needed again, it was anticipated that it would have at least three weeks' notice to get into a state of preparedness.[1]

On 26 September 1944, the Home Secretary, Herbert Morrison, spoke to the House of Commons, explaining the release of certain detainees on the basis of 'the success of arms of the United Nations and the certainty that the forces of evil arrayed against us are doomed to complete overthrow'.[2]

On 19 October 1944, Sir David Petrie, Director-General of the Security Service, wrote to Sir Alexander Maxwell, Permanent Under Secretary at the Home Office and responsible for the police, to thank them for their help with internal security, saying:

> 'Although the war is not yet ended, one can but look upon the "stand down" of the Home Guard and the easing of black out restrictions as a tacit acknowledgement that the last serious risk to internal security has been removed. The brunt of this struggle, now successfully ended, has fallen upon the Police and the Security Service, each with their separate responsibilities but partners in the main one. I feel therefore that the time is appropriate for me to pay some tribute of thanks to Chief Constables (and through them to their respective forces) for the unfailing support and co-operation they have afforded the Security Service throughout the war. I would prefer to do so at this stage, as my connection with MI5 has been a war-time one only and, in the nature of things, cannot last much longer.'[3]

By December, Germany appeared to be exhausted and just hanging on. Mussolini's Fascist Republic, created and sustained by Hitler's Germany, was cowering behind the Gothic Line in northern

Italy. Although many men were still dying in the bitter fighting in Europe and the Far East, and although Germany's V-1 and V-2 rocket bombs were falling regularly on British soil and killing hundreds of British civilians, the mood remained one of optimism. The dark days of 1940–2 were gone. So confident were the Allies of victory that General Eisenhower had bet Field Marshal Montgomery back in the summer that the war against Germany would be won by Christmas 1944.

How different was the atmosphere now to that of June 1940 after Dunkirk, when Hitler's Germany had thrown British and Allied troops out of Europe, and then Mussolini's Italy had joined the war, hoping to seize British territories in North Africa, and to take control of Greece. The Battle of Britain and the Blitz had followed, but the expected German invasion had never come. For years, the British had fought on with their backs to the wall.

When, on 10 May 1940, Churchill replaced Chamberlain as British Prime Minister, one of the great concerns was that Germany would activate a 'Fifth Column' in Britain. It had used this tactic very successfully in the other European countries upon which Hitler had set his sights. Fifth Columnists, as they were known, were those whom Hitler, or once Italy had joined the war against Britain in June 1940, Mussolini, had introduced to Britain in peacetime, to act as 'sleepers' against a time when their help might be needed by their mother country – they could be Germans, Italians or native pro-Nazi or Fascist sympathisers operating covertly. Native Britons were hugely suspicious in the early days of the war of anyone in their country who was of German heritage, and after June 1940 Italians too fell under suspicion. Those who were British-born generally escaped the net, but all enemy nationals were detained. They might have been living peacefully in Britain for many years, but the British authorities simply could not take the risk that foreign nationals might secretly be working against them within their shores. Throughout the 1930s, many Germans and Austrians had fled to Britain to escape the Nazis, including both Jews and political opponents of the regime. Britain had a long history of accepting refugees from persecution for political or religious reasons. In September 1939, sadly, that had to change, since it was felt inevitable that some German Fifth Columnists would have entered Britain pretending to be refugees, or as businessmen, or tradesmen plying their craft.

Thus it became necessary to arrest and intern enemy aliens. There can be no doubt that the vast majority of the Germans and Austrians interned in the early stages of the war were not Fifth Columnists, or even Nazi sympathisers. A large number of those who were interned had nothing but the best of intentions towards their British hosts. A number of them, after their release later in the war, joined the British forces, usually the Pioneer Corps to start with, and then moved on to other units. There were 'Free Germans' who joined the Special Air Service and the Special Operations Executive.

When Prime Minister Chamberlain finally resigned on 10 May 1940, he had lost the confidence of parliament, and his health was failing (he died later that year). Winston Churchill took over with Britain facing what seemed to be insuperable odds though the large and far-flung British Empire gave hope. Shortly after Churchill took office, the hugely significant defeat at Dunkirk followed, and only the 'miracle of the little ships' saved many of the country's servicemen from capture or death. Britain had been thrown out of Europe, and with the capitulation of France within weeks, stood alone against the Nazis.

Until now, Mussolini, the Dictator of Italy and the Grand Old Man of Fascism (he had taken control of Italy in 1922), had stayed out of the war. After Dunkirk, however, Mussolini declared war, in the hope that Italy could seize Britain's North African territories whilst the British were hopelessly weak and preparing for an invasion by Germany. Britain's reaction was to intern all Italian nationals in the United Kingdom. There was a fear that if this was not done, Italian Fascist sympathisers living in Britain would help Britain's enemies. Churchill's approach was robust – if action was necessary for the protection of Britain he would take it. He regarded Germany as waging an all-out, no holds barred war, in which it would do anything necessary to win, including bombing civilians as a terror tactic. In response, Churchill was prepared to use any methods available to fight back and protect his country. Chamberlain's government had detained Germans, Austrians and some British Fascists, but Churchill was much tougher, particularly on the British Fascists. In late May, his government began to intern people of this sort – British citizens, men and women, who were believed to be a threat to national security because of their pro-Nazi/Fascist views.

Many Italians who had run small businesses in the UK for many years therefore found themselves in detention camps. There was a large Italian population in Great Britain and Northern Ireland. With work and money scarce in many parts of Italy, villages would send their young men to look for work in England, Scotland, Wales and Ireland. Many would return home to Italy when their fortune was made, some would stay. During the Second World War, often the sons, if they were British-born and British nationals, would be called up to serve in the British Army, whilst the fathers were arrested and interned.

Having interned many thousands of enemy nationals, the obvious difficulty was where to keep them. Many were detained on the Isle of Man, where it was felt that they could be more easily contained. However, at home in Britain, detainees would tie up manpower (as did all prisoners of war), and in the event of a German invasion, they would constitute a threat to internal security. In 1940, with the threat of an imminent invasion, Britain could ill afford to keep thousands of potential enemies within its shores – a lesson it forgot as the years went by, and the threat of invasion faded.

Great Britain had an empire, and it was decided to send many of its internees to distant parts of that empire. There was plenty of space in Canada, British India, British Africa or Australia to keep suspect German or Italian nationals. They were to be transported by sea, despite the obvious danger to all British shipping posed by German U-boats. One of the ships employed to carry detainees was the *Arandora Star*, a pre-war luxury passenger liner that had been commandeered by the British government as a troop carrier, and now as a prison ship. On 1 July 1940, the *Arandora Star* left Liverpool carrying 1,295 prisoners, 200 British military guards and a British crew. The prisoners comprised 730 Italian civilian detainees, many of whom were small businessmen, 479 German civilian detainees, and 86 German prisoners of war. The *Arandora Star* sailed alone, not as part of a convoy, and was bound for Canada. On the second day of its voyage, it was spotted by the German submarine *U-47*, commanded by Günther Prien. Prien had only one torpedo left, and decided to use it on the *Arandora Star*. He was a U-boat 'ace', and wanted to increase his score. He did not of course know that 565 of his fellow countrymen were on board. He sank the liner with his last torpedo, causing the loss of 773 lives – 243 Germans, 470 Italians and 60 British. The tragedy struck hard in many villages and towns in Italy. Pontremoli, a *comune* in northern Tuscany, lost seventeen of its citizens. Many of these were from families who later proved to be courageous supporters of escaped Allied prisoners of war in Italy.

The prisoners who survived were deported to Australia, again by sea. Happily, on this occasion, after some narrow scrapes, their ship got through and they survived the war. Notwithstanding that tragedy, the British government continued to pursue a policy of internment. There was a constant search for any possible 'enemies within'.

But all this was almost forgotten in December 1944. As Home Secretary Herbert Morrison had said, and Sir David Petrie had confirmed, the war in Europe was effectively won – it was now only a matter of time before Germany collapsed – and the threat to internal security had been removed.

Little did MI5 and the British government realise that they were about to face the most serious internal threat of the war.

Chapter 4

The Enemy Within
The British Fascists

Before the outbreak of World War Two, and for a surprisingly long period after the beginning of that war, Fascism was public and lawful in Great Britain. It was a political belief, and providing its proponents did not break any British laws, they could preach the tenets of Fascism to the British people. The opposite extreme to Fascism was Communism, and there were plenty of Communists preaching their gospel too. However, Fascism in Britain had become not only pro-Nazi, but anti-Jewish. There was a surprisingly large number of people in Britain who found the Nazi–Fascist message attractive, embodying as it did a hatred of both Communists and Jews.

To understand the appeal of Fascism after World War One, it is necessary to remember that in 1917, the rule of the tsars in Russia was terminated by revolution, and shortly thereafter the Bolsheviks seized power. A civil war between the anti-Bolshevik White Russians and the Bolsheviks followed, with Britain supporting the White Russians. British forces were for a while involved in Archangel and other parts of northern Russia in support of the White Russians. In September 1919 that involvement ended, but the threat of Bolshevism continued to be felt throughout Europe, with many states fearing a Bolshevik take-over similar to the one in Russia. It must be remembered that democracy was still restricted in many European countries. In Britain, the enfranchisement of women was vigorously fought for and won. However, it was not until 1921 that women in Britain were allowed to serve on juries, trying their fellow citizens – most often men.[1]

Also, following a number of years of military service during World War One, many men were not troubled by the prospect of a militaristic regime, which would provide order and discipline, and get things done. In the early 1920s, therefore, the concept of a Fascist dictator opposed to Communism bringing calm to a troubled country did not appear so totally unattractive as it does to most today. Benito Mussolini, in Italy, invented Fascism. Italy, under King Victor Emmanuel III, had fought alongside Great Britain and its allies against the Germans, Austrians and Hungarians in World War One. Like other countries, Italy had suffered heavy casualties, and the war had cost its economy dearly. Victory brought little compensation for Italy; its spoils of war were limited. Benito Mussolini was born in 1883 in Romagna. In December 1912 he became the editor of the Socialist paper *Avanti!* ('Forward!'). In late 1914, he split from the Socialists, and founded his own paper, *Il Popolo d'Italia*. It seems that Mussolini first began referring to his followers, and others of like mind, as Fascists in 1915. The Fascist movement grew, one of its tenets being a vigorous patriotism.

At the end of the war, with Bolshevism on the rise, Italy was impoverished, King Victor Emmanuel was passive and non-interventionist, and politics were confused. The historian R. J. B. Bosworth comments:

> 'To be sure, within a few short years, a Fascist "revolution" proved that Mussolini and his friends were those armed with the most effective immediate replies. Proclaiming a totalitarian "last word", the Fascists sought to silence all debates and to impose on Italians "unity" and the obedience of the parade ground (even if the appearance and intent of the regime should not be assumed to be identical with its reality).'[2]

The term Fascist was taken from the traditions of Ancient Rome. *Fasces* was the Latin word for the bundle of sticks, and usually an axe, bound together with rope, which was carried in a ceremonial procession before a Roman consul. The Fascist creed was that the *fasces* symbolised the unity of all sectors of Italian society in the national interest – no class, gender, regional or other division could weaken the strength of a Fascist state, for all were locked together in National Unity – in patriotism.

After years of political confusion following World War One, and rising internal violence and disorder, Mussolini was invited to become Prime Minister of Italy in late October 1922 as the head of a coalition government. Thereafter, he consolidated his power until his regime became a Fascist dictatorship, allowing no dissent. In the 1920s, Mussolini brought order to Italy, adopting a 'gloved fist' approach, backed up by gangs of black-shirted bully boys. However, initially, there appears to have been little hatred of the Jews in the Fascist manifesto. There were many well-established and prosperous Jewish communities in Italy, and some of them were supporters of the early Fascism. Adolf Hitler is said to have admired Mussolini, and what his Fascist party had achieved in Italy, in the days before Hitler himself came to power in Germany. However, Hitler's Nazi strain of Fascism was far more extreme than Mussolini's. Hitler always intended that Jews were to be exorcised from national life in Germany.

A fear of Communism led many people to support Fascism. It was argued that Fascism was the opposite side of the coin to Bolshevism – and Mussolini's success in bringing order to Italy showed that Fascism could deal with the Communist threat. In the 1920s and 1930s, many believed that Bolshevism was a far worse fate than Fascism. Even Winston Churchill, who would become an implacable enemy of Fascism and Nazism, had flattering words to say about Mussolini in the early 1920s. He was far from alone.

In the United Kingdom, freedom of speech and democracy were both highly valued, and protected by law. Thus, it was lawful for both Communists and Fascists to establish political parties within the UK, and to preach their respective gospels, provided that they did not, for instance, turn to violence. With Communism in Britain on the increase, a number of Fascist parties grew up in Britain. The earliest was the British Fascisti (later the British Fascists), who became active in Britain shortly after Mussolini took over Italy. Its members

believed that Fascism was the effective antidote to Communism.
When Communist MPs were elected to the House of Commons, and
when the first Labour government took office in 1924, the concerns
and activities of the Fascists in Britain increased.

The British Fascisti campaigned on the basis that they were a
democratic party which would protect Britain from a Communist
dictatorship. A pamphlet in November 1924 asked:

> 'Are you willing to accept the chains which Bolshevism offers
> you, and to fight under the Red Flag, whose only battle honours
> and distinctions are murder, famine and disaster? Will you join
> those who in hatred and envy seek to destroy the Empire which
> your ancestors helped to build? If you believe in a free England
> you will join the National Fascisti, you will work for us for the
> cause of Fascism and Country, and with us you will fight for
> the ideals of Monarchy, Empire, Progress, Liberty, Prosperity
> and the maintenance of Law and Order upon which Fascism
> is based. The National Fascisti is essentially a democratic
> body, in which every active member is entitled to vote on the
> conduct of affairs, and in which any undue personal influence
> or any form of Dictatorship is impossible.'[3]

The Membership Oath for the British Fascisti read:

> 'In the name of God I solemnly swear to uphold His Most
> Gracious Majesty King George V, his heirs and successors
> and the British Empire. I undertake that, without personal
> consideration, I will render every service in my power to the
> British Fascisti in their struggle against all treacherous and
> revolutionary movements now working for the destruction of
> the Throne and Empire.'

The enrolment form was in similar terms, promising to uphold
the King and the established Constitution of Great Britain and the
British Empire.

As time went by, and other Fascist leaders emerged onto the
European stage, such as Hitler in Germany and Franco in Spain,

the Fascists in Britain increased in number, and fragmented into a variety of different groupings. Many of the Fascist leaders in Britain were vehemently anti-Jewish, and regarded Hitler as the only European leader prepared to deal with the 'Jewish Problem'. Also, as the outbreak of World War Two threatened only twenty years after the wholesale slaughter of World War One, there were many pacifists who preached that Britain should not go to war against Hitler's Nazi Germany.

The most famous British Fascist leader of the time, and still today, was undoubtedly Sir Oswald Mosley, Baronet, leader of the British Union of Fascists (BUF). Mosley, himself an ex-MP for both the Conservative and Labour parties, adopted an overtly militarist, pro-Nazi stance, and had many supporters, particularly in the East End of London. He openly supported Hitler's Germany, and was vehemently anti-Jewish. His supporters favoured the Nazi Salute, and the greeting: 'Hail Mosley'. However, the British Union of Fascists was not the only significant pro-Hitler organisation in the United Kingdom. By 1939, as Britain's Security Service MI5 was aware, there were numerous other Nazis/Fascists within Britain's borders who were prepared to resort to violent action to support Hitler's Germany, and to enable a Nazi/Fascist take-over of Great Britain and Northern Ireland when the time was right.

In Scotland and Westminster there was a serving Member of Parliament who had long been an ardent Fascist. Captain Archibald Maule Ramsay led a secret organisation called the Right Club, into which he recruited a number of other MPs, members of the House of Lords, prominent persons and people working in important organisations. Although its objectives were much the same, the Right Club was significantly different to the BUF. Mosley's organisation was a very public political party. It was known for its violent actions. Mosley's Fascists wore black shirts, and were populist rabble-rousers, backed up by thugs. Not surprisingly, Ramsay and Sir Oswald Mosley did not get on too well together, but at one stage Mosley offered Ramsay the post of 'Gauleiter' of Scotland, the equivalent of Military Governor, once Mosley's Fascists ruled in the United Kingdom.

Ramsay refused, preferring to run his own secret organisation, infiltrating the British establishment. As an MP he was well placed to do this, and had access to much sensitive material not available to those outside Parliament. However, once war had broken out in September 1939, Mosley and Ramsay were in regular contact.

In Berkhamsted, Hertfordshire, there was a local businessman called Ben Greene. He was a Justice of the Peace, but also a rabid Nazi. His mother was German, his father British. His sister worked in Berlin, and was well connected with the Nazi establishment.

In Guildford, Surrey, there was a retired veterinary surgeon called Arnold Leese. He was the leader of the Imperial Fascist League. He was virulently anti-Jewish, and regularly published works vilifying Jews. He had solid support from his circle of Imperial League Fascists, although they were far fewer in number than Mosley's BUF and less well known. In September 1936, Leese had been tried and convicted at the Old Bailey of effecting a public mischief by publishing a newspaper accusing the Jews of practising ritual murder. He served six months' imprisonment.

Chapter 5

Maxwell Knight

MI5's Spy Chief

Against the British Fascists were ranged the agents of Britain's
MI5. When war broke out in September 1939, MI5 was under the
command of Vernon Kell, the veteran who had been in charge of it
throughout World War One, and before that from its very beginning.
However, Kell was replaced by Churchill when he became Prime
Minister in May 1940, and in due course Sir David Petrie took over.
MI5 had long been interested in Britain's Fascists. Its investigation
team was headed by an expert spymaster called Maxwell Knight,
who ran a network of secret agents, many of them women, tasked to
infiltrate British Fascist circles. He was an intriguing character who
had once been a Fascist himself. The information that his agents
gathered became vital to Britain's fight against Hitler and Mussolini.

Maxwell Knight was, by all accounts, a most unusual man. Born
on 9 July 1900, from his earliest years he was a naturalist with a great
love of animals and birds. He was almost too young for World War
One but, having been a naval cadet, served briefly as a midshipman.
His father had died when he was fourteen, and his brother Eric
was killed in the last year of the war. After the war, Knight led an
unsettled life, changing jobs regularly. He got into jazz, and collected
quite an extraordinary menagerie of pets, including a bushbaby and
a bear, all of which lived with him in the family flat in a mansion
block in Putney. He ended up teaching games at a preparatory school
nearby.

In 1923, Knight was recruited by an extremely wealthy Scottish
baronet called Sir George Makgill. Makgill was a strong patriot, who
had set up a privately funded intelligence service (to be used by the

business world) to combat what he saw as a Bolshevik infiltration of Britain after the end of the First World War. In 1920, Liberal MP Lieutenant Colonel Cecil John L'Estrange Malone declared himself a Communist, and left the Liberal Party. In 1924, the first two Communist MPs were elected to parliament under the banner of the Labour Party. Makgill felt that the British government did not appreciate the danger of this. He worked with a number of industrial and financial backers to gather as much information as possible on Communist activity in Britain. There was a constant fear that Communism might bring the factories to a standstill, and thus Makgill's agents would seek information on what the Bolsheviks were planning. Makgill would then report to his industrial backers, and also to Vernon Kell, the head of MI5.

The most obvious opposition to the Bolsheviks came from the emerging British Fascists, known in 1923 as the British Fascisti, and Knight was instructed by Makgill to join them. At that time, Mussolini was the only European leader believed to have totally eliminated the Communist Party from his country, for which deed he attracted much praise from those who feared the world-wide influence of Bolshevism. Knight himself appears to have been sympathetic to Fascism at that early stage of his life, and did well within the British Fascisti. He was soon promoted to be their Director of Intelligence, whilst all the time working secretly for Makgill. He continued to teach at the prep school in Putney, but in his time off he now had access to all the information that the British Fascisti had gathered on Communist activity in Britain, in particular their personnel files on suspected Communist agitators. It was a splendid coup for his boss, Makgill. For Knight, however, it meant constant exposure to Fascism, its principles and its literature. It also meant that he met and gained knowledge of many Fascists who would later become wartime enemies of the British government. One of these was the American-born William Joyce, who would eventually defect to Germany and become the leading broadcaster (known by the nickname 'Lord Haw Haw') of Nazi propaganda to Britain during World War Two.

The British Fascisti developed a para-military wing called 'K'. This squad of younger men decided that it was their job to attend meetings where there were likely to be groups of Communist thugs, and to confront and 'deal with' such groups. Knight became a member of the K section's inner circle. William Joyce was an active, and very physical member. The K section was regularly involved in physical violence against their equivalent in the Bolshevik movement. On one occasion, Joyce, in the thick of the disturbance, had his face severely slashed, causing a scar that he bore for the rest of his life. Suffice it to say that during his involvement with the K section of the British Fascisti, Knight inevitably committed some illegal acts himself.

By 1925 the British Fascisti had anglicised their name to the British Fascists, and Knight had fallen in love with one of the leading women in the movement, Gwladys Poole. They married in Sherborne Abbey, Dorset, in December 1925. The following year, in May 1926, came the General Strike. There was no accompanying Communist uprising in Britain, and the strike itself was relatively short-lived. Five months later Sir George Makgill collapsed unexpectedly and died. Soon after, Knight found himself out of work. Mr and Mrs Knight decided to leave London and move to Exmoor in the West Country.[1] Gwladys, who was a lady of means, decided to buy the Royal Oak Inn in the remote village of Withypool, which she and her husband would run. Knight looked forward to the country life, where there would be ample room for his exotic pets, but the move was not a success. Knight's marriage seems to have become increasingly unhappy during the Exmoor years, probably because it was never consummated.

However, Knight still had his contacts amongst the Fascists, and a network of low-key agents working in the Communist Party. From time to time during his Exmoor years, Desmond Morton of MI6 asked for Knight's assistance, and in late 1929 Morton offered him a full-time job as one of MI6's agents. Knight accepted, and brought with him his network of agents. His job was again essentially that of obtaining information about Communist activities in Britain. In due course, Knight moved from MI6 to MI5 because of a decision that all Communist activities should come under MI5's jurisdiction. His work against British Fascism would not start until after 1932, when Sir Oswald Mosley founded what became the British Union of Fascists. MI5 did not initially regard the BUF as a threat, but as their activities became more extreme, and it became clear that British Fascism was being supported by funds from Italy and Germany, MI5 reluctantly began to take an interest. Happily, it had as one of its most experienced spymasters Maxwell Knight, who still had many contacts amongst the British Fascists, and who understood the workings of Fascism very well. Increasingly, as war approached, it became clear that the new breed of Fascists posed as great a threat to Great Britain as the Communists. Whilst Knight continued to run his network of agents within the British Communists, he now began to recruit agents to penetrate the inner circles of the various Fascist organisations in Britain.

There is no doubt that Knight was a good recruiter and handler of agents. Probably, he regarded his agents in much the same way as he did his selection of exotic pets – he cared about them, understood them, and looked after them. The work of his agents in identifying the most dangerous of British Fascists, and finding out what they were up to, was undoubtedly a major contribution to Great Britain's survival and eventual victory in World War Two. He, like Major General Sir Colin Gubbins, the head of the wartime Special Operations Executive, believed in the use of women agents 'on the front line'. Knight would approach someone who he thought would make a satisfactory agent, generally from amongst his acquaintances, and would ask them to help him. So charming was he that they generally did. The technique that he recommended to his agents was that they should never go hunting for information, but once they were mingling with the right people (their targets), they should simply be patient and let the information came to them. It almost always did.

Knight and his wife Gwladys led mostly separate lives after his return to London in 1929. She continued to run the Royal Oak;

he would go down at weekends when possible. In 1936, Gwladys, staying at the Royal Overseas League in London, took an overdose of painkillers and died. Knight was not with her at the time. The coroner returned an open verdict, being neither satisfied of suicide or accident. Knight re-married in 1937 to a lady called Lois Coplestone, but the marriage did not last. He married his third wife, Susi Barnes, in 1944, and she survived him, after a marriage of more than twenty-three years.

When war eventually broke out in September 1939, Knight was given an Army commission on what was called the General List – used for those who were not attached to a regiment. He ended the war as Major Maxwell Knight. Thereafter, Knight worked on at MI5 until a problem with angina caused his early retirement. He wrote numerous books about animals and wildlife, became a popular radio broadcaster, and eventually died of heart failure on 24 January 1968, seven years after his retirement.

However, it was with the coming of war that the challenge really began for Maxwell Knight. Throughout most of his career as a spymaster, the Communists had been his target. Only over the few years before the war had he become involved in spying on the British Fascists. Yet he, his agents and MI5 were really the only weapon that Great Britain possessed against the Fascist extremists within its borders. Knight's agents assumed a vital importance, and their intelligence would in due course make the difference between freedom or imprisonment for many leading British Fascists. Only in 1944, when Knight was busy courting and marrying his third wife, did MI5 let its guard down. Everyone relaxed, thinking that the war was won for the Allies – except Adolf Hitler.

Knight's agents will variously appear later in this story, and this book is not concerned with his infiltration of Communist circles, only Fascists. Mrs Marjorie Norah Mackie née Amor,[2] a very ordinary middle-aged single mother, was one of his most successful agents. Mrs Mackie was separated from her husband, and had lost touch with him. In 1931, she had taken part in a political and religious organisation called the Christian Protest Movement, which condemned the persecution of religious bodies in Soviet Russia. She remained with the movement until 1935, and then left.[3] As a Christian and anti-Bolshevik group, the Christian Protest Movement attracted support from a number of British Fascists, including Captain and Mrs Ramsay, whom Mrs Mackie had met. In late June 1939, when Captain and Mrs Ramsay were becoming a threat to security through their Fascist activities, Knight approached Mrs Mackie, and asked for her help. Because she was known to the Ramsays, Knight suggested to Mrs Mackie that she might be able to re-establish her contact with them, and penetrate their Fascist organisation on his behalf. Quite how Knight persuaded her is not clear, but Mrs Mackie agreed to become his agent, and became one of his best. Knight would always make friends of his agents once they started to work for him, and would carefully build up his relationship with them. Over the years that followed, Marjorie Mackie brought Knight a broad selection of very useful information. Her very ordinariness – she was a cookery demonstrator in her working life – opened many doors.

Another key agent was Eric Roberts, a bank clerk. Whilst Marjorie Mackie, in her work as an agent, played herself – a chatty middle-aged mum – and simply added on some fiercely pro-Nazi views, Eric Roberts took on a very different role. From bank clerk, he became a supposed Gestapo agent working covertly in Britain, using the false name of 'Jack King'. Roberts carried off the role with great success, entrapping a number of would-be German Fifth Columnists and spies, the most prominent of whom was a certain Marita Perigoe, a woman of mixed Swedish and German heritage, whose husband was interned on the Isle of Man as a member of the British Union of Fascists.[4] 'Jack King' received regular information from Perigoe and her friends over a long period. It was information that they thought he was passing back to Germany, but of course in reality it went to Maxwell Knight at MI5. Perigoe and her associates collected all sorts of intelligence that might be relevant to Britain's enemies – the position of anti-aircraft guns, the defences of airfields and the like. When the Germans dropped bombs in the area of targets they had named, Perigoe and her circle always presumed that they had been aiming at the targets that they had supplied to 'Jack King', and lamented their inaccuracy. A report from Roberts on 19 April 1943 of a meeting that he had with Perigoe, and two other Fascists called Nancy Brown and Eileen Gleave (a contact of Arnold Leese's), reads:

'Nancy Brown said the attempt to get the A.R.P. [Air Raid Precautions] Headquarters next to the municipal market, described as a suitable target on one of her previous visits, failed by a narrow margin. One fire engine or A.R.P. transport vehicle was wrecked by a splinter. A nearby school clinic was hit and Nancy Brown said with a grin that one expectant mother was killed, two girls badly injured, and a clerk and two children killed. I looked in vain at the faces of these three women for any signs of contrition. Nancy Brown looked a fine, healthy, specimen of an English woman, but it was obvious that the deaths of these people meant absolutely nothing to her. I thought of the excellent impression that this woman would make on an Advisory Committee [for Detention] or the Home Office or a Jury. She sat there pleased and happy to think that the news she had given me had resulted in the deaths and damage of that last raid . . . Brown next gave some news about Hastings with great satisfaction. She said that in Hastings and St Leonards 1,000 people were homeless and 400 houses were uninhabitable as a result of a recent raid. Eastbourne, particularly in the Victoria Place area, had also suffered heavily.'[5]

There can be no doubt that these Nazi women were exulting in the belief that their information had brought about these deaths and this suffering. In fact, the information they supplied to 'Jack King' went nowhere.

The large and well-known German firm of Siemens-Schuckert had subsidiaries in many countries, and it was generally believed within MI5 that Siemens ran a vast international espionage operation on behalf of the German government. In Britain its subsidiary was Siemens-Schuckert (Great Britain) Limited. In August 1939, before the actual outbreak of war, most German nationals working for Siemens had returned to Germany, and after the outbreak of war, others, together with some dual nationals, were interned. All pro-Nazi activity at Siemens went extremely quiet but Knight still targeted Siemens, and began to gather, through his agents, valuable information about those who remained there.

The information gathered by Roberts (described in one report as a 'genius') and other agents made quite clear that, whatever the British government might feel about the war, even in the summer of 1943, four years into the struggle, the British Fascists still intended to take over by force when the time was finally right. The Fascists believed that anti-Semitism and anti-Communism were on the rise in Britain, and that it would eventually be realised throughout Europe that Germany was right in its battle against 'Jewish Bolshevism'. An Allied victory would, they argued, be a victory for the Jews. Thus, even if Germany lost the war, the British Fascists hoped that their time would still come.

Chapter 6

Captain Archibald Maule Ramsay

Head of the Right Club

Under the Defence Regulations passed at the outbreak of war, there was a power to detain British citizens under Regulation 18B if there was 'reasonable cause to believe that a person had recently been concerned in acts prejudicial to the public safety or the defence of the Realm, or in preparation or instigation of such acts, and that by reason thereof it is necessary to exercise control over him'. Captain Archibald Maule Ramsay, MP,[1] was arrested on 23 May 1940, shortly after Churchill became Prime Minister, and was held in Brixton Prison for more than four years.

Captain Ramsay's country home was Kelly Castle, near Arbroath in Scotland. His London home was at 24 Onslow Square. Born on 4 May 1894, at the time of his arrest he was therefore forty-six years old. He was described by the press as a 'tall, handsome, eagle looking man, scion of one of the oldest families in Scotland'.[2] Ramsay had been commissioned into the Coldstream Guards before the First World War, and served until, in 1916, he was seriously wounded and sent home. He was eventually formally invalided out of the Army in 1920. It is of relevance that he was a military man, who knew what military action entailed, and had undergone military training. Captain Ramsay was known to his family and friends as 'Jock'. He was married and had four sons. In 1931, he had been elected as a Member of Parliament for the Conservative and Unionist Party in South Midlothian and Peebles, Scotland, and had been re-elected, and remained the MP for that constituency when war broke out.

Ramsay had for a long time held right-wing views, and in May 1939, with war looming, he formed an organisation called the Right Club. The objects of the club were said to be directed against Jews, Freemasons and Communists. However, according to what was said against it at his Detention Appeal Hearing, the Club was designed 'to spread subversive and defeatist views amongst the population of Great Britain, and to obstruct the war effort of Great Britain'. In reality, the club was intended to do far more than that. It aimed to overthrow the British government when the time was right, and replace it with a pro-Nazi Fascist government. Ramsay appealed against his detention, and when he appeared before the Appeal Committee that had been set up to consider the cases of those who challenged their detention, Ramsay said that he had been convinced for ten years that international Jewry was a real menace to the peace and happiness of the world.[3] However, he denied that the Right Club was subversive or intended to undermine the war effort.

In truth, Ramsay hoped one day to lead a Fascist government in Britain.[4] He was quite happy to work with any fellow Fascist, and indeed, according to one of them, Oliver Gilbert, he also worked with a Japanese spy called Eguchi.[5]

The Right Club was an intelligence organisation, infiltrating the military, government departments, and the government itself. Once war broke out, the club went underground, and kept its activities totally secret. The membership of the club was kept entirely confidential by Ramsay, there were no public meetings, and there was no literature explaining the objects of the Right Club, or confirming its existence. It was therefore the very opposite of Mosley's British Union of Fascists or Leese's Imperial Fascist League, and was more dangerous than both because of its secrecy. The membership list for the Right Club was kept by Ramsay in a locked leather-bound book. Some of the members' names indicate the true nature of the organisation. Members were divided into Wardens (the most senior), Stewards, Yeomen, Keepers and Freemen. William Joyce was a 'Warden member'. Amongst the other members known to MI5 were men called Richard Findlay and H. W. Luttman-Johnson, both of whom were known to be strongly pro-German. Ramsay sought secretly to penetrate both government departments and rival right-wing organisations, so that he would have club members strategically placed for the coming overthrow of the British government.

When Marjorie Mackie was tasked to penetrate Ramsay's organisation, she began with a phone call to Mrs Ramsay, reminding Mrs Ramsay of who she was, and asking for a meeting with her husband. Mrs Ramsay invited her round to tea a few days later. Only Mrs Ramsay was at that tea, not her husband. It was a form of screening. Mrs Ramsay was the Honourable Mrs Ismay Lucretia Mary Maule-Ramsay, a daughter of Viscount Gormanston and also a dedicated Fascist. She was born on 29 October 1882, and was some twelve years older than her husband. She was particularly well connected in British society. She had two children by a previous marriage and four by Ramsay. She, like Ramsay himself, was extremely anti-Jewish, and may have been partly responsible for indoctrinating Ramsay with Fascist views. She was convinced that the United Kingdom had been deliberately manoeuvred into war by 'the hidden hand of Jewry', in the hope that a war between Germany and the British Empire would remove the two main obstacles to a plan for world domination by 'International Jewry'. She favoured the Nazis because Hitler was committed to doing something about the Jews.[6]

Marjorie Mackie reported that Mrs Ramsay's conversation was 'violently anti-Semitic and anti-Masonic'. Mrs Ramsay described the Right Club, saying that its purpose was to propagate the extreme views that she had been expressing. She confirmed that the membership list of the Right Club was kept in a special locked book, and that Mrs Mackie's connection with the Right Club, if she joined, would not become known – its membership was secret. At Mrs Ramsay's suggestion, Mrs Mackie attended some meetings of the equally right-wing Nordic League, and in August 1939 she joined the Right Club. Knight had successfully infiltrated his agent. Between then and the outbreak of war on 3 September 1939, Mrs Mackie attended two further meetings of the Nordic League, and one of the Link, the right-wing organisation of which Admiral Sir Barry Domvile (of whom more later) was chairman.

When the war against Germany began, Captain Ramsay claimed that he had closed the Right Club, but in truth he continued to hold secret meetings at his home, and kept trying to infiltrate government departments. Ramsay used the false name of Freeman when he felt the need for additional secrecy, as did his wife

Mrs Mackie finally met Captain Ramsay again in late September. They met at his mother's house at 17 Sussex Square. Ramsay confirmed to Mrs Mackie that the Right Club was working on, and had not closed, but said that he had now stopped having any public meetings. He stressed the secrecy of the membership list, and said that he was the only one who held a copy. Ramsay asked Mrs Mackie what work she had done in World War One, which led to a statement by him that he had Right Club members in most government departments. He also asked Mrs Mackie if there was any chance of her getting work in the Censorship Department or the Foreign Office, since they were the two departments in which the Right Club had no agents. Mrs Mackie said that she had many friends in military circles, and she would try.

Before leaving, Mrs Mackie asked Ramsay whether, in the event of a right-wing revolution breaking out in Britain, Right Club members would be asked to follow Sir Oswald Mosley. Ramsay replied: 'Certainly not, before such a situation arises, I shall be in touch with all the members and you will then be told who is to be your leader.' He clearly intended to be 'the Leader' himself.

Mrs Mackie had succeeded in penetrating the Right Club, and her reports back to Maxwell Knight became of the greatest importance. Knight duly arranged that she should be given a job in Military Censorship, and she started there on 4 October 1939. Mrs Mackie reported to the Ramsays that she had got a post in Military Censorship, and they were delighted. She was invited to attend meetings each week of the Inner Circle of the Right Club, which met at the Ramsays' house in Onslow Square. The excellent Mrs Mackie had got to the centre of the Right Club.

When Ramsay was finally arrested and detained in May 1940, a poem was found at his home which it seems he himself had written, and which reflected his view of Britain when war broke out in September.[7] There was a note on the document: 'Written the day after war was declared on Germany.' The poem was written on House of Commons embossed notepaper, and is a parody of the patriotic song 'Land of Hope and Glory'. It reads:

> Land of dope and Jewry,
> Land that once was free,
> All the Jew boys praise thee,
> Whilst they plunder thee,
> Poorer still and poorer,
> Grow thy true-born sons,
> Faster still and faster,
> They're sent to feed the guns.
>
> Land of Jewish finance,
> Fooled by Jewish lies
> In press and books and movies,
> While our birth right dies.
> Longer still and longer,
> Is the rope they get,
> But – by the God of Battles
> T'will serve to hang them yet.

No doubt Ramsay hoped that it would be sung by his 'patriotic' supporters, when hunting down the Jews, and the British government that embraced and supported them. The last couplet of the poem speaks for itself – Ramsay clearly contemplated violence (the 'God of Battles'), and hoped to hang the Jews, but also, it seems, hoped to hang those in the British government who had supported war with Germany.

A pamphlet entitled 'War Alphabet' identifies those whom Ramsay and his Right Club selected for particular hatred. Winston Churchill was one of them. The 'Alphabet' lists both those that Ramsay supported (H is for Hitler) and those that he would no doubt have liked to have hanged: 'C stands for Churchill, B better describes this blood-thirsty braggart, his boasts and his jibes.'

Another crude pamphlet[8] gives the words of another song:

Oh! England's heroes show your grit
The LEADER calls to fight the Jew,
The hour has struck: so do your bit
To prove that you are Freemen true.
We're free at last: We're free at last:
We've crushed the snake within our land.
We're marching on: We're marching on:
Saluting with our outstretched hand [the Nazi salute].

Ramsay was aware that MI5 was watching him, and took all possible steps to hide his activities. Nonetheless, Maxwell Knight had managed to infiltrate Ramsay's organisation with relative ease. Marjorie Mackie was code-named M/Y – the M was a reference to Knight's own Christian name, the Y was what identified the particular agent, Mrs Mackie. Mrs Mackie's reports persuaded Knight that it was necessary to take the Right Club very seriously, and with Mrs Mackie's help, he infiltrated two other agents into the Right Club set-up. These were both young ladies: Joan Miller and Helen de Monck, who was Belgian. From what he learned from his agents, Knight knew that both the Fascists and the Communists were clearly contemplating an uprising to overthrow the British government, of which Ramsay, as an elected Conservative and Unionist MP, was a part.

Although Ramsay had always disagreed with Oswald Mosley, when Mosley held a meeting of all the extreme right-wing leaders on 9 November 1939, with a view to discussing means of collaboration in their common aim, Ramsay attended. He was quite prepared to use Mosley's Fascists for his own purposes, and indeed needed them, but he was not prepared to accept Mosley's leadership. Ramsay had told Mrs Mackie that in the event of an invasion of England, or a Bolshevik uprising, the Right Club would take over and govern the country. Ramsay clearly hoped for a British civil war, saying on one occasion: 'I would welcome civil war, with shots in the streets.' As an ex-soldier who had served in World War One, Ramsay knew exactly what war meant, and saw a civil war as his way to power.

Once Mrs Mackie was embedded in the Military Censorship Department, Ramsay asked her to try to find somebody who was working in Military Intelligence, which was housed in the same building as Censorship. In due course, with Knight's help, Mrs Mackie was able to do this. Mrs Mackie's own flat was used from time to time for meetings of the Inner Circle of the Right Club, and in early March a flat was rented at 24 Manson Mews, with Mrs Mackie as the tenant. Mrs Mackie witnessed open discussions between the Ramsays and their friends about the possibility of MI5 monitoring their activities. They discussed with Mrs Mackie who amongst their circle might be working for MI5, and Mrs Mackie suggested: 'We ought to be more discreet in our activities.' It was then agreed that whenever referring to Captain Ramsay, they should use the name of Freeman for him. Ramsay himself said that he had no intention of allowing MI5 or Scotland Yard to know anything about his activities! Mrs Ramsay was worried about the interception of post about the Right Club when she was at the family home, Kelly Castle, Arbroath. It was agreed by Mrs Ramsay and Mrs Mackie that 'secret' post for Scotland would be addressed in the fictitious name of 'Mrs R. Mackie, c/o GPO, Dundee', and that an innocent letter would be sent to Kelly Castle including a coded sentence: 'Give my love to Dundee', to indicate that there was a letter to be collected.

On 5 April 1940, for the first time a meeting of the Right Club was held at 24 Manson Mews, the flat rented for Mrs Mackie. This was now to be the Club Room for the Right Club, and a password had been invented: 'Freeman' (the same as Ramsay's false name). About twenty-five people attended the first meeting.

Marjorie Mackie was able to pass on to Maxwell Knight the details of Ramsay's more significant associates. He was in regular contact with Anna Wolkoff, a White Russian exile living in London who was strongly pro-German and anti-Jew. Mrs Mackie reported that Wolkoff spoke very freely to Ramsay, although she (Wolkoff) insisted that he did not pass on to his wife what she told him, or: 'We shall all end up in the Tower' (meaning in the Tower of London as traitors). Wolkoff was working actively for Nazi Germany and in the early part of the war, while the Italians remained neutral, it was believed that Wolkoff was passing information to Germany via Italy. Another possible line of communication was through the German Legation in neutral Eire. Wolkoff was arrested in due course, and in October 1940 she was convicted and sentenced to ten years' penal servitude for her treachery. One of the things that she did was to pass on confidential information to William Joyce, for use in his propaganda broadcasts to Britain. Joyce, of course, was also a member of the Right Club.

On Saturday 20 April 1940, at a meeting of the Inner Circle of the Right Club, Mrs Mackie asked Ramsay to explain the policy of the club. Ramsay stated that penetration in every direction was the keynote – he wanted cells of his members everywhere, in all government departments, and in every right-wing movement, so that whoever eventually took power, the Right Club could take things over from them. 'For example, if Mosley came to power we should have someone in his movement who could take over control from them [the BUF].' Ramsay said that it was never his policy to let his right hand know what his left hand did. Because of these policies, said Ramsay, he had been able to lead MI5 and Scotland Yard quite astray, so that neither knew anything about his real activities. There is no doubt at all that Mrs Mackie had the Ramsays totally and utterly fooled

In early May 1940, Anna Wolkoff, still at liberty, introduced Ramsay to Tyler Kent, a young American coding officer working at the US Embassy in London. The United States was still neutral at this point. Kent, however, was believed to be entirely pro-Nazi and anti-Jew. For some time he had been stealing confidential documents from the embassy, and had shown many of them to Anna Wolkoff. He was also known to have met a man believed to be a Gestapo agent, Ludwig Ernst Matthias, when Matthias had visited England. Matthias was known to MI5 as a German spy, and was closely watched. Kent met Matthias in a room at the Cumberland Hotel,

London, in October 1939. Matthias was followed by an MI5 agent, and was seen to leave the hotel room carrying a bulky envelope. What Kent told, or handed, to Matthias is not known. Evidence has subsequently emerged that Matthias (and Kent) may not have been working for the Germans but for the Russians, who in 1939 were still a threat, and not yet an ally. In any case, as a US Embassy employee, Kent enjoyed diplomatic immunity, so that although he could be observed, he could not be interfered with.

Following his introduction to Kent, Ramsay visited Kent's flat, where presumably he was given access to some of the documents that Kent had stolen. He left in Kent's custody the locked secret ledger that contained the names of the members of the Right Club, believing that Kent would be safe from arrest because of his diplomatic immunity. It is to be inferred also that Kent could, if necessary, pass the list of members (who were presumably all good Fascists) to the enemy. However, after his arrest, Ramsay was to say that he had only left the register of members with Kent because he was afraid his home might be raided by Jews or Communists, and that the register of members might be stolen.

In due course, MI5 presented its case against Tyler Kent to the United States Embassy, and to the US Ambassador, Joe Kennedy (father of John Kennedy, who much later was to become President of the United States). Confronted with what MI5 had discovered about him, the United States waived Kent's diplomatic immunity and he was arrested. He stood trial with Wolkoff in October 1940. He was convicted and sentenced to seven years' penal servitude.

When Tyler Kent was arrested, his flat was searched, and the locked ledger of Right Club members which Ramsay had left there was found. It was still locked, but was opened, and examined. Presuming that it was accurate (and it carefully recorded the membership fees paid or promised by each member), it demonstrated the power of the Right Club. There were a number of peers of the realm listed, including the Duke of Wellington, Lord Carnegie and Lord Semphill, and many others in significant positions in British society and government, as well as a number of military men. At the back of the book there was an extract, which listed Members of Parliament who had signed up to the Right Club. There were eleven of them: Peter Agnew, Sir Samuel Chapman, Sir J. Edmondson, Provost Hunter, Sir Ernest Hunter, Lord Colum-Stewart, C. I. Kerr, John McKie, Harold Mitchell, the Honourable John Stourton, and Mrs Tate.[9] It is a fair assumption that all the members of the Right Club shared Ramsay's right-wing views. Hopefully not all would have been prepared to use violence against the legitimate British government, but no doubt the MPs who had signed up to the Right Club hoped to take office in a Fascist government. The outbreak of war reduced the number of members of the Right Club serving in the House of Commons. Colonel C. I. Kerr left the House of Commons in 1940, moving to the Lords as Baron Teviot. Peter Agnew (later Sir Peter Agnew, Baronet), a Conservative representing the Camborne constituency, returned to the Royal Navy in August 1939, and served throughout the war, before resuming his seat in the House.

Ramsay's wife and three of his sons, Robert (Bob), Alexander and George, were listed as members, as was William Joyce. Ramsay's cousin Mrs Newenham was also a radical Fascist, who listened regularly to a Nazi radio station called the 'New British Broadcasting Station', and passed on its propaganda and intimidating broadcasts until her detention under Regulation 18B on 2 July 1940. Such was the secrecy of the Club that, with the possible exception of the Inner Circle, an individual member of the Club would not be told who the other members were, but would only be put in contact with those working close to him or her. Many women were members. Both sexes could work for the overthrow of the British government.

One of the obvious dangers to security was that Ramsay, as an MP, enjoyed parliamentary privilege in relation to anything that he said publicly in the House of Commons. Thus, any sensitive and confidential information stolen by Kent and shown to him could be disclosed with impunity by Ramsay in the House of Commons. The correspondence Kent stole included communications between Prime Minister Churchill and President Roosevelt, which were highly confidential.

On 23 May 1940, Ramsay was arrested and detained under Regulation 18B (1A) of the Emergency Powers (Defence) Regulations. Amongst the things that he said to the police officers who arrested him was that Hitler was pursuing the right policy against the Jews, and that Churchill (whom he hated, and who was responsible now for his arrest) was Jew-ridden. He appealed against his detention, but his appeal was dismissed, and he remained in custody under the detention order. He was held in Brixton Prison.

Maxwell Knight's excellent agent Marjorie Mackie remained in place after Ramsay's arrest, masquerading as a friend of both Mrs Ramsay and of Ramsay himself. It very soon became clear that Mrs Ramsay was in no way prepared to sit back and accept her husband's imprisonment. She immediately began to plan his escape. Brixton Prison was and is an impressively secure facility, which the author has visited many times, but nonetheless Mrs Ramsay expected that before long she would be able to take advantage of one of three things to free her husband: disorganisation as a result of German bombing; a German invasion; or a 'revolution' in Britain aimed at overthrowing the elected government. Clearly, she expected to be able to use members of the Right Club to help her break into the prison, and also talked of being supported by some of the British Army, a comment which suggests that the Right Club had penetrated the British armed forces. She planned that at the right moment she and her supporters would blow open the gates of Brixton prison with bombs – to which she and Ramsay's followers clearly had access, perhaps through their Army contacts. Mrs Ramsay's only concern was that the authorities would send all the detainees to Canada, as they were doing with many enemy aliens, before she could get her husband out. As she put it: 'My only hope is that they will not have time to do that before the Germans are here.'

Mrs Ramsay and her son Bob were allowed to visit Ramsay in his cell in Brixton, and she commented: 'Bob and I have taken note of every detail on the way to Jock's room, and of everything we can see on our visits. We shall not fail, and I long to see the Home

Office people swinging and hanging from lampposts.' Mrs Ramsay's desire to see public lynchings echoes the Vehmic justice of Hitler's hangmen. She clearly longed to be an executioner herself. Those who had caused Ramsay's arrest and detention were to be killed, if Mrs Ramsay got her way. Happily, neither the Blitz on London, nor the bombing that followed it, gave Mrs Ramsay the opportunity that she was looking for, and Ramsay remained in Brixton prison for more than four years, becoming more embittered by the day.

There is chilling confirmation of the real aims of the Right Club in a book written by Joan Miller, one of the three agents that Knight had inserted into the club, which was published in 1986, shortly after her death.[10] She said that, in the summer of 1940

'   The Right Club was becoming increasingly incautious about expressing its views. With a German invasion expected at any moment, those who had all along supported Germany's claims believed themselves in a strong position. The Society was engaged in compiling a list of prominent opponents to the Axis cause: if you got your name on this list you could expect to be strung up from a lamppost once the country was in German hands. I was consulted, I remember, over the question of who was to be classed as a fit for lynching candidate.'

Brixton was the prison used for many of the leading figures who were detained under Regulation 18B, and the detainees were allowed periods of association there. Thus, Britain's enemies had the chance to gather and to discuss their dreams regularly. Ramsay came to know some of his fellow Fascist detainees very well, including Arnold Leese and Ben Greene. It is often said of young criminals in our prison system today that to gather them together in custody simply enables them to learn from each other how to defeat the law. The gathering together of the Fascist detainees probably served the same purpose.

The intelligence on Mrs Ramsay's activities after her husband's arrest, supplied by Marjorie Mackie, makes clear that Ramsay's detention had not brought the activities of the Right Club to an end. Clearly the club still had a number of active members, and access to explosives and probably firearms. They were hoping for a German invasion or an internal revolution or civil war. Both Mrs Ramsay's reference to Home Office officials swinging from lampposts, and Joan Miller's account of the Right Club's list of those to be lynched, make clear the sort of justice that the new Fascist government of the Right Club would mete out – the justice of the lynch mob, a British version of Nazi Vehmic justice.

Mrs Ramsay was surprised that she herself was not detained along with her husband, since several other female members of the Right Club had been arrested. She made sure that those of the Right Club who were still at liberty remained united in their aims, and that the Club did not fall apart. She visited those in custody regularly. She kept the secret papers of the Right Club safely hidden, so that they were not discovered when MI5 searched her home. She remained entirely pro-German, despite the dreadful German Blitz of London and other British cities. She talked openly about her belief that Britain could not survive much longer, saying on 17 October 1942 that Britain could not last out for more than another year, that there would be a terrible crisis, and that then her husband and his friends would take over the reconstruction (along Fascist lines) of the country.

Mrs Ramsay was extremely well connected in high society as a result of her father, the late Viscount Gormanston, and her first husband, the late Lord Ninian Crichton Stuart, a younger son of the Marquess of Bute. Her second husband, Ramsay, had, of course, very many political contacts in the House of Commons and the House of Lords. Those who had joined the Right Club were in position, both before and after Ramsay's arrest, throughout the various departments of state. Mrs Ramsay canvassed all her contacts in an attempt to have them bring pressure upon the Home Office to release her husband from detention, but her attempts were to no avail. However, even with Ramsay and several of his 'Inner Circle' in prison, Mrs Ramsay made sure that the Right Club remained active and very secret. The club was ready to help any German forces who might invade Great Britain.

As with all detainees, Ramsay's position was reviewed from time to time. Ramsay did not help himself. Having lost his appeal against detention, he decided to take legal action against the *New York Times*, through the British courts, claiming that it had defamed him in an article it published about the Tyler Kent case. The *New York Times* claimed that Ramsay had transmitted treasonable information held by Kent to the German Legation in Dublin, and thus was a traitor himself. Ramsay sued for libel. He fought his case in the High Court of England and Wales in front of Mr Justice Atkinson, and as a result of the action and the evidence given in court, much of his past activity was made public. Mr Justice Atkinson dismissed his case, saying, amongst other things, in his judgment:

> 'I am convinced that Captain Ramsay's claim to loyalty is false. He shared many of the political views of the Nazi regime, approving their propaganda, endeavouring to persuade [British] people that they were fighting only in the interests of and at the dictation of Jewry . . . I am convinced that Hitler would call Captain Ramsay a friend. He was disloyal in heart and soul to our King, our Government and our people.'[11]

Despite all this, Ramsay remained an MP. The *Daily Record* newspaper, in commenting on Mr Justice Atkinson's judgment, remarked '. . . and we are still paying Captain Ramsay MP £600 a year [his MP's salary]'. When the German invasion finally came, he no doubt wanted the advantage of being able to say that he was an elected member of the House of Commons as he seized the reins of government.

In June 1941, Ramsay received one of a number of regular visits from his secretary Ruth Erskine. These meetings were recorded and reported to MI5. On this occasion, Ramsay told Erskine that a German Blitz, followed by an invasion of Britain, was imminent, adding: 'When we 18Bs [detainees] get out, we shall have Churchill and his crowd before a tribunal, then they will know about it!' In a later meeting on 17 January 1942, Ramsay told Erskine that although he expected to stay in prison until the end of the war, when he was released the Home Secretary would take his place. Ramsay obviously still believed that the Germans would win the war.

In mid-1943, Ramsay's detention was reviewed. Others had been set free, on the basis that, bearing in mind the improved military situation, they could no longer be regarded as a genuine threat to Britain's security. However, a report on him reads: 'This man, though he sincerely regards himself as the most loyal and patriotic of British subjects, is led by a morbid obsession with British Jewry and international finance to adopt views and courses which in effect are both traitorous and dangerous. He should remain in detention.'[12] Comment was made that Ramsay was a conspirator who believed that it was the part of a loyal British subject to purge the country of Jews, and that Hitler had no designs on the British Empire, but only wished to destroy Jewish control in the world. T. M. Shelford of MI5 wrote in a memorandum dated 29 September 1943 that Captain Ramsay would come out of detention a very embittered man.

However, finally, on 26 September 1944, Home Secretary Herbert Morrison (whom Ramsay no doubt would have liked to have seen hanging from a lamppost, or at least locked away in Brixton Prison) decided that it was at last safe to release Ramsay. Ramsay was, after all, still a serving MP and he had been convicted of no crime. When he was interned in May 1940, Ramsay had resisted demands for him to resign as an MP, and despite later calls during his detention, he had always refused. Thus, he was still, four years later, an Honourable Member of Parliament. Vigorously attacked in the House of Commons for his decision to release Ramsay, the Home Secretary said:

> 'Hitherto, I have not felt I would be justified in ordering his
> release, but the success of arms of the United Nations and the
> certainty that the forces of evil arrayed against us are doomed
> to complete overthrow, have created a situation in which I, as
> the Minister responsible for internal security would be justified
> in taking this step, which would not have been justifiable but
> for the improvement in our national fortune.'[13]

Ramsay's release came as a complete surprise to him. He reached home in Onslow Square in the evening of 26 September 1944. Some others still remained in detention, but Ramsay was the last of the Fascists highlighted in this book to be released. Ramsay, Greene, Leese, Beckett and Mosley were all free men again by the end of September 1944. Time would show how wrong Herbert Morrison was to feel that victory was secure.

Because Ramsay was still an MP, he enjoyed certain rights and privileges which made it difficult for MI5 to fully monitor his activities. He was entitled to confidentiality in his parliamentary work, and because of this, MI5 did not apply for a Home Office warrant to intercept his mail or his telephone calls. However, they had in place a number of intercepts on other leading Fascists, and were therefore able to monitor some of Ramsay's contact with them – because of incoming phone calls and incoming post at their addresses from Ramsay.

Although his wife claimed that Ramsay's health was broken, Ramsay made immediate contact with many of his old Fascist friends. One of them, Ben Greene, was tremendously excited at Ramsay's release, saying that it had come at 'exactly the right moment'. Greene referred to Ramsay as a 'Man of Destiny', and 'the natural leader whom everybody had been waiting for'.

A significant question is how Ramsay now regarded the British government? Did he still want to bring 'Churchill and his crowd' before a tribunal to answer for their deeds? Did he share his wife's views that those responsible for his detention should be left 'swinging and hanging from lampposts'? All the indications are that Ramsay had in no way softened his Fascist views, and agreed with every word that his wife had said.

The day after his release, on the morning of 27 September, Ramsay went straight down to the House of Commons, where an MI5 report later recorded that he received a more favourable reception than he had anticipated.[14] He later wrote to a fellow Fascist: 'On the whole they have been very nice to me, and some have gone out of their way to be so.' Ramsay estimated that about 20 per cent of the House were very sympathetic, about 20 per cent hostile, and the rest indifferent. However, Ramsay had always been a master of secrecy, and there appears to be no record of what was really important – how many of the eleven MPs who were listed as having joined the Right Club were still in the House, and still secretly sympathetic to the Fascist cause? It is necessary to remember that the House of Lords Chamber (in which the Commons was still sitting) is not large. Once a free man, Ramsay was able to sit within yards of Prime Minister Churchill, Home Secretary Morrison, and the rest of 'Churchill's crowd'. He would be physically extremely close to the men whom he hated, and who had been responsible for his four years of impotent imprisonment.

Chapter 7

John Beckett

Another dangerous Nazi was John Beckett, an ex-MP who had become disillusioned with left-wing politics, and had veered violently to the right. Born on 11 October 1894, Beckett had served in the 1st King's Shropshire Light Infantry in World War One, was wounded twice, and discharged as unfit for further service in 1917 with a very excellent character. Beckett worked for a time alongside William Joyce in Mosley's British Union of Fascists, but then left to found what he called the National Socialist League. That did not last long. In April 1939, Beckett and Ben Greene, launched yet another pro-Nazi party in Britain, this one known as the British People's Party (BPP). The President of the British People's Party was the Marquis of Tavistock, later the Duke of Bedford. The BPP launched a manifesto entitled the 'Campaign against War and Usury' – opposing the war with Germany and vilifying Jews. Ben Greene was the party's treasurer. The handbill advertising the first meeting of the campaign included the statement: 'Every effort must clearly be made now if any effective alternative is to be provided to the warmongering politician by whom we are now misgoverned.'

In June 1939, the BPP put up a candidate in a by-election in Hythe, but he polled only 516 votes out of 22,000, and the BPP forfeited their deposit. Democracy was clearly not the way forward for the BPP.

On 5 September 1939, Great Britain having declared war on Germany, Beckett wrote to one of his supporters in Scotland, Captain Luttman-Johnson: 'It is vitally necessary that all those who remain sane should be organised and ready for the moment when a real fight for truth and justice may be made.'

Later, Beckett became Secretary of the pro-Nazi British Council for the Christian Settlement of Europe, which was run by Admiral Sir Barry Domvile. He was involved in intensive efforts to obtain contacts in the British armed forces, in order that, when the time was ripe, they would: 'turn their rifles in the right direction'.[1] Beckett was entirely ruthless. A report dated 9 January 1940 states that: 'Beckett wants the Duke of Bedford (aged 92) to die as quickly as possible so that [the Marquis of] Tavistock would inherit about half a million pounds and get a seat in the House of Lords.' It was not very long before Beckett got his wish. According to Katherine Greene, Ben Greene's sister, the British Council for the Christian Settlement of Europe was intended to be the organ used to stop the war, and then the British People's Party was to obtain political power. The British People's Party was to be the 'machine for altering the present system of Machiavellian economy and government'.

The name of Lady Clare Annesley appears in Beckett's MI5 file in January 1940, as a supporter of another new organisation called the Parliament Christian and White Brotherhood. Beckett and Tavistock were invited to sit on its council. Lady Clare was not a member of either the People's Party or the British Council for the Christian Settlement of Europe, but did send in a contribution of fifteen shillings. She was in touch with Beckett on many occasions, and attended some public meetings. She will feature again later in this book.

A report of a meeting of the British Council for the Christian Settlement of Europe on 13 January 1940 says of Beckett:

> 'It is quite certain that he has been in communication with highly-placed members of the German Government and is now engaged in getting [peace] terms which would be accepted in Berlin and which might be swallowed by the British Public, and he wants it done before the big [German] offensive starts. He keeps referring to the "time factor". I am quite certain it is not mere propaganda, he is quite definitely negotiating first and then he will use the British Council and the People's Party

to put the terms already discussed over, and stage a situation where, the public being willing, there will be an organised uproar if negotiations break down. I think his activities are at present confined to direct negotiations on these lines. He could get communications backwards and forwards through his channels.'

Beckett succeeded in making contact with an armourer in the Royal Air Force called Dick Sheppard, who was stationed at Croydon. Sheppard, however, is described by MI5 as seeming sincere and straight, connected to Beckett because of his political ideas rather than through any fondness for Hitler. Nonetheless, Sheppard was an armourer, and Beckett and his fellow Fascists, having hooked Sheppard, no doubt wanted to exploit him for revolutionary purposes.

On 28 January 1940, Beckett was recorded as speaking, at a public meeting, of 'the corruption in the conduct of the war and the necessity of ultimately removing the people with the power to commit evil'. A few days later he made what is described as a 'short ranting speech', in which he frequently referred to 'international financiers and exotic and debased scum'. Such was the level of hatred in the meeting that one of the speakers, Professor Darwen Fox, suggested that the British government was perfectly capable of painting swastikas on British planes, and then bombing the East End with those planes, in order to bamboozle the British public into believing that the Germans had done it. This was only months before the London Blitz began.

In mid-February 1940, Beckett began to write and publish a newsletter called *Headline*. He did so under the name of John Stone. The purpose of the newsletter was to put across a pacifist, anti-government message. However, an intelligence report in early March 1940 states that Beckett had admitted that his views were pro-Nazi, and that he was working 'day and night for Germany'. On 9 March 1940, a Home Office warrant was granted to intercept his post and telephone.

Beckett was undoubtedly a clever man, and at this time he wanted to restrain any public excesses by members of the British Council for the Christian Settlement of Europe. There is a report in Beckett's MI5 file emphasising the difficulties that he was having keeping Ben Greene under control. It says of Greene: 'They want to stop him talking. He is being very difficult. He makes anti-British and therefore damaging utterances, and is most restive at being kept in the background.' Beckett played a more subtle game than most of his pro-Nazi colleagues. He did not want to give the impression of being pro-German, but of being a good and reasonable British patriot. He kept his desire to overthrow the British government and install a Fascist government instead largely to himself. The truth was that he wanted to arm and rise up. On 15 May 1940 Beckett said privately that he was actively considering joining the 'anti-Parachutist Corps' (an early form of Home Guard) because he thought: 'It would be too marvellous if one were able to obtain a revolver and ammunition at the present time.' The general tenor of his remarks left no doubt that he would, if given the opportunity, actively assist the enemy in the event of an invasion. According to Beckett's son's interesting biography of him, Beckett joined the Home Guard after this.[2]

On 18 May 1940, with the defeat in France looming, Beckett and Greene were reported to have been discussing the formation of an ex-servicemen's organisation:

> '. . . to be put into operation at the close of the present war. It is to be run like the British Legion and is to have people at the head of it who are, to quote John Beckett, "above suspicion", and he himself would not appear on the list. Their idea is to get an organisation together with the object of collecting dissatisfied ex-servicemen and exploiting their grievances.'[3]

In other words, with British defeat looming, Beckett and Greene were planning, like other Fascists, to create their own private army. Another report on the same date reveals that Beckett and a man called Captain Robert Gordon-Canning (of whom more later) were ready to help pro-Nazi Germans if they were on the run in Britain.

On 22 May 1940 Beckett wrote to the Marquis of Tavistock asking him if he was prepared to head an 'alternative' government, which he called a possible 'Government for National Security'. Tavistock was to become Prime Minister; Mosley would be Leader of the House and President of the Council; Beckett himself would get the Home Office and the ominous sounding National Security ministry; Gordon-Canning would be Minister for the Dominions; Ben Greene would be Minister of Education, and have responsibility for the Post Office; and there would be jobs for Beckett's other friends and supporters. On the same day, Beckett gave a speech at Holborn Hall, Gray's Inn Road, London, in which he decried the weaknesses of democratic government, and extolled the benefits of a dictatorship. The British system of voting was out of date, he said, and would be replaced by the British People's Party. Beckett was clearly planning for a German victory and a puppet Fascist government, apparently under Lord Tavistock, but actually run by himself and his cronies. It is interesting that Beckett had no place in the Cabinet for Captain Jock Ramsay, MP. No doubt this was because Ramsay wanted to be prime minister himself.

The very same day as the meeting and Beckett's letter to the Marquis of Tavistock, the Home Secretary, Sir John Anderson, signed an order under Regulation 18B of the Defence Regulations 1939 for Beckett's detention. He was arrested next day. Once in Brixton Prison, Beckett's visits and conversations were monitored. Also Maxwell Knight, who had had at least one agent inside Beckett's organisation, received a report on 27 May 1940 which confirmed the justness of Beckett's detention. In conversation, Beckett openly referred to himself and his associates as Fifth Column, and said that it was absolutely definite that the names and addresses of all Fifth Column people had been sent to and received by the Germans (Beckett had been working with Ben Greene, who had strong contact with Germany). These names and addresses were, said Beckett, being listed and put into notebooks for future reference 'on arrival' by the Germans. Only names of thoroughly reliable people had been sent. What Beckett was confirming was that he and his organisation had indeed been working for Germany, and that the Germans would know upon invasion who their friends in Britain were from the notebooks. He was later to say that the notebooks contained 'everything we know' about friends and sympathisers. Whilst Beckett was in Brixton Prison, Ramsay was in a cell close by, and he also became close to Arnold Leese.[4]

After his appeal against his detention had failed, Beckett was moved to Stafford Prison, where he was regarded as a troublesome prisoner, and then to the Isle of Man. According to his son, the accommodation there was in the seaside resort of Peel, in old-fashioned boarding houses behind barbed wire.[5] Each house had a 'house leader', and Beckett became the leader of his house. He became part of an escape attempt which involved a tunnel, as so many escape attempts did. The escape was organised by a joint team of members of the British Union of Fascists and some Irish Republican Army (IRA) detainees. The objective was to steal fishing boats and to make for the neutral Republic of Ireland. If true, it is an interesting example of co-operation between the IRA and British Fascists, which is said to have endured throughout the war. The IRA were seeking to throw the British out of Northern Ireland, and the Fascists to overthrow the British government. According to Beckett's son, this team successfully tunnelled out of their house and under a road at the back of the camp. A number of men successfully escaped through it, but their plan was frustrated because the fishing boats had had their engine spark plugs removed as a security measure by the owners. Beckett himself did not, in the end, escape. He withdrew because money was needed to fund the escape to Ireland, and he had none. However, his son records that Beckett was one of the leaders of a riot that started three days after the escapers had been recaptured, which resulted in the guards firing on the rioters.

The idea of escaping to the Republic of Ireland, and of creating an organisation there, cropped up regularly in Fascist circles. Information gathered by MI5 suggested that there had been a number of successful escapes there by those whom the authorities were hunting. According to a memorandum dated 7 June 1940 the

Fascist intention was that 'eventually, there will be a legion formed in Ireland (by those who go over by the secret route) who will return to fight when the revolution starts'![6]

Beckett was eventually released from detention in October 1943, after more than three years' imprisonment. By this time, he was said to be ill, suffering from a heart condition. After a few weeks staying with a friend, Beckett came under the patronage of the former Marquis of Tavistock, now finally the Duke of Bedford, and was provided with a cottage to live in. Beckett seems to have overcome his heart condition, since he was soon back in action as a British Fascist. He did not abandon his Fascist principles. He eventually died of stomach cancer in 1964.

Chapter 8

Ben Greene

Ben Greene[1] was a Fascist with strong German family connections. His mother was German (and still living). He had been born in Brazil, where there was a German community, on 28 December 1901, and had spent his early years there, before going to England for his schooling. His English father had a coffee business in Brazil. Ben Greene was apparently a physically very impressive man, 6 feet 8 inches tall, and heavily built. He was just too young to fight in the First World War. Whilst at Wadham College, Oxford, he apparently underwent a religious conversion, and became a Quaker. He left university before graduating, and worked until 1923 with the Quakers on relief work in Germany, Poland, Czechoslovakia and Russia. He married a British woman in 1924. He then worked for a time for his father's coffee business in Brazil, then also in the United States, and in 1927 took over a business called Kepston Limited. The business, and Greene's home, were in Berkhamsted, Hertfordshire, where his father owned significant property. When his father died in 1938, Greene inherited a number of properties. Greene was initially a Labour politician. He stood unsuccessfully for parliament as a Labour candidate in 1931 and 1935, and for a number of years was the secretary of his local Labour Party.

Greene's business, Kepston Limited, made wooden pulleys, and, ironically, the outbreak of war brought the company a lot of work. Most wooden pulleys had previously been imported from abroad. With a war on, and German submarines stalking the seas around Britain, few imports got through. Kepston became very busy working on government contracts.

However, MI5 had received information that, as of April 1936 Greene, had become a paid agent for the Nazis, and had received £10,000 for propaganda purposes – selling the Nazi message to the British people. Thereafter, he became openly pro-Fascist. Together with ex-Labour MP John Beckett, he founded and became a leading light in the British People's Party, one of many emerging British Fascist organisations. Greene became the treasurer, the Marquis of Tavistock was the chairman, and John Beckett was the honorary secretary. A man called Robert Gordon-Canning was also prominent in the party. As we have seen, the British People's Party mounted what it described as a 'Campaign against War and Usury', and John Beckett, using the alias of John Stone, published a pro-German propaganda newsletter called *Headline*. Greene's sister Katherine worked for Beckett, calling herself Katherine Gray. Ben Greene's wife was described as 'thoroughly pro-German and pro-Nazi'.[2]

Greene was a Justice of the Peace in Hertfordshire, until he was stripped of that office because of his pro-German opinions. His passport showed that he paid several visits to Germany before the war began. The British People's Party had an off-shoot called the British Council for the Christian Settlement of Europe (in other words it was anti-Jewish). On 14 October 1939, after war had been declared against Germany, Greene spoke at a Christian Settlement meeting. He told the meeting that the British government's policy was one of bluff and treachery, sneered at those who said Britain could not trust Hitler, and declared that Hitler had been justified in all that he had done, using phrases such as: 'those of us who admire him'.

An MI5 report dated 19 February 1940 records that Greene had another sister, Barbara, who was working as a translator in the German Foreign Office in Berlin. His sister Katherine, and a brother called Edward, were living in London, in Overstrand Mansions, Battersea. The British People's Party had its head office at Greene's business premises in Berkhamsted.

Greene was being watched by MI5, partly as a result of the information that it had received some years before, but also because of his now openly Fascist activity. Maxwell Knight instructed one of his agents, a young German refugee called Harald Kurtz, to get to know Greene. Kurtz did so, posing as a German who had recently been released from detention. Kurtz reported that it was clear that Greene was in contact with the Nazis, and Greene had even gone so far as to recommend to Kurtz (whom he believed to be pro-Nazi as well) that if he wanted to send messages to Germany, he should go through Eire, or through the medium of one of the Reuters news agency correspondents in neutral Switzerland. Greene instructed Kurtz to tell his friends in Germany that: 'There were men in this country [Great Britain] ready to take over the government after a German victory, men trained in and filled with the proper spirit of National Socialism – a British National Socialism.' He indicated to Kurtz that he was in contact with his sister in Berlin 'in a very informal way'. He also claimed to know many routes which enabled a man to cross on foot from Northern Ireland to neutral Eire.

Whatever his Fascist views and intentions for Britain, Greene's greatest importance was probably as a communications link to Germany – he was able through family and other contacts to get news to, and, more importantly from, Germany. Looking towards the end of this book, it is interesting also to note that the Greene family had a detailed knowledge of, and contacts with Brazil, where there was already, as noted, a significant German community. Greene's brother Edward once wrote that: 'The Greenes are Brazilian people.'

Because of the number of government contracts which were coming in to Kepston, and also, apparently, because his bank manager threatened to withdraw the bank's support for his business unless he withdrew from right-wing politics, Greene gave up his role as treasurer of the British People's Party in October 1939. His sister Katherine took over the job. Greene's resignation from the role made no practical difference. He continued his activities, and addressed a number of meetings in the first half of 1940. Two days before Greene's eventual detention, on 22 May 1940, MI5 came into possession of a letter already referred to, written by John Beckett to the Marquis of Tavistock, proposing a 'Possible Coalition Government of National Security'. At this time the German blitzkrieg was rolling across the

Low Countries and France, and Britain was facing defeat on the Continent. The proposed 'government' was clearly intended take control of Great Britain in the near future. Greene was to be the Minister of Education. It is clear that Greene's ambitions were the same as Beckett's and Ramsay's – to get rid of the current British government and to replace it with a Fascist one.

Greene was arrested and detained under Regulation 18B on 24 May 1940. Sir John Anderson signed his detention order. His representations, at his appeal hearing before the Advisory Committee to Consider Appeals against Internment, that he was merely a Quaker and a pacifist and not a Nazi, were disbelieved. The Committee expressed the view that although Greene would not be disposed to assist German armed forces to defeat the British, he expected the Germans to win, thought a German occupation of Britain probable, and hoped that he would be able to secure a position of influence under the new German regime. The Committee rejected Greene's appeal, and confirmed his detention under Regulation 18B. It is suggested, however, that they were wrong about Greene not being disposed to help German armed forces

Ben Greene did not give up. He was valuable to the Nazis and, using funds from an undisclosed source, he chose to follow a legal route. Through a solicitor, Oswald Hickson, he applied for Habeas Corpus, claiming that he had been illegally detained. He fought his case in the High Court, the Court of Appeal and House of Lords – losing all the way until the House of Lords, who, although disallowing his appeal, recommended that he should have a fresh hearing before a differently constituted Advisory Committee. That soon followed.

In Greene's case, Maxwell Knight's agent Harald Kurtz had lost his anonymity, apparently through error or mismanagement at the original Advisory Committee hearing. Kurtz therefore became a named witness at the new hearing before the differently constituted Advisory Committee. Having been identified, he was ambushed one day by Greene's solicitor, and, not knowing whether to preserve his cover (as a pro-Nazi) or to tell the truth, he gave an account of his dealings with Greene contrary to the one that he had given in evidence to the committee. When Harald Kurtz gave evidence before the new committee, he not surprisingly found himself under heavy cross-examination and his evidence was not believed. He was in fact a good agent, who had proved himself many times in other secret work that the committee were not, and could not, be aware of for security reasons. Later, Kurtz himself was very frank about his failure as a witness. He commented that when his whole life as a secret agent involved lying, it was very difficult to go on the witness stand, and persuade people that the truth was the truth. In late 1941, the committee recommended Greene's release, and his detention was finally suspended on 7 January 1942. He was unwell at that time, suffering from acute sciatica, and was in the process of being moved to St Mary's Hospital, Praed Street, Paddington, for treatment. From there, once fit enough, he had his liberty restored. Greene was one of the first of the key Fascists in Britain to be released.

Despite his release, Ben Greene, together with his sister Kate, brother Edward and German mother Eva, remained on what was known as the Censorship Black List. They were to be carefully watched. Not surprisingly, a Home Office warrant was obtained to monitor Ben Greene's post and telephone calls. The product of the warrant showed that Ben Greene got in contact with Mrs Maule Ramsay only two weeks after his release from Brixton Prison. He wrote to her on 21 January 1942. The letter no longer exists, and its exact contents are unknown, but he was apparently trying to arrange a meeting with her. Greene had, of course, just spent over eighteen months in Brixton with Ramsay.

After a number of exploratory visits to Scotland during 1942, Ben Greene moved his family to Braefoot Farm, Crook of Devon, Kinross, at the end of the year. The overt reasons for doing so were that Mrs Greene wanted to get away from Berkhamsted (where the Greene family's reputation was now unsavoury), and that the family would be safer from German air raids in Scotland. MI5 was informed that Ben Greene might also prefer his family to be out of the way so that he could conduct extramarital affairs in his wife's absence. He spent most of his time in the Home Counties, but visited Kinross occasionally, and also went to Kelly Castle to see Mrs Ramsay. He had 'cleared the decks' at his home in Berkhamsted, but whether that was for romantic or political reasons is arguable.[3]

Greene was not satisfied with merely being a free man again. He decided to take legal action against the Home Secretary who had imprisoned him, Sir John Anderson. He sued the former Home Secretary for wrongful imprisonment (on the grounds of bad faith), and for libel in relation to the allegations made against him. The trial began on 5 April 1943. Greene abandoned his case after four days, before the defence had even started. He was ordered to pay the costs, which were substantial. However, it seems that he was prepared for this, and was intending to go bankrupt, having transferred everything into his brother Edward's name.[4]

One result of the trial was that MI5's view of Ben Greene grew more critical. He was described in one report by Maxwell Knight, who had studied him throughout the whole of the trial, as 'an unscrupulous scoundrel. He has that touch of egotism which is noted in many persons of abnormal size . . . on the whole he is clearly a man of very little courage of any kind. I unhesitatingly describe him as highly dangerous.'[5]

Following his unsuccessful court case, Greene remained quietly active. He became the principal of the English National Association, yet another Fascist organisation, and liaised with many other British Fascists regularly. The approach of all the Fascists was to appeal to national patriotism, and to emphasise the threat to the country from Jews and Bolsheviks. No doubt Greene maintained his covert lines of communication to Germany, and to German sympathisers in Brazil. He had met many of Britain's Fascist leaders whilst in detention, and had formed the view that Ramsay should be the leader of a united Fascist party in due course. However, Greene believed that the government would not set Ramsay free until the war was over. Ramsay believed the same himself.

Greene obviously knew something of the German plan for December 1944 – an uprising and break-out in the United Kingdom, timed to coincide with the major German counter-attacks in the

Ardennes and Italy, which is an indication of how much he was trusted by the Nazis. Without that knowledge, at a time when everybody thought that it was only a matter of weeks or months before Hitler lost the war, the release of Ramsay in late September would have been of minor significance to a Fascist such as Greene. Yet Greene greeted Ramsay's release as coming at 'exactly the right moment . . . the Man of Destiny . . . the natural leader whom everybody has been waiting for'. MI5 had been of the view that Greene was in contact with Germany, even whilst in custody, and the developments in the autumn of 1944 proved them to be right.

Having welcomed Ramsay's release, Greene became Ramsay's main lieutenant in what was to follow. Ramsay came to live with Greene in Berkhamsted, and became accustomed to spending half of each week there. When he was away from Berkhamsted, or Greene was, they would be in contact by post or phone.

But it was not just Ramsay and Greene who were working together in the autumn of 1944. MI5 files show that, on 31 October 1944, Ramsay was in touch with Arnold Leese by telephone, and on 2 November he wrote to him. The copies of the intercepts no longer exist, but presumably they were of themselves innocuous as both Ramsay and Leese were aware that MI5 was watching them. Ramsay wrote again to Leese on 29 November and 10 December 1944.

Ramsay himself told the *Sunday Express* on 21 October that he had no intention of resigning his seat in parliament until the whole matter of his detention had been thoroughly aired. Ramsay was preparing himself to return to the fray – to finally achieve that for which he had founded the Right Club.

Buried in an MI5 file on Ramsay, and apparently recorded months after the event, there is a highly significant piece of evidence.[6] It records that there was a Regulation 18B social gathering on 16 December 1944. Ramsay did not, in the event, attend. The significant question is: 'Why?' Why were all the ex-detainee British Fascists meeting on 16 December 1944, the day that was scheduled to be the beginning of the big German break-out from the British prisoner of war camps?

Chapter 9

Arnold Spencer Leese

Arnold Spencer Leese came from a rather different background to Captain Jock Ramsay, Sir Oswald Mosley, Bt, and Ben Greene. Born in 1878 at Lytham in Lancashire, Leese had been an Army veterinary surgeon before and during the First World War. He was commissioned in September 1915, and reached the rank of captain, serving in India, East Africa and Somaliland. He described himself in a letter in 1929 as an experienced and successful camel re-mount officer. After the war, he went into private practice in Lincolnshire, but retired early in 1928 at the age of fifty, apparently not having enjoyed his work. Leese moved to live in Guildford, Surrey. In 1929, he offered himself to the Ministry of War for re-employment as an experienced military vet, but his offer was not accepted.

Leese had long been a Fascist, acting in the 1920s as a district officer for the British Fascist Party, before resigning in order to found the Imperial Fascist League in the late 1920s. The only European Fascist ruler then had been Benito Mussolini of Italy. By the late 1930s, Mussolini had been joined by Hitler of Germany and Franco of Spain. The Imperial Fascist League was registered as a business name on 23 May 1932.[1] It was believed that Leese had some private means, which enabled him to give up work and concentrate on his Fascist beliefs.

Leese was married to May Winifred Leese, who was an equally virulent Fascist. The Imperial Fascist League made every endeavour to ingratiate itself with the Germans and to make contact with the Nazi Party. The badge that the League adopted was a swastika imposed upon a Union Jack.[2] In July 1936, the British Ambassador

to Berlin sent a report saying that there was evidence that an agent
of the Imperial Fascist League was operating in Munich, and trying
to persuade British and other foreign visitors to Munich to join the
Imperial Fascist League, and the war against 'international Judea'.

Leese was fanatically anti-Jewish, and initially his main weapon
was propaganda. In 1936, he was tried and convicted at the Old Bailey
of publishing and printing a seditious libel in his newspaper *The
Fascist*. The British government took the case so seriously that the
Attorney General, Sir Donald Somervell, KC, led for the prosecution,
and a High Court Judge, Mr Justice Greaves-Lord, tried the case.
Leese defended himself.

The prosecution quoted from an article in *The Fascist* that Leese
had written, where he said:

> 'The Jews are not wanted anywhere on earth. Unfortunately,
> they are on earth and all over it, destroying everything good
> and decent by their contaminating influences. The alternatives
> are: (1) to kill; (2) to sterilise or (3) to segregate, and our policy is
> the last one, conducted and maintained at their own expense.'[3]

There were other equally racist and inflammatory passages. Leese
was convicted, and was sentenced to six months' imprisonment.

Upon release, Leese continued to publish Fascist propaganda,
and to lead the Imperial Fascist League. Once war broke out, he
operated the League from his home, 'The White House', Pewley Hill,
Guildford. Once Britain was at war with Germany, Leese claimed
that: 'The first watchword of our creed is King and Country.' However,
he argued that the war was the fault of the Jews. He announced:
'Britain has been shoved into the war by the Jews, like a dirty dog
is shoved into a bath.' He campaigned for peace on that basis, with
the slogan: 'Leese for Peace'. In his publication *Weekly Angles,* and
in propaganda pamphlets, he argued that: 'Hitler is the Jews' enemy,
he was never the enemy of the British people. We are fighting the
Jews' chief enemy, for the Jews.' His pitch was always that Hitler
had no battle to fight with *Angles*, the Anglo-Saxon British, but that
the British government was being run and manipulated against the

interests of the British people by Jews. Hitler was the only leader who had the courage to take on the Jewish conspiracy.

According to an MI5 informant, after the outbreak of war Leese came into possession of a number of revolvers, and ammunition for them. These he distributed in batches amongst his supporters, with instructions that they should keep them hidden. Leese advised his supporters that should any sort of internal disorder break out in the event of a German invasion, he expected them to co-operate with other Fascists and give whatever support they could to the invaders. Put bluntly, 'Leese for Peace' was merely a propaganda ploy – in reality, Leese was arming his men ready to support a German attack.[4]

Although he was not on friendly terms with Sir Oswald Mosley, Leese appreciated the value of Mosley's Fascist party, the British Union of Fascists. In a letter to Leese dated 8 November 1939, a fellow Fascist, Henry Duke, told him: 'As I see it, he [Mosley] is the only living Force in the Fascist movement. I know that his team is, or has been, a mob of opportunists.' Leese, like Ramsay, would not have been happy with a British Fascist government led by Mosley, but their aims were similar, and because of his rabble-rousing tactics, Mosley had a large following. It was partly because of the diversity of Fascist leaders that Ramsay was telling his Right Club: 'Wait until it is time [for the revolution], and I will tell you who the Fascist leader will be.' Leese was very disappointed by the German–Russian non-aggression pact as the war started in 1939, because he hated Bolshevism as all Fascists did, but he was reconciled to Hitler when Germany tore up the pact and invaded Russia in 1941.

Once Churchill became Prime Minister, Leese knew that he would be a prime candidate for detention under Regulation 18B, and so he went into hiding, supported by his wife and family, and using his network of Fascist sympathisers. An order for his arrest and detention was made on 28 June 1940, but it was not until October that the police were able to find him. Police officers, acting on information, raided his house in Guildford, at 2.30 in the afternoon on 9 October 1940. Two officers, led by Acting Detective Inspector Percy Bowes, who had previously searched the house without result in June, and an Inspector Hayward, entered the house, leaving two other officers stationed in the garden. Having gained entry, they found Leese upstairs near the bathroom. For some reason he had come home. Leese had armed himself with a stick, and was prepared to fight. His wife was equally aggressive, and called out to the officers: 'You ought to be ashamed of yourself, you filthy swine, you scum, taking their filthy money for this work. Why don't you go back and tell them you won't arrest a patriotic Englishman?' There was also another female family member present.

Inspector Bowes grabbed Leese's stick, and Inspector Hayward went to help him, but Leese fought back vigorously, and was joined by the two women, who punched and clawed at the officers. It was only when the two officers outside, hearing the disturbance, also entered the house that Leese finally gave up, saying to his wife: 'All right my dear, I give in to superior force.' His wife shouted at Bowes, whom she had scratched: 'I am glad I marked him, I hope he will keep the mark for the rest of his life!' Leese was taken to Guildford Police Station, where he was still so violently angry that he smashed up his cell. Leese showed his true character on 9 October 1940. So much for 'Leese for Peace'! Leese and his wife were quite happy to resort to violence against the representatives of the British state (which the arresting officers were) if it served their purpose.

When 'The White House' was searched, three books containing the names of hundreds of subscribers to *The Fascist* newspaper were found, from many countries all over the world. Leese clearly had a large following. Also found, which is significant to this story, was an identity card in the name of John W. Lovell, of 125 Gloucester Avenue, London NW1. Leese claimed that Lovell was a friend who had accidentally left his identity card there. The truth probably was that, as with guns and ammunition, Leese was able to obtain false documents. Leese's Fascist paper and his anti-Jewish books required printers, and it may be that those anti-Jewish printers (because nobody else would touch his publications) were able to forge documents for him.

During his time in Brixton Prison, Leese came into regular contact with Captain Jock Ramsay, younger than himself and much higher on the social ladder. Leese did not stop working for the Nazi cause simply because he was in detention. As has been seen, Knight's spy Eric Roberts ('Jack King') was masquerading as a Gestapo agent and was busy intercepting information intended to be sent back to Germany. In the course of his work he also found evidence relating to Leese. Some of a bugged conversation recorded on 17 May 1943 referred to Leese by name.[5] It was said that Leese had compiled a list of 2,000 Jews and converted Jews from his home area. They were to be exterminated when the Nazis arrived and the revolution took place. The conversation continued:

> *Marita Perigoe*: 'Leese apparently has all these persons' life histories and everything written down, all their crimes and everything. A good beginning isn't it? The first two thousand a complete wipe out – I mean they're not even deported these people . . . Bakker [a Dutch fellow Fascist] . . . takes a more personal view. He says he's got his own private list and when the time comes he wants to bump them off personally.'
> *Jack King*: 'I'd like to see that list very much. We've all got to face danger or death sooner or later.'

It seems, however, that Roberts never got either Bakker's list or Leese's list of the Jews that they wanted to lynch.

After more than three years of detention, Leese became genuinely ill with a prostate problem that required surgical intervention. He was now sixty-five. Leese underwent a suprapubic drainage followed by a prostatectomy in hospital between December 1943 and January 1944. On 19 January 1944, his detention under Regulation 18B was suspended, subject to certain conditions, including residence at 'The White House', and an order not to travel more than ten miles from his home without permission of the police. When discharged from hospital in February, he returned home. The prognosis was that Leese would not be able to resume an active life for at least six months after the operation, but despite his age he recovered quickly.

Leese had lost none of his fanaticism. He may have been sixty-five, but his violent resistance when the police came to arrest him showed that he retained a remarkable energy, no doubt spurred on by hatred – and his original organisation was still intact. Once he had regained his strength and health, he was able to plan for the future. He still had caches of arms, and a number of fanatical followers. He now knew Ramsay well, and had kept company in custody over the years with a number of other dedicated Fascists. No doubt many of the rivalries between competing British Fascist organisations had evaporated during the years of mutual detention. In any event, it had always been Ramsay's objective with his Right Club to unite British Fascism under his leadership. Since Hitler had attacked Russia, Leese's faith in the German Nazi Party had been restored, and he now worked tirelessly to further the common cause – the elimination of the 'Jewish threat' and the overthrow of the British government which had imprisoned him.

Chapter 10

Sir Oswald Mosley

Oswald Mosley was the most public and populist of Great Britain's pre-war Fascist leaders. He appealed to the mob, whilst remaining overtly upper class. His first wife was the daughter of Lord Curzon, his second was the daughter of Lord Redesdale (Diana Mitford, one of the well-known Mitford sisters). Although his own inherited title was only that of baronet, he was thus connected to Britain's nobility by marriage, was arrogant, vain and bombastic. He knew, like other unscrupulous politicians, that it was not difficult to please those of a much lower station in life than his, providing his ideas were pitched in an attractive way. His appeal was specifically aimed at the working classes, and he commanded a significant following. Like both Hitler and Mussolini, he was a populist. Diana was also an enthusiastic Fascist.

Mosley was himself an ex-soldier, having been commissioned into the 16th Lancers, and served with them and with the Royal Flying Corps in the First World War. After the war, he had become the MP for Harrow, firstly on behalf of the Conservative Party, and then as an Independent. He had then joined the Labour Party, and had been Chancellor of the Duchy of Lancaster in the 1929 Labour government. However, he fell out with the Labour Party, as he had with the Conservatives, and then set up the British Union of Fascists. There he gave himself autocratic power of the type that he had always sought.

Mosley differed from both Ramsay and Leese in that he sought to use mindless thugs as his 'foot soldiers'. He was expert (like Adolf Hitler) at whipping up a crowd into a frenzy, and clearly enjoyed the power of his own oratory. His style was described at a meeting in March 1940: '[He] adopted a forward crouching posture, clenched his hands, and his voice gradually increased in volume until he was almost shouting.'[1]

His critics would say that he believed in 'mob rule'. He was the most public Fascist in Great Britain, but probably because of his arrogance many of the other educated Fascists found it difficult to work with him. Indeed, as stated above, the existence of so many separate Fascist organisations in Great Britain was probably the result of Mosley's abrasive character. However, within his own British Union of Fascists, he was known as 'The Leader' (which was the translation of Adolf Hitler's title of *'Führer'*) and enjoyed fanatical support. The greeting 'Hail Mosley' (a parallel of *'Heil Hitler'*) was common amongst the BUF.

A speech that Mosley delivered on 30 January and 1 February 1940 illustrates his style. He emphasised to his audiences that:

> 'Our time is approaching. After long years of struggle in the face of unprecedented odds, when only the spirit kept you going, reward and victory are in sight. You must now mobilise people for "peace" and the British Union of Fascists . . . you must bring in new members . . . to take their place in the ranks when the time comes for the sweep forward, which the movement will make, as their brother parties in mother countries have made when their hour of destiny struck . . . The river of history is generally like a placid stream and floating on top one may see funny things like Baldwin, Churchill and Chamberlain, being full of wind they keep on the surface. But when the hour of destiny strikes, when the placid river turns into a torrent and the lightning strikes down from above, these floating objects are whirled away, battered and broken . . . the coming fight is a fight which might mean great effort and sacrifice, perhaps the supreme sacrifice.'[2]

Mosley was telling his supporters that violence was to come, and that they might have to sacrifice their lives. The target, of course, was what Mosley regarded as the Jew-infiltrated British government.

Mosley (and many other Fascists) regarded Winston Churchill as Britain's greatest enemy (alongside, of course, the Jews). In early 1940 (before Churchill became prime minister), Mosley published a handbill aimed directly at Churchill and entitled 'WHO?' It was a series of questions such as: 'WHO hates the German people so much that he does not care how many British lives are sacrificed in attempting to work off his personal hatred'; and 'WHO is Britain's greatest enemy because he is the biggest WARMONGER of them all?' The handbill finished with: 'AND WHO MUST BE THE NEXT TO GO IN 1940?'

About this time, Mosley hoped to visit Eire. The Irish Republican Army was still active in Eire, and was anti-British, and therefore, by convenience, pro-German. In wartime, it was necessary to obtain a permit to travel to Eire from Britain, and MI5 made sure that no permit would be granted to Mosley without reference, first of all, to themselves. The presence of an independent country so close to British shores was highly significant to the British Fascists, as will become clear later in this story.

Mosley continued to preach what was a common British Fascist doctrine – that the war was the result of a Jewish conspiracy, and their vendetta against Germany. Great Britain being enamoured of freedom of speech, Mosley and his fellow Fascists were permitted to continue their pro-Fascist campaigning, even when the war against Germany was well under way. On 1 March 1940, at a lunch at the Criterion Restaurant attended by 480 supporters, Mosley delivered a speech in Hitlerian style attacking the British government and Jewry. He preached in favour of German expansion into Eastern Europe. He maintained that the British government was the tool of Jewish financiers. He spoke of the British Union of Fascists as being the only possible solution to the current situation, saying that the British people had to choose, and that the battle for Fascist supremacy in Britain had started, and must be fought to the bitter end. Amongst those present were Bob Ramsay, Captain Jock Ramsay's son, and Anna Wolkoff, who would introduce Jock Ramsay to Tyler Kent.

On 13 March 1940, Mosley held a private meeting for his south-west London members. In his speech, Mosley expressed his determination to defeat 'the enemy' (the Jew) if not at the ballot box, then by 'other and more drastic means'. He was roundly cheered when he said this. The report of the meeting in Mosley's MI5 file reads: 'I rather feel that he [Mosley] is relying upon calling on British Union members to provide eventually an armed force which will effect revolution . . . it was not what he said, but what he meant.' It is important to remember that British Union members were liable to be called up into the armed forces like everyone else. The military would train them in the arts of war, and no doubt Mosley hoped that eventually he would be able to call upon loyal British Union of Fascist members of the British armed forces to join his British revolution. He himself was, of course, an ex-soldier.

Mosley was finally detained on 23 May 1940. His wife, Lady Diana Mosley, was also detained (they both claimed to be personal friends of Adolf Hitler), and in due course, Sir Oswald and Lady Mosley were allowed to live together in Holloway Prison.[3] Thus Mosley did not spend a long time in Brixton with the likes of Ramsay, Greene and Leese. But, as with others, as the years passed the government's attitude towards the interned Mosleys relaxed.

The Home Office was responsible for all final decisions in relation to detainees, and on 18 November 1943, decided (without consulting MI5) that Mosley should be released on medical grounds. He had been complaining of, and had been treated for, thrombo-phlebitis – an inflammation of a vein in his leg that could lead to blood clots. Lady Mosley was released at the same time as her husband. Some of his leading colleagues in the British Union of Fascists had already been released from detention – Captain Gordon-Canning, Admiral Domvile and John Beckett amongst them. When T. M. Shelford of MI5 learned of the decision to release Mosley, he was furious, but could do nothing about it. He wrote:

> 'It is quite impossible to prophesy with certainty what the
> result of Sir Oswald Mosley's release will be. If he is genuinely

ill – and it is apparent that the Prison Doctor has doubts about this – it will of course be unlikely that he will engage in anything active . . . Even if Mosley is not genuinely ill, he may well think it the path of prudence to refrain from any kind of political activity. He has been so anxious to obtain his release that I think that this is even probable. There is no doubt that the Fascists will be much encouraged, but Fascism of the British Union variety is now so thoroughly discredited that such encouragement as the Fascists may feel is, in my view, unlikely to have a serious effect on the general situation. I am not optimistic about our being able to keep watch on Sir Oswald Mosley's activities very efficaciously. Fascists are now being released thick and fast and I am afraid our defences are rapidly becoming saturated.'[4]

When Mosley was released, restrictions on his movements and activities were imposed. He was to reside at a notified address, not to travel more than seven miles from that address, and not to contact the press. Home Office warrants were imposed for the interception of his mail and his telephone calls. However, the Mosleys were experienced at avoiding surveillance. Mosley arranged that his incoming mail was not sent to his address, but under cover to a different address in the same village, from which he could collect it. Happily, MI5 found out, and thereafter monitored that address, as well as his mother's.

Chapter 11

Yet More British Fascists

There were many Fascist organisations, and many other Fascists in Britain. One thing that united many of them was the catch phrase 'Perish Judah' ('Death to the Jews'), or simply 'P. J.' Often this would be preceded by *'Heil Hitler'*. Once Great Britain and Northern Ireland had declared war on Germany, the primary aim of British Fascists was to stop the war. If that was impossible, they must help Germany to win it. However, stopping the war was the first objective, and, usefully, the Fascists could join with pacifists in a campaign to achieve this. It was only a little over twenty years since the horrors of the First World War had come to an end, and many non-Fascists of any or no political persuasion wanted to bring the new war to a close as soon as possible. However, for the Fascists, always lurking under the surface was the real objective, to overthrow the British government by force, and to replace it with a Fascist one.

A potentially very dangerous Fascist was Sir Barry Domvile, KBE, CB, CMG.[1] Domvile had been born in 1878. He joined the Royal Navy, and rose to the rank of vice-admiral. He was Director of Naval Intelligence towards the end of his career, and retired in 1934 at the age of fifty-six. In 1937, he founded an organisation called the Link, which ostensibly was designed to encourage German–British friendship, but in reality was completely pro-Nazi. After founding the Link, Domvile visited Germany several times, and he met Hitler, Reichsführer-SS Heinrich Himmler, Goebbels and other prominent Nazis. He visited the Dachau Concentration Camp in 1935, which, he said, contained Jews, hardened criminals, persons who had tried to return to Germany from abroad, and political dissidents. Domvile said that the inmates had 'very pleasant work to do, and the camp was very comfortable, and the food was very good'. He said that he would rather be a prisoner there than in Brixton Prison. His second wife, Lady Alexandrina, whom he married in 1916, was almost certainly German, although she pretended to be Dutch. She was also an enthusiastic pro-Nazi. Domvile's organisation, the Link, was largely controlled from Germany, and dedicated to German propaganda. It published a regular magazine called the *Anglo-German Review*. MI5 was later to report that Domvile had attended meetings with Mosley, Ramsay and others after war had broken out, when the co-ordination of future Fascist activities was discussed, with the object of achieving a Fascist revolution in Britain.

As a recently retired former Director of Naval Intelligence Domvile would obviously have been an important member of any possible revolutionary plot. The British Admiralty expressed the view: 'If there are to be any British Quislings [traitors], then there are few more likely candidates for the role than Admiral Domvile and his wife.' Domvile was described as being apparently infatuated with Nazi and Fascist doctrines.

Domvile was extremely confident that Hitler's Germany would win the war. As a result of his rank, he was a governor of the Star and Garter Services Retirement Home in Richmond. In late May 1940, Domvile spoke to the residents. He stated that Hitler was going to win the war, but there was no reason to worry about that because he would bring the Duke of Windsor over as King (from Bermuda), and everything would be better than it was then. Very soon, Adolf Hitler would be in Britain, and that would be for the benefit of everyone. The Director of the Star and Garter Home reported what Domvile had said to MI5.

After war was declared, Domvile's activities had become less public. The Link closed down, and was replaced by a body called the 'Information and Policy Group'. Domvile also became one of the moving spirits behind a new organisation, already referred to, called the British Council for Christian Settlement in Europe. The Marquis of Tavistock was the public face of this organisation. Tavistock was a declared pacifist, but was closely associated with a number of leading Fascists. Tavistock paid a visit to the German Minister in neutral Dublin, in order to discuss possible peace terms between Hitler and Britain. Obviously, war between Germany and Britain was a disaster for British supporters of Hitler's Germany, who blamed 'World Jewry' for the war.

Sir Barry and Lady Domvile were both arrested and detained on 7 July 1940. When their home was searched, the Domviles' address book was found, containing the addresses and telephone numbers of Ramsay and Gordon-Canning. Like so many others, after several years in prison, the Domviles were released once it was thought that the danger of Germany winning the war had passed.

Captain Robert Cecil Gordon-Canning[2] was born in 1888. He joined Mosley's British Union of Fascists in 1934 or 1935, and became one of Mosley's inner circle. Gordon-Canning had served in the Army in World War One, and had won a Military Cross for his heroism. He had previously been a member of the British Fascists. He was described in an MI5 file as an adventurer, who had been involved in gun-running in the past (during the Rif War in Morocco in the 1920s), a useful skill for a British Fascist who was thinking of armed revolution. Once war came, Gordon-Canning made clear to his own inner circle that he was prepared to provide active support to the Nazis. At a party on Christmas Eve 1939, in the presence (unknown to him) of an MI5 agent, Gordon-Canning announced that he would not be doing the right thing by mankind if he did not do all he could to help the Nazis. He praised the Nazi regime and said that if a submarine came and needed refuelling or re-victualling, they would know where to find a friend – in other words, Gordon-Canning himself.

Gordon-Canning was detained on 10 July 1940. He was released just over three years later on 6 August 1943, subject to strict conditions. These were relaxed on 12 October 1944, by the then Home Secretary Herbert Morrison.[3] The reasons given were that due to the war situation, the Home Secretary no longer feared that there might be a revival of the British Union of Fascists, and that Gordon-Canning was no longer a danger. His post and phone calls were monitored, however. On 15 August 1944, he wrote to Admiral Domvile: 'If the heterogeneous masses known as the "Allied Armies" have not forced a capitulation by 1 October, there may arrive some kaleidoscopic changes in the fortunes of war.'

Another Fascist, Charles Geary,[4] was forty-eight years old when he was eventually made subject to a Detention Order on 8 August 1940. He had been a Fascist in the 1920s, but by the early 1930s did not belong to any official Fascist organisation. He had tried to form his own anti-Jewish and anti-Communist groups but they came to nothing. What troubled MI5 and Special Branch was that Geary clearly wanted to form an armed, quasi-military Fascist band. In early 1935, Geary was trying to obtain unlicensed firearms, including Lewis and other machine guns. In late 1935, he was discovered to be trying to recruit ex-servicemen from the Fellowship of the Services organisation who would be prepared to resort to violence in the event of a political upheaval in Britain. Geary is described as being a very cautious individual, but the authorities found out about a private shooting range that he and his cronies apparently used for training. In March 1940, it was learned that Geary was seeking to recruit from the British Union of Fascists, that he was trying to obtain weapons from the Enfield Small Arms Factory, and that he was encouraging his men to join the Territorial Army with the object of stealing piece by piece all the small arms that they could get their hands on, and, if possible, some Lewis machine guns. Happily, Geary's organisation was penetrated by an agent, probably one of Maxwell Knight's.

By July 1940, Geary was claiming that his organisation had about two dozen motor vehicles which patrolled about the country with four men in each car, finding positions for military strongpoints when the revolution came. There was a suggestion that these men would disguise themselves as Home Guard. Geary's organisation is described in the report supporting his detention as being pro-German and anti-Semitic to the point of being prepared to commit acts of violence against Jews. There was no desire for peace behind his actions.

Geary was said to be a great admirer of Captain Ramsay, and was apparently hoping to join the Right Club. Together with a colleague, he produced a news sheet called *The Liberator* which was extremely anti-government, anti-war and pro-Fascist. The title of the news sheet gives away what the object of his organisation was – the armed overthrow of the British government. The author has not discovered Geary's release date, and it is not clear whether he was free at the time of the big break. If he was, there is no doubt that he would have joined in with enthusiasm.

Oliver Conway Gilbert,[5] born on 1 July 1903, was the chairman and treasurer of the Nordic League, a Fascist organisation which has already been mentioned. He was also a member of the British Union of Fascists. Because of his extremism, and a belief that he was unbalanced, he was one of the relatively few Fascists detained in 1939 under Chamberlain's government. He was arrested on 23 September 1939, only weeks after the outbreak of war. Gilbert was virulently anti-Semitic, anti-Communist and pro-Nazi. He was also pro-Japanese, and supplied information (as he eventually admitted) to a suspected Japanese agent called Eguchi about Communist and Jewish activity in Britain. He sent copies of his reports to Captain Ramsay, who, he was later to state, was in touch with Eguchi too. According to Gilbert, Eguchi was also working with Arnold Leese. There was some evidence to suggest that Gilbert was in contact at one time with a German agent called Kruse.

It is interesting to note that in October 1941 Gilbert wrote to Mrs Leese, wife of the now interned leader of the Imperial Fascist League, saying: 'I shall always remember how the I.F.L. boys took such an energetic interest in my case, and tried to obtain justice for me when I was first arrested.' Although there were many different British Fascist organisations, they were all connected, and shared a common goal.

Of note, when considering whether revenge entered into the mindset of these detained Fascists when they were finally released, is a letter on Gilbert's file dated 26 October 1941, which he wrote to the Advisory Committee who were reviewing his continued detention after two years. He said:

> 'I was arrested on 23 September 1939. Since then over 15 months of my imprisonment, in defiance of constitutional law, has been spent in bug-ridden, vermin-infested prisons, sometimes locked up in a gloomy cell for 23 hours a day . . . 23 hours a day in cells for innocent men is more punitive treatment than even that meted out to the most dangerous criminals.'[6]

The complaint of many of the detainees was that they had not been convicted of anything, and they had had no proper trial. In time of war, the security of the state takes precedence, and once an order for detention had been signed by the Home Secretary, the only hearing would be an appeal before the Advisory Committee, which was held in private, and concerned only with the question of risk to the public that would be occasioned by the restoration of the liberty of the subject before them.

In October 1941, the Advisory Committee commented: 'He is intensely embittered by his detention,' and that he was unstable. Gilbert's detention was further reviewed in 1942 and 1943; it was discovered that he had become a Christian Scientist, and eventually it was thought that he was no longer a danger and would not revert to Fascism. Gilbert wrote to his mother in February 1944 saying: 'Now I realise the utter futility of idealism . . . I have utterly finished with politics.' He was finally released on 18 February 1944. He remained a free man until the end of the war. However, a report dated 3 May 1945, shortly after Hitler's suicide, revealed his true feelings.

> 'Gilbert took Hitler's death very seriously, and referred to it as: "This tragic drama . . . this modern Twilight of the Gods". He shook his fist in the air, and demanded vengeance against the Jews and their friends in Whitehall . . . He stated that those left behind must not fail, they must set their hands to the task of undermining the Jewish colossus the world over. All

anti-Semitic movements in all countries were henceforward friends. The cry of the future was Vengeance. Adolf Hitler had died a hero and a martyr . . . Although the world's greatest leader was dead, he lived for ever in the hearts of the people.'[7]

Gilbert's fanatical Nazism and anti-Semitism had not changed at all. In November 1944 he was out, and available to support any revolution in Britain. Although he was regarded by some of his fellow Fascists as unreliable, there is little doubt that he would have been in contact with many of his fellow ex-detainees in the autumn and early winter of 1944.

As late as 17 April 1946, Gilbert attended a meeting with Ramsay, Gordon-Canning and other Fascists, which is discussed later in this book. Reports in October 1946 record Gilbert's hysterical fury at the Nuremberg war crimes trials, which Gilbert said must be avenged. He said that if he had had an automatic pistol in his possession he would go to the East End and shoot up a few Jews. He talked about the possibility of murdering Churchill, Field Marshal Montgomery and Prime Minister Attlee. At some stage Gilbert learned that Montgomery had a flat in Latymer Court, Hammersmith. He announced a plan to wait until the Christmas holidays, when Montgomery would be at home, and to place a time bomb disguised as a bundle of laundry outside the door to his flat. Gilbert suggested that a girl should deliver the bomb, as she would be less conspicious than a man. A few weeks later, in November, Gilbert decided to target Norman Birkett, KC, who had been the chairman of the Review Committee that had confirmed his detention, and more recently a judge at the Nuremberg Trials, saying that if he had the opportunity he would kill Birkett and gladly suffer the consequences.

Gilbert was yet another very dangerous British Fascist, and as with all the others listed in this chapter and the last, he was free and available in the autumn of 1944 to help Hitler and his Nazi forces in Britain to overthrow and kill Churchill and his government.

Chapter 12

Theodore Schurch

A Fascist Soldier

One question that arises in this book is whether Hitler, Mussolini, or the British Fascists had agents within the British armed forces. When Churchill imposed his crack-down on British Fascists in late May 1940, there were a great many of them. Mosley, in particular, had a large following. However, generally speaking, it was only the more prominent (and therefore more dangerous) Fascists who were detained. Regulation 18B required that any candidate for detention be assessed as being a threat to the security of the state, and the foot soldiers of Fascism were not of individual concern. Without their leaders, it was believed that they posed no real problem. Therefore, many of those who had supported Mosley, Leese, Beckett and Greene remained free, as did many members of the Right Club. The mere presence of a name in the Right Club register of members was not enough to prove that its owner was dangerous. However, it is highly likely that some of the Fascist foot soldiers did not change their views, and it is clear that a large number of them ended up in the armed forces – some conscripted and some as volunteers. It is to be remembered that British Fascists were patriots, even if they felt that Britain was being manoeuvred into a war with Germany by a Jewish conspiracy. Extreme patriotism was a part of the public face of Fascism – 'Britain First' was the slogan, then as now. Mrs Ramsay was undoubtedly right to say she believed there were those in the armed forces who would support a Fascist coup.

There is evidence that when Churchill imposed the detentions in May and June 1944, it was already too late to prevent the infiltration of the British armed forces by Fascists. It had been going on for some time. The case of Theodore John William Schurch is a good example.[1] Born in Marylebone, London, on 5 May 1918, to an English mother and Swiss father, Schurch was a little over 5 feet 8 inches tall, weighed 135 pounds, had fair hair and blue eyes. He spoke with a strong Cockney accent. Schurch joined the British Union of Fascists at the age of sixteen in 1934. He was later to say that he had been persuaded to join by a young woman at his place of work – however, this was proved to be a lie, and it must be presumed that he joined the Fascists because he shared their political views. Schurch was an extremely skilled and convincing liar, and reading his interviews after his eventual arrest, it is difficult to know whether anything he said was true.

In 1936, Schurch applied to join the Regular Army. He was a volunteer. Since he had a Swiss father, he had to be vetted, but he passed his vetting without difficulty, and became Private Schurch of the Royal Army Service Corps, Army number T/61711. Schurch later said, and this is quite likely to be true, that he had been asked to join the British Army by the Italian Military Intelligence Service (SIM) in 1936, and claimed that they suggested that he enlist as a Regular not a Territorial, specifically in the Royal Army Service Corps. The object was that he could spy for them as a driver. In November 1937, Schurch volunteered for service in Palestine, and in due course joined the Staff Car Section of 68th Company, General Command, Palestine – perhaps an ideal job for a Fascist spy, since he would be driving British staff officers around. Again, Schurch was to say much later that he had been instructed to volunteer for work in Palestine by SIM. His handlers in London, he said, were an Italian called Bianchi and an Englishman called King. It seems likely that he was supplying information to Britain's enemies, but just how that came about is in doubt – whether he approached them, or they approached him.

When war broke out, Schurch was still in the Middle East. Under interrogation in 1945, he said that he worked through an Arab contact called Homsi, who passed on his information to SIM and the Germans. He said that he supplied information on the movements of senior officers such as General Wavell, and on troop deployments. In 1940, Schurch became a Transport Clerk in the Operational and Control Office in Sarafand al-Amar in Palestine, but in 1941 he was transferred to the No. 6 Mechanical Supplies Depot in Egypt. Schurch said that in order to liaise with his handler Homsi in Palestine, he forged papers in the name of Captain John Richards, and went absent without leave for a time, before returning to give himself up. Captain Richards was an alias under which he would operate later in the war. No doubt his performance as an officer was enhanced by his experience of having officers as passengers in the vehicles that he drove. Schurch was transferred again in June 1942 to 201st Guards Brigade of the 7th Armoured Division, and was in Tobruk that month when it surrendered to the Germans. Schurch told his interrogators in 1945 about all sorts of things he had claimed to have done, but it is impossible to say how many of them were true.

Whatever his activities may have been whilst serving initially in the Middle East and North Africa, once in enemy hands there is no doubt that Schurch began working energetically for the Italians. He also claimed to have worked for the Germans, which is probably true. Using the assumed identity of 'Captain Richards', Schurch worked as an informant and spy from June 1942 until his final arrest in La Spezia, Italy, in April 1945. It was not until October 1943 that information reached the British suggesting that Private Schurch had changed sides, and that he had acted as a 'stool pigeon' on behalf of the enemy at Prison Camp 158, Tarhuna, North Africa, which was an interrogation centre. However, in October 1943 Schurch's whereabouts were unknown. He was in fact in Italy.

Schurch, masquerading as Captain Richards, was introduced to a number of camps in Italy in order to obtain information from as many Allied prisoners of war as he could fool into accepting him as genuine. In February 1943, Schurch was placed in the Special Interrogation Centre so that he could pass time in the company of Lieutenant Colonel David Stirling, the founder and erstwhile commander of the Special Air Service (SAS). They would meet at meals and during exercise sessions. Schurch was put into a cell next to Stirling. However, Stirling was suspicious of him, and although they had a number of conversations, Stirling told him nothing. 'Richards's' Cockney accent was strong so he told some of those that he spoke with that he had started the war as a private, and had been commissioned on the field of battle. After the Allied invasion of Italy, Schurch continued to work for the Fascists, now becoming a full-time spy, endeavouring to penetrate Allied commands, and to learn confidential information that he could pass back. Very near the end of the war, Schurch was operating in La Spezia on the north-west coast of Italy south of Genoa. He was working with a Fascist Italian radio operator. Having successfully penetrated the British HQ in La Spezia,[2] and photographed significant personnel there, Schurch was eventually captured by US troops who became suspicious of him. Schurch was subsequently tried by a British military court for treason, and was convicted and condemned to death. He was hanged at Pentonville on 4 September 1946.

Schurch is a particularly interesting example, because he was introduced to the British Army as early as 1936 to obtain information for his Fascist masters (whether at that stage they were British Fascists, Italians or Nazis) and became a professional spy. He had the quickness of mind to lie and lie well. However, there were plenty of Mosley's toughs who would never have been able to do what Schurch did, but were in due course called up into the armed forces, trained how to fight and to use various weapons to greatest effect. No doubt a number of Leese's Imperial Fascist League, Ramsay's Right Club and Beckett and Greene's British People's Party also joined the forces. The evidence is that, surprisingly, some of them retained their Fascist convictions throughout the war and beyond it – even when the horrors of the Holocaust became known.

The significance of the Schurch example is this: there were British Fascists in the armed services who had not forsaken their Fascist views, and who could be called upon, even in 1944, to support the Fascist cause. Just because a man wore a British Army uniform did not mean that he was not a Fascist.

Chapter 13

Italian Prisoners of War

To shoot an enemy who has surrendered and is therefore a prisoner of war is murder. But if you do not shoot him, what do you do with him? Various international conventions sought to control the actions of those who went to war, with variable success, and the rules regarding prisoners of war during the period 1939–45 were set out in the Geneva Convention of 1929. The intention was to protect those who had surrendered or been captured from abuse, cruelty or death. Inevitably in war, both sides would have men taken prisoner by their enemies, and in order to safeguard the well-being of their own prisoners in enemy hands, the Geneva Convention had been signed by many nations, although not by the Soviet Union or Japan.

In practical terms, this often imposed great difficulty on the captors. Small units operating away from the main body of their force would not want to be burdened with prisoners, who would simply become a nuisance and slow them down. Countries involved in war would often be exhausted, short of manpower and short of food. They would not want to waste food on enemy prisoners, or indeed deploy the manpower required to guard them. Camps would have to be built to hold the prisoners of war, and this required labour and money. It was a problem that any government at war would rather do without. However, whatever the practical difficulties, Britain, Germany and Italy all generally tried hard to abide by the rules of the Geneva Convention with regard to each other's prisoners. Battlefield success inevitably led to the capture of significant numbers of prisoners, and these prisoners had to be housed somewhere. Taking the example of the surrender of Tobruk

in June 1942, about 35,000 Allied prisoners were taken, and all had
to be found accommodation in prison camps. Since the Italians
had started the campaign in the North Africa and the Middle East,
it was Italy's responsibility to house these Allied prisoners. They
struggled to find enough accommodation for them.

The same was true of Great Britain after the successful invasion of
France in June 1944. Before that time, the majority of the prisoners
of war, taken mainly in North Africa, were shipped to parts of the
British Empire where they could be safely contained – in the same
way as detainees had been at the beginning of the war. The purpose
of deporting detainees to far-flung corners of the Empire, at a time
when Britain expected to be invaded imminently by Germany, was to
'clear the decks' of potential enemies within Britain's own borders. It
was as close to a 'no risk' policy as Churchill's government could get.

However, the Geneva Convention allowed for 'other ranks' (not
officers) to be put to work in their 'host' country. Other ranks could
be required to work for a living on farms or in factories outside their
camp. As the war progressed, and thousands of civilians volunteered
or were conscripted into the armed forces, Britain became increasingly short of labour. Women took over many of the men's jobs, but
still there was an acute shortage. Thus, Britain looked for ways of
expanding its civilian work force, and one obvious solution was to
use prisoner of war labour. Having taken extreme measures to get
rid of enemy aliens in 1940, a little later in the war that policy began
to change.

By the summer of 1941, the immediate threat of an invasion of
the United Kingdom had passed. The British armed forces had regrouped, the Battle of Britain had been won by the Royal Air Force,
and the war in North Africa against the Italians was going reasonably
well. Many thousands of Italian prisoners had been taken, often
because the conscripted and ill-equipped Italian soldiers had no
will to fight in an overseas war for Mussolini's 'Italian Empire'. At
home, the fear of a Fifth Column seems to have lessened with the
passing of the threat of immediate invasion, and in total contrast
to government policy in the previous years of the war, a decision

was taken to import enemy personnel into Britain. Faced with the shortage of labour, it was decided to bring some 50,000 Italian prisoners of war into the United Kingdom, so that they could be put to work, and thereby ease the increasingly acute labour shortage. Indeed prisoners often welcomed work to alleviate their boredom. Working parties of prisoners would normally be supervised by armed guards, and would work where required in the community.

The decision to use Italian prisoner labour no doubt seemed a sensible one when it was taken, and by June 1941 the first 3,000 prisoners of war were on their way from Libya and the Near East. Amongst them, there would no doubt be some hardened Fascists, but those (it was believed) could be adequately guarded and controlled. Those government departments thought appropriate were informed of the decision, including the Prisoners of War Branch of the War Office. Camps were prepared or built in various parts of the country where it was intended that the prisoners should work. One such camp was at Comrie, in Perthshire. The camps were given numbers, and Comrie became Camp 21. It was built for and used by Italians, until later in the war when it was needed for German prisoners.

Then, in the middle of June 1941, it was suddenly realised that the Italian prisoners carried with them a serious threat to Great Britain. Nobody had considered the dangerous infectious diseases that they might bring into the country. Through an oversight, nobody had seen fit to inform the Ministry of Health of the scheme until it was too late to stop it. Only on 17 June did a Brigadier Richardson telephone the Ministry of Health. Richardson had realised the problem. The memorandum recording his call, and a subsequent visit by Dr P. G. Stock to Richardson's office in Hobart House, London, reads:

'[Richardson] informed me that it was proposed to bring to this country from the Near East some 50,000 Italian prisoners of war, who would probably be employed as labourers . . . the first 3,000 Italian prisoners of war are now on their way and are due to arrive on July 8, but the port of entry is not known. The men will go to two transit camps – one near Sheffield and the other at Press Heath, Shropshire – and from these camps they will be distributed all over the country. From the information in his possession, Brigadier Richardson anticipated that malaria, dysentery, typhoid fever and pediculosis had been rife amongst prisoners.'[1]

The Army authorities would do their best to provide hospital accommodation where necessary, and disinfestation treatment, but the Ministry of Health was invited to advise on further precautions.

On the face of it, the decision to bring thousands of Italians to British shores was a gift to Hitler and Mussolini. Germ warfare was against the rules of war (as it remains today), but on this occasion the British could not blame their enemies. Any illness or fatality that resulted from the presence of the Italians would be no one's fault but the British government's. Although 50,000 Italian prisoners of war would undoubtedly help to solve the labour crisis, if even a small percentage of these prisoners proved to be carriers of potentially fatal diseases, and typhoid or malaria, for example, took a grip on Britain in the summer of 1941, a disaster would follow. To make things worse, they were to arrive in midsummer, when the weather was likely to be warm, and the indigenous mosquitoes would be active. The Geneva Convention also demanded that prisoners of war should receive the same rations as their captor's soldiers. British soldiers received better rations than civilians, and thus the Italian prisoners of war would do so as well. Civilian victims of any diseases that they carried would not be as well nourished.

On 24 June 1941, the Ministry of Health wrote to the Director at the Prisoners of War Branch at the War Office:

'The Minister apprehends that certain infectious diseases may be prevalent amongst these Italian prisoners of war, and is anxious that all possible steps should be taken to prevent any spread of such diseases, especially malaria and dysentery, in consequence of their arrival in this country. It is understood that the Army Medical Authorities will undertake certain measures by way of inoculation, disinfestation etc. at the

Transit Camps, but the Minister is particularly concerned to ensure that precautions are taken in districts to which these prisoners may be sent to work as labourers ... the risk of spread of malaria is greater in some parts of the country than in others, and the Ministry would be prepared to furnish you with information on this point if it is agreed that steps would then be taken to avoid, as far as is possible, sending any Italian prisoners of war who may be carriers of malaria to a district where there is the most risk of spreading this disease.'[2]

The prisoners of war began arriving on 8 July 1941. There was competition as to who could use their labour, and a note on the same day from Dr Stock reads: 'The Ministry of Agriculture and Fisheries particularly wants men at Doddington [in the fenland of Cambridgeshire], and asked whether we would agree if prisoners from Libya, born north of the River Po, and apparently free from malaria, could be sent.'[3] The Ministry of Health was clearly not happy with the request, but wrote: 'We would not press our objections to this first contingent.' A later memorandum explains that Italian prisoners captured in Abyssinia (where the danger of contracting infectious diseases was apparently greater) must not be sent to Doddington.

The question of which districts were most in danger of the spread of malaria was carefully examined. The expert advice was that there was only one type of mosquito which constituted real danger – *Anopheles maculipennis* (var. *stroparvus*). This mosquito was found in sufficient numbers to carry malaria in coastal areas along the south coast of England east of Wareham in Dorset, and up the east coast as far north as the River Humber. This included the Thames estuary, the Isle of Grain, the Isle of Sheppey, Harwich, Ipswich, Great Yarmouth, the Isle of Ely, and parts of Norfolk and Lincolnshire. Doddington labour camp, four miles south of March in Cambridgeshire, was in this area.

The difficulty for the Ministry of Health was that there were strong competing interests. Following the guidelines that had been issued, a prospective site for a labour camp on the Isle of Ely was inspected

by the local Medical Officer of Health and military hygiene experts
at the end of July 1941. They rejected the site as unsuitable because
of 'the general conditions prevailing at the site and the possibility
that the site may be flooded in winter, together with the evidence
found of the existence of mosquitoes which might act as malaria
carriers'. The Isle of Ely had, of course, been certified as one of the
danger areas. Despite this, plans for the camp went ahead, and by
the end of August the camp was up and running with Italian prison
labour on site.

Mr P. G. Shute noted in a memorandum dated 1 September 1941:
'Dr Banks . . . states that the Ely site is being used. You will remember
that anopheles [mosquitoes] are breeding on the site. I suppose there
is nothing we can do about it, but it is to be hoped that the local
doctors will at once notify any cases of fever in the village (especially
children) where the cause of the fever presents any difficulties.'[4] Shute
went on to recommend spraying the animal houses on a nearby farm
with an insecticide called Flit, both in October and March, to try and
reduce the population of *maculipennis* mosquitoes.

The Ministry of Health's Malaria Laboratory at Horton Hospital
in Epsom, Surrey, was busily trying to find a solution to the problem.
They were not concerned about those who were openly exhibiting
signs of malaria or other diseases. They could be isolated and
treated. The Ministry was concerned to identify the carriers of the
disease who might pass it on to others. If a carrier was bitten by
a *maculipennis* mosquito, that mosquito would drink his infected
blood, and would thereafter pass on the infection to others that it
bit. Shute wanted to take blood from the prisoners for examination.
The Ministry of Health said that he could not do so without the
permission of the military authorities in whose care the prisoners
were – a classic 'red tape' problem. On 8 September 1941, it was
confirmed that the military would be responsible for screening the
blood of Italian prisoners.

However, 'proper procedures having been satisfied', the Royal
Army Medical Corps, which provided doctors for all of the camps,
invited Shute to attend the Ely camp and examine the prisoners'

blood screens. The results were encouraging, and by November 1941, Shute had examined 100 blood screens. He reported that he had found no parasites, but that the absence of parasites was not evidence that a person had not had malaria, and might not relapse.

With precautions now in place, and with the coming of autumn and winter, it seems that the danger of a major outbreak of disease was averted. Many more Italian prisoners of war duly followed the first 3,000, and the majority settled happily down to work. There were rabid Fascists amongst them, but where identified, these were usually segregated from the workforce, and held in a separate camp.

Nonetheless, the vigilance of the Ministry of Health, and Mr Shute of Horton Hospital, continued throughout the following summer. For instance, on 21 July 1942, Shute paid a visit to a camp at Horsham in Sussex. He liaised with the camp medical officer, a Dr Hope Gill, and examined the site. He reported: 'A few Anopheles larvae and some Culex were found in a ditch near the pump. Here the sides of the drain have caved in and if this was remedied the breeding would stop.'

So, happily, disaster was avoided, and no 'Italian plague' swept through Great Britain. If there were cases of British nationals catching malaria, or any other unpleasant disease from Italian prisoners of war, they were few in number, and were kept confidential. Most of the Italian prisoners worked well, and many seemed quite content with their new role in life. There had long been a natural friendship between the British and the Italians – until Mussolini imposed his regime on Italy.

As the Allies invaded and fought for control of Sicily in July 1943, Mussolini was finally deposed by his own Fascist Grand Council. In the Italian prisoner of war camps in Britain, morale fell sharply amongst the Fascists. In many of the camps, there were pro-Fascists who had tried to maintain the Fascist ideals, and to run the camps on Fascist lines. Most of them now fell silent.[5] Generally, the news came as a great shock, and for a time many Fascists refused to believe it. As the truth sank it, many prisoners were relieved that Mussolini had finally gone, but remained afraid to express their feelings, because they were still frightened of the Fascists who had, for so long, ruled their lives.

However, in the autumn of 1943, a complication arose. On 3 September, Italy signed an armistice agreement with the Allies, and nominally withdrew from the war. The armistice was announced on 8 September. The reaction in the camps was one of distress and depression at the defeat of their country. However, after the announcement of the armistice, the Germans, who had been fighting with the Italians against the Allied invasion, refused to leave Italy. After the invasion of Sicily in July, when Mussolini had been deposed, control of Italy had been handed back to the King, Victor Emmanuel III. He had appointed an old Army chief, Marshal Badoglio, to be his prime minister, and Mussolini had been arrested and imprisoned in the Gran Sasso mountains. Germany rescued Mussolini from his mountain prison, using paratroopers amongst whom was Otto Skorzeny, whose exploits have already been described. Mussolini was restored to the 'throne' of Italy as Hitler's puppet, and created a new Fascist Republic in the north of Italy with Hitler's support. This caused a hardening of divisions in the camps – prisoners now became starkly pro or anti the new Fascist regime. The royalist Italian government then declared war on Germany, and became a co-belligerent of the Allies. There were now Italians fighting for and against the Allies – for the Italians, it had become a civil war.

Inevitably, the status of Italian prisoners of war taken in the conflict before 3 September 1943 had now to be considered.[6] Italy's co-belligerence with the Allies in Italy was not unimportant, since the new government supplied a number of divisions to fight alongside the Allies in Italy, and intelligence of considerable value. Partisan groups were co-operating with the Allies, and caused considerable damage behind enemy lines. The Allied armies in Italy had a tough campaign to fight, and with the preparations for D-Day, many troops were transferred from Italy, leaving the Allies there short of men. The support of the Italian royalist forces was of value, as was the entry of Brazil into the war on the Allied side in 1942 – something which Ben Greene, in particular, must have lamented because of his connections to the German community in Brazil. In 1944 Brazil supplied thousands of troops to fight with the Allies in Italy.

The Italian prisoners of war whom the Allies held had been captured fighting for Fascist Italy – and there was now a new Fascist Italy under Mussolini. With the war still ongoing, Britain was reluctant to release or otherwise change the status of the Italian prisoners it held. Prime Minister Badoglio, however, pressed for an amelioration in relation to the welfare and conditions of the Italian prisoners. As he put it in early April 1944, he was 'anxious to do everything in his power to enable Italian prisoners of war to contribute a greater share in helping the war effort against the enemy'. Many of the Italian prisoners of war in the British camps were keen to fight the Germans, and to throw them out of Italy.

The Italians were divided into two categories – Co-operators and Non-co-operators. The Non-co-operators were usually keen Fascists, and sometimes dangerous men. They would be kept in separate camps, and properly guarded, whereas the Co-operators would be sent out to work and were increasingly allowed freedom of movement. Italian Prisoner of War Pioneer Companies were set up. A report in 1944 assessed that only 15 per cent of the Italian prisoners now supported Fascism and the Germans.[7] The possibility of recruiting Italian prisoners of war into a special regiment of those who wanted to fight for the King of Italy was considered but, in the end, rejected.

In the event, Britain's attitude to its existing Italian prisoners did soften somewhat. Those who had been working in Britain since the summer of 1941, and those who had arrived subsequently, were doing valuable work, and many had settled down happily in the communities where the camps had been placed. Indeed, when the war finished, many Italians decided to make their future in Britain, rather than return home. The camp at Beechbarrow House Farm, Pen Hill, near Wells in Somerset was one of a number where that happened. So happy was the relationship between the Italian prisoners of war and the local people on whose farms they worked that they erected a monument (architect Gaetano Celestra) on the boundary wall beside the road to Wells, depicting Romulus and Remus, the mythological founders of Rome, suckled by a she wolf. The monument was dedicated to the bond of friendship between prisoners and those they worked for. These prisoners were, of course, those classed as Co-operators.

There were Italian prisoners being captured every day – soldiers of the new Fascist Army. Although these included hardened Fascists, they also included many who had simply been caught up in the tide of history, and who, once in imprisonment, were happy to become Co-operators, and go out to work.

The assessments of the position of Italian prisoners of war by the British Political Warfare Executive, who monitored their reactions to events in Italy carefully during the armistice period, suggest that the Italians were never considered a threat. They were believed by the British authorities, really upon the basis of their performance in North Africa, not to be good soldiers, and were generally viewed quite differently from the Germans. Ardent Fascists were regarded as a problem, but not, apparently, as any real danger. Italian Fascists were, where possible, placed in special Non-co-operator camps, such as Camp 14 at Doonfoot, just south of Ayr in Scotland. By December 1944, Italian prisoners of war were continuing to be of considerable use to the British economy, and nobody worried very much about the Non-co-operators.

Chapter 14

Colonel Scotland and the London Cage

All prisoners of war who arrived in Britain were screened by Military Intelligence 19 (MI19), which was responsible for what was described in internal correspondence as a 'comb out'. A memorandum of 25 May 1944 records that all German prisoners of war would be interrogated as to their views on Nazism, and would be classified on the basis of their replies as Black (pro-Nazis) or Black plus (vehement Nazis), Grey (uncertain) or White (anti-Nazi). The Whites might be sent to Lingfield Camp, described as being a special camp for intelligence and political warfare purposes.[1] They would be further interrogated, and then, if thought suitable, would be transferred to a 'friendly' camp at Ascot. One of the objects of this process was to cultivate potential informants, who could later supply information on what the Black Nazis were getting up to. Many camps contained mixed Black, Grey and White Germans, and an effort was made to ensure that the Senior Officer in each camp was a White. In theory, he himself might inform on the activities of the committed Nazis, and there would be informants in most of the camps. It was of great importance to know what was going on inside the camps. Covert recording devices were installed in certain parts of some camps, but the best intelligence came from informants. Thus it was often necessary to leave an informant who was in fact an anti-Nazi in a camp which contained a preponderance of Black prisoners.

Working against the intrigues of enemy prisoners of war was an intelligence operation run by a section of MI19, the Prisoners of War

Information Service (PWIS). It ran a number of interrogation centres, the most important of which was the London Interrogation Centre (known as the London Cage) run by a Lieutenant Colonel Alexander Paterson Scotland, the head of the PWIS. It was the responsibility of Scotland and his team to interrogate all of the most important prisoners of war on their arrival in the United Kingdom. Scotland was a man in his sixties, fluent in the German language, who had the unusual distinction of having served in the German Army many years before. As a young man in 1903, he had been working for a trading company known as South African Territories Limited in a town called Ramonsdrift on South Africa's border with the German colony of South-West Africa. When the Hottentots rose in rebellion against the Germans, Scotland, who had by then learned to speak German, was involved in the supply of provisions to the German troops seeking to subdue the rebellion.[2] Because the Germans were short of officers, Scotland was offered an appointment as a supply officer in the German Army. He accepted the role, and as a result, he came to learn a lot about how the German Army worked. He remained with the German Army for four years. Thus not only did Scotland speak good military German, but he knew the workings of the German Army well, and understood the mentality of the German officer and soldier.

Thereafter, Scotland was recruited by British Intelligence to keep an eye on what was going on in German South-West Africa. When the First World War broke out, he was arrested by the Germans and imprisoned for a year. He was regularly interrogated, in lengthy and arduous sessions. When finally released, Scotland made his way back to Britain, and it was not long before he took up intelligence duties in France – interrogating German prisoners of war. With his experience as a German officer, and a prisoner of war of the Germans, Scotland was able to produce most impressive results. He developed a very effective style of interrogating German prisoners. Between the wars, Scotland visited various parts of the world including Germany, where he retained many friends, and parts of South America. On one occasion in Germany, Scotland met Adolf Hitler.

Thus, over many years leading up to the eventual outbreak of World War Two, Scotland, through his personal experiences, his visits to Germany, and his numerous German contacts, had built up a very detailed knowledge of the German Army and of interrogation techniques. At the outbreak of war in September 1939, Scotland was appointed to command the London Cage – the interrogation centre based at 6–8, Kensington Palace Gardens, London. There he ran a very effective team of German-speaking interrogators, many of them Jews. As is obvious, the information that could be gained from prisoners of war was potentially extensive and highly useful. The difficulty was persuading the prisoners to supply it. Scotland used a variety of techniques, and produced a lot of very valuable information.

Scotland, an old-fashioned soldier, undoubtedly viewed the techniques that he and his interrogators employed as fair and pro-portionate. He clearly believed that he could treat German prisoners of war in the same way that their own German officers would treat them, using physical force where necessary to bring them into line. However, modern-day human-rights lawyers would have protested at many of his methods, as became clear when, in the 1950s, Scotland wrote a very revealing book about his time at the London Cage. His manuscript was submitted by his publishers to the War Office for approval, but they did not get it.[3] Eventually, a much-edited version was published under the title *The London Cage* in 1957. The original manuscript remained banned by the War Office for many years, but is now available for all to read in the National Archives at Kew, London

Comparing Scotland's methods at the London Cage to those of the Gestapo in Germany perhaps puts them into perspective. Scotland did not pull out finger nails, administer electric-shock treatment or order regular beatings. However, because the London Cage was a transit camp, and men were not held there for very long, it did not fall under the Geneva Convention regime of regular inspections by the Red Cross. Scotland also argued that many of those held there were being held on suspicion of crime (usually war crimes), and therefore did not fall under the jurisdiction of the Red Cross anyway. Scotland, with his experience of the German Army and its methods, clearly believed the things that he did to break the will of an arrogant and self-opinionated Nazi prisoner were justified and were not torture. He complained in his manuscript that he had been accused of far worse things than he had ever done, particularly during the post-war Nuremberg Trials. In summary, his technique appears to have been to break the will of a prisoner, and to interview him once he was compliant, usually on a different occasion.

The London Cage was made up of three houses in Kensington Palace Gardens, all of them of three storeys plus basements. They were surrounded by a single barbed-wire fence. Number 8 was detached and Numbers 6 and 7 were semi-detached. Number 8 was used as accommodation for the guards, who were posted inside and out throughout the compound. Scotland had his office in Number 7, and prisoners were held in Numbers 6 and 7, some in single rooms, others in dormitories. Scotland was in complete charge. In his unpublished manuscript, he gives a number of examples of how he broke down awkward 'customers'.

One 'customer' he described as a 'stocky, bullet-headed, arrogant young Nazi'. The Nazi told Scotland that he would not answer any questions. He announced that he refused to speak, and nothing could force him to do so. Scotland ordered the Nazi to stand up straight and keep silent, and then simply got on with his work, ignoring the Nazi completely. When Scotland had finished his paperwork for the day, he ordered that the Nazi should be kept there, in his office, standing up. He would be supplied with meals, taken to the toilet when necessary, but otherwise totally ignored until he said he was ready to speak to Scotland. The light was kept on in the office during the night, and the Nazi was not allowed to sleep. The Nazi endured this treatment for twenty-six hours, and then gave in and talked. Physically, he was undoubtedly tired from standing; psychologically, he had been totally ignored for twenty-six hours, which had knocked the Nazi arrogance and 'strutting' attitude completely out of his system.

The first edition of Sir Oswald Mosley's British Union of Fascists paper, dated February 1933. Note the slogan 'Britain First' and the attack on parliamentary democracy.

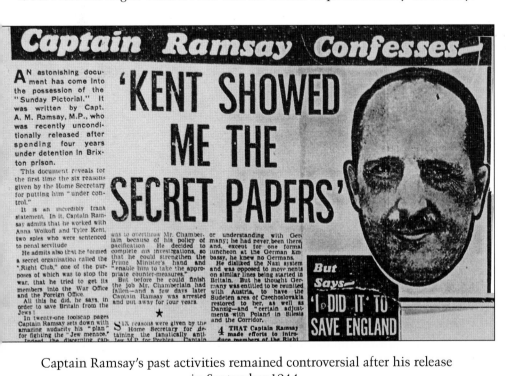

Captain Ramsay's past activities remained controversial after his release in September 1944.

Arnold Spencer Leese, in the uniform of
the Imperial Fascist League
which he founded and led.

Oliver Conway Gilbert, Chairman and
Treasurer of the Nordic League,
yet another Fascist organisation.

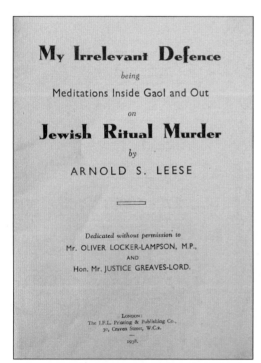

After serving a prison sentence in 1936,
Leese published this account of his trial,
in justification of his cause.

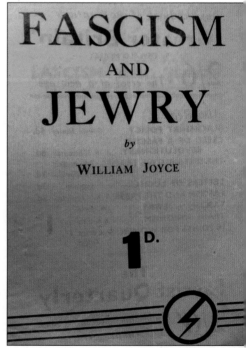

William Joyce, 'Lord Haw Haw', published
this anti-Semitic pamphlet whilst a
Mosley supporter before the war.

The result of Vehmic Justice: the body of Werner Drechsler, murdered at Papago Park Camp, Phoenix, Arizona.

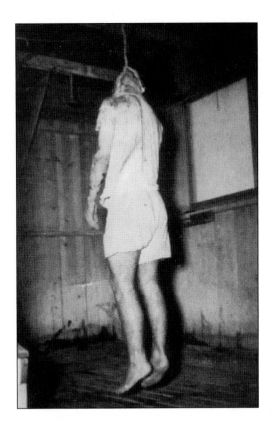

The shower block where Werner Dreschler's body was displayed.

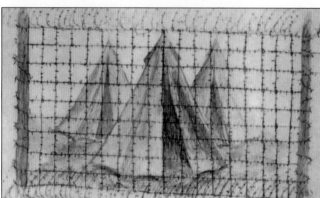

Above, left & below: Views of Camp 23, Le Marchant, Devizes, drawn by Hermann Gensler.

Right: The former armoury building of Camp 23.

Top, far right: The keep of Le Marchant Barracks, Devizes, in December 2018. It is now converted into a block of flats.

Der Tag....

Contrasting camp styles of British and German prisoners. Tidy bunks and military discipline at Camp 23 (*above right*), as drawn by Hermann Gensler. A sketch of Camp 21, Chieti, Italy, drawn by Lieutenant Jack Hodgson Shepherd (*right*).

A Corner of a Living Quarter for 20 Officers P.G. 21
Size 45' x 18'

Above: Much of Camp 21, Comrie, remains unchanged today. These are huts from Compound C photographed in February 2019.

Above left & left: Drawings by an unknown German artist depicting a section of the camp's Polish guards and his impression of the camp and its location as seen from a nearby hill.

A contemporary police photograph of Hut 4,
where Wolfgang Rosterg was beaten and tortured before his death.

Camp 17 at Lodge Moor, Sheffield, drawn by Heinz Georg Lutz, prisoner of war.

Camp 17, Lodge Moor, Sheffield – all that remains today. The photograph shows the base of one of the many huts which held prisoners of war.

With an older Nazi prisoner, Scotland describes using a different method. The man had been causing a lot of trouble, and was apparently trying to provoke the British guards in the London Cage to attack him. Scotland paraded all the officers and other ranks of the guard in one of the rooms, and then, sitting behind a desk, had the prisoner brought in. He ordered the prisoner to kneel in front of him, and then boxed his ears. Scotland then explained to the Nazi that this was how a German commanding officer would deal with a troublesome soldier under his command, and that it was a German form of official reprimand. According to Scotland, this treatment had the desired effect, and the prisoner caused no further trouble. Scotland had, of course, assaulted his prisoner, but justified his actions on the basis that what he did was standard disciplinary action in the German Army.

Scotland said in his manuscript:

'In both these cases, I used a modicum of physical force to discipline a prisoner, but, I repeat, it was never used to obtain military information. It was apparent to us from time to time that Nazi prisoners expected to be beaten up; after all, they were past masters in this treatment, and probably expected some of their own treatment to be meted out to them.'

Scotland clearly specialised in ways to break down Nazi arrogance and pride, after which interrogation would become easy. He gave an example of a group of U-boat men:

'Many of these U-boat men prided themselves on being tough, and three of them, all officers, had to be shown that we were indifferent to their posing. When they arrived at the cage they used to lie in bed and order the guards around. (A deliberate tactic designed to impose psychological supremacy over their guards.) I was asked what should be done about them, and I replied that they should be treated the same as anybody in the British Service who refused to get out of bed. The next thing the U-boat officers knew was that their beds had been turned right over and that they were underneath. We took their uniforms away and set them to work in denim suits on cage chores for three days. We found the ruling of the Geneva Convention that prisoners may be employed on various duties and chores in a transit camp to be useful on many occasions for not only were we short-staffed at times, but it was a salutary exercise in discipline when awkward prisoners found themselves put to work with a bucket and scrubbing brush.'

Another, more dramatic example that Scotland gives is of an occasion when he had three Germans in front of him, all of whom claimed to be doctors, and therefore entitled to that status as prisoners of war. Having questioned them, Scotland was of the view that one of them was not a qualified doctor at all, but only at best a medical student. However, all three men supported each other. Scotland's solution was to announce that, in order to test their stories, he demanded that one of the genuine doctors was to have his perfectly healthy appendix removed by the 'doctor' whom he suspected was not qualified. That called their bluff! Of course, one advantage that Scotland would always have in an interrogation scenario was that he could threaten to do something which was obviously outside his power in Britain, but which would have been entirely possible in Nazi Germany, and thus his subject would believe him.

Scotland emphasised that he never used physical force 'to obtain military information', but would only use it to break the will of a troublesome prisoner. It seems that the London Cage gained a reputation for sorting out German troublemakers, and that a number of particularly difficult prisoners were sent there from the permanent camps simply so that Scotland and his team could impress upon them the importance of compliance with the prison camp rules.

The difficulty with any interrogation is that once a prisoner has 'talked', what he has said has to be evaluated. Those prisoners who supplied information to Scotland and his team might to do so for a number of reasons – most often to curry favour and seek to get better treatment or some advantage whilst prisoners of war. Sometimes they would lie, sometimes they would tell a part of or all the truth. Some lied well, some lied badly. Private Schurch, for example, was an extremely plausible, very practised liar.

It is generally accepted that confessions obtained through torture are unreliable – a victim simply tells his torturer what he thinks the torturer wants to hear to make the pain stop. Scotland would argue strongly that he did not torture any of his prisoners into making a statement. He and his team built up a detailed background knowledge of all the matters that they investigated, and could often prove a liar to be telling lies – but not always.

As we have already seen, one difficulty about interrogations of German prisoners of war was the Nazi Vehmic law system. If a prisoner under interrogation was more frightened of the Vehmic *Rollkommando* teams of thugs than of his British interrogators, then he was unlikely to tell the truth, or if he told it, might well have second thoughts and retract it later.

Chapter 15

Camp 21 at Comrie
British Colditz, Nazi Hell

Even with 'White' anti-Nazi Senior German Officers, the German prisoner of war camps were generally run internally by pro-Nazi, 'Black' prisoners. Nazi culture and discipline was to be maintained at all times, Nazi songs were regularly sung en masse by the German prisoners, and the Nazis imposed a savage discipline on those who did not behave in the way that good Nazis should. Punishments of various kinds, including beatings, were commonplace. They were very difficult to prevent, since the prisoners spent much of their time inside their accommodation unsupervised. Usually the Nazis conducted 'disciplinary proceedings' in the early hours of the morning, in Vehmic-style 'courts'. If the victim was warned of his fate, or a White Senior Officer found out in time, a request could be put in for a transfer to an anti-Nazi camp, but there were dangers even in that. A 20 May 1944 memorandum reports that approximately 600 German prisoners had been transferred to a special camp because their safety could not be guaranteed in the camps where they were.[1] That was before the flood of prisoners that followed the D-Day invasion of Normandy had begun.

Camp 21, Cultybraggan, Comrie, Scotland was regarded as the British equivalent of Colditz – it was a high-security camp, from which escape was extremely difficult. The camp was situated in a fairly remote part of Scotland, and was purpose-built, constructed in 1941. It stood (and still stands today) on a plain surrounded by mountains and moorland. It had the security advantage that it had been constructed on ground that had been raised and levelled. The soil was therefore loosely packed, and totally unsuited to tunnelling.

Tunnels were attempted, but nobody tunnelled out of Comrie Camp. However, it was always very difficult to control what the prisoners did amongst themselves, and to each other. The camp was split into four individual compounds, each wired off from the others, and each nominally a separate community. Each had a Senior Officer, and each hut had an appointed Leader.

In the autumn of 1944, intelligence was gathered as to what was going on in Camp 21. In mid-December 1944, a memorandum already cited was circulated by MI19. It read:

'In the officers' sections of [Compounds] B and C at Comrie, the SS and paratroops had organised a regular system of spying on other officers. In B, which was the worst, there was a sort of Vehmic organisation i.e. a secret police with executive powers. If, for instance, they recognised a man who had ever made an anti-Nazi remark, they maltreated him under cover of darkness. They were careful to note for punishment those who did not give the Nazi Salute. Their activities became those of organised terrorism. They had spies in all the huts and compiled lists of anti-Nazis, which were to be smuggled into Germany by means of exchanged Prisoners of War. There is a regulation in Germany that, if a Prisoner of War does anything against the Government, or opposes it, the Government has the right to take steps against both his private property and against the lives of members of his immediate family. A copy of the list of Officers selected for the anti-Nazi Camp 13 is said to have been made by a supposed Unteroffizier working in Compound B at Comrie, and to have come into possession either of the spies or out-and-out Nazis, who openly threatened those included on that list that, if they went to Camp 13, the Nazis would see to it that the German Government and the Security Service in Germany heard that they had moved to an anti-Nazi Camp, and the members of their family and property would be treated accordingly. If this list could not be smuggled into Germany, it was intended that some Prisoner of War who was going to be exchanged should inform the S.D. [Security Service] in Germany that everyone in Camp 13 was friendly to England and anti-National [Socialist].

A number of Nazis wormed their way into Camp 13 and immediately started to stir up political trouble as before. When the War Office turned out these spies, they threatened those remaining that if they did not get turned out quickly too, they would make it public [in Germany] that they were in Camp 13. The ringleader at Comrie was Obersturmbannführer Jaeckel.'[2]

One of the devices used to gather intelligence was to covertly record the conversations of German officer prisoners of war when they were talking together. Often the content would be useless, but sometimes it was of real value. If the information did seem valuable, it would often be followed up by an interview of those who had been involved in the discussion. The report above was based on information from a Major Zapp, who had been captured in Brussels on 4 September 1944, and who had been imprisoned at Comrie in early October.[3] By mid-December he was no longer there. Judging by what he said, he almost certainly left before the death of Major Willi Thormann on 29 November 1944, or he would have mentioned it. He was speaking with an Oberst Wachsmuth, who had been the Commandant of the Military Hospital in Brussels, and had been captured the day before Zapp on 3 September 1944. On 14 December, Zapp had said to Wachsmuth:

'I don't know whether I should tell the Intelligence Officer this. At the Comrie Camp there was a whole "Kompanie" – [the camp] was divided into separate "Kompanien" with separate hutments – in which there were only parachutists, who were very tough, and SS men. They had organised a proper Vehmic court, and at night they stuck up threatening posters, signed: "The Vehmic Court". They had their confidential men in all the hutments and had compiled lists. Those lists were to be smuggled into Germany with exchanged prisoners of war.'

Zapp went on to say that when there was a move by the British to transfer 200 prisoners from Comrie to Camp 13, the list of proposed transferees was obtained by Jaeckel, who then proposed to send it with a disabled prisoner, who was to be exchanged, back to Germany. Apparently, there was a *Sturmbannführer* of the Todt Organisation who had a wooden leg, and the plan was to conceal the list of anti-Nazi prisoners in his leg when he was sent home. Zapp repeated that it was made clear to all German prisoners that the Nazis knew that Camp 13 was the anti-Nazi camp, and that they had informed the censor in Germany to that effect. That meant that any letters home, which had to carry the prisoner's camp number and address, would be intercepted by the Sicherheitsdienst (the SS Security Service) if they came from Camp 13, and the families of the prisoner would be punished. Zapp said that as a result nobody dared write a letter home from Camp 13:

'Of course a lot of officers are scared stiff, and they are justified ... An order was issued a little while ago that any prisoner of war occupying a special position, or coming under special arrangements, or collaborating with the enemy, shall pay for this with the lives of all his family and with his entire fortune ... that's the sort of terrorism there is in that camp! You can't imagine the terrorism that is there.'

Wachsmuth asked about the Camp Leader, a White anti-Nazi German called Prince Urach. Zapp replied:

'He's scared stiff as he himself has a lot of relations who were arrested in connection with 20 July [the bomb plot to assassinate Hitler]. He was terrified that something would leak out, and that others in the Camp would denounce him by means of letters to Germany, saying that he had advocated those ideas with the Camp Commandant; then he might be identified with the 20 July "putsch" and his wife liquidated as a result. Obersturmbannführer Jaeckel is a frightful fellow, he is the terror of the whole hut ... he organised a spy organisation and had a spy in every hut and always made notes, about every individual there.'

On 15 December, Zapp and Wachsmuth were interviewed together by a British Intelligence Officer. Zapp referred again to what was going on in Comrie as terrorism, and to the system of Vehmic courts. He explained that the officers' part of the camp was divided into two compounds, B and C, separated only by some barbed wire. Each sector contained about 1,000 officers. Zapp said that Compound B was the worst sector for Nazi terrorism, but C, where he had lived, was similar. Sturmbannführer Jaeckel was in Hut 1 in C, and controlled the Nazi 'spies' who reported back on perceived anti-Nazis.

Zapp himself had courted trouble when he saluted a British officer with a normal military salute. Although his act was noticed by the Nazis, he got away with it. Others were not so lucky. Zapp said that six or seven officers had to be taken out of Compound B into protective custody, because otherwise 'they would have been more or less murdered'. He said that violence was regularly used against suspected officers. He explained that the Vehmic police had tried to throttle two officers at night. He added: 'Then there were those proper Vehmic courts. There were posters with headings like "Regulation so and so of the Camp Police".' There was a hut exclusively occupied by German paratroopers, and the violence was meted out by them.

Zapp said that a rumour had circulated at Comrie that the British intended to set up special camps for non-Nazis. Then, according to Zapp, a list of about 200 officers (out of a total of 2,000 in the camp) was compiled by the British authorities. The list included all of the officers whom they believed to be anti-Nazi. They were to be moved to Camp 13, one of the special, non-Nazi camps. The list came into the hands of Jaeckel's Vehmic organisation, and threats were immediately issued to everyone on the list: 'If you go to a camp like that, we will see to it that the German government and the Security Service in Germany hear that you have moved to an anti-Nazi camp, and the members of your family in Germany or your property will be treated accordingly.' According to Zapp, the British list had been badly flawed, and sixty-two of the alleged non-Nazis were in fact vehemently pro-Nazi. They were identified and removed by the British, but yet more still remained in Camp 13. The problem was, said Zapp, that the sixty-two Nazis who had been kicked out of Camp 13 had seen exactly who else was there. Hence the threat: 'Get out of Camp 13 or else you will be black-listed as an anti-Nazi!' As Zapp put it:

> 'All those in Camp 13 are caught in a trap and their relatives and property are in the greatest danger. Things have gone so far we in Camp 13 – I was in Camp 13 too – haven't written a single letter from Camp 13. They are all too much afraid.'

Zapp said that the officers' compounds at Comrie, Compounds B and C, had now been disbanded, and only 'other ranks' were billeted there. All the officers were taken away on the same day, in five separate batches. It later transpired, as we shall see, that the Nazi other ranks were as bad as their officers. The Vehmic system was an essential part of a Nazi-controlled camp.

It is, in fact, no surprise that recently captured Nazis sought to exert the same rule of terror in their prisoner of war camps as they had within Germany and its occupied territories earlier in the war and before. Fear and the Vehmic courts were very effective ways of ensuring that most prisoners of war obeyed Nazi orders, and they enabled Nazis to maintain a far greater control over their fellow prisoners, and to order them to take part in escape schemes. The fact that a prisoner's family back in Germany might be executed because the prisoner was suspected of no longer being a good Nazi was a strong incentive to obedience. Being taken prisoner in wartime is always the most demoralising experience – a serviceman is rendered powerless, unable to fight any longer for his country or to protect and support his family. In that state, a threat to one's family is devastating. For a prisoner of war to feel unable to write home to his family, and to forgo that vital personal contact, as Zapp describes, is a cruel sacrifice.

Chapter 16

Escapers and Accomplices

The Prisoners of War Assistance Society

It was a part of the accepted duty of any prisoner of war to try to escape and rejoin his own forces. From mainland Britain, that was particularly difficult because Britain was an island. From Northern Ireland, it was in theory considerably easier, because of the land border with Eire, which was a neutral country. However, what the British government feared most were not escapes aimed at getting home, but those aimed at committing sabotage. They were concerned that prisoners might escape in order to damage important installations, communications or military equipment. In fact, little if any of that seems to have happened.

To fully understand the prisoner of war escape mentality, it is necessary to consider the situation in which a prisoner of war found himself, particularly an officer. Capture was usually a shock – one minute you were fighting for your country and for your family's well-being, the next you were an impotent prisoner, totally under the control of your captors, with your future in their hands. However, once the shock had passed, a prisoner would either accept his imprisonment, give up and wait for the end of the war, or dedicate most of his time and effort to the possibility of escape. In the case of the Allies, there were a number of prisoners who gave up, and decided simply to sit out the war. Others often became obsessed by the idea of escape.

Allied prisoners in enemy hands were usually divided up into camps containing their own service – Army, Navy or Royal Air Force

– and a prison camp would hold perhaps thousands of initially fit, mostly young men, who between them had a vast array of skills. The officers, who were not allowed by the Geneva Convention to be used as labourers, had nothing to do all day and every day. If they wished, they could dedicate all their skills and all their energy to escape. Many did. However, although discipline was maintained as best the Senior Allied Officer in each camp could, it was not reinforced by the threats against prisoners' families or the physical brutality of the German camps. An illustration is the difference between the messy and somewhat chaotic barrack rooms of British prisoners (as illustrated in the paintings of Lieutenant Jack Hodgson Sheppard) and the military order of the German prisoners, who had to make their beds tidy and clean their barrack room every morning. Nonetheless, British escapes from camps in Germany and Italy were regular and often very ingenious. It was a constant challenge for the various organisations who were allowed to send parcels and letters to the British prisoners in the camps to try to smuggle in to them escape aids – maps, compasses and so on. The Red Cross was in no way involved in this, because its parcels were too important to the health and welfare of the prisoners to be tampered with, but those of the YMCA or other welfare organisations (some entirely fictitious) might contain a variety of items useful to escapers.

The British camps for Germans were different in some ways, similar in others. In the autumn of 1944, with enemy prisoners of war flooding into Britain, there was no attempt to segregate the prisoners according to which branch of the German armed services they had been serving in. Thus, in a camp such as Camp 23, Le Marchant, Devizes, the compounds contained a mixture of infantry, gunners, tank commanders, aircraft pilots, seamen and, importantly, members of the Todt Organisation. The Todt Organisation is probably now best known for its forced labour camps, where many Russians, Poles and the like were compelled to carry out slave labour for the Germans, but the Germans who worked for the Todt Organisation did so on a military basis. The Todt Organisation was responsible for building many U-boat bases and other military installations. The

Todt men were very good engineers, ideal for designing and building escape tunnels. Because of the mixed disciplines all available in a single camp, a German escape party would usually include men with a variety of relevant skills – a pilot who might fly a stolen aircraft from a nearby airfield, a sailor who might navigate a boat across the Channel or the Irish Sea. If the escape was to be through a tunnel, the Todt Organisation would design it. German officers, like their British counterparts, were not allowed to work, and therefore had an enormous amount of time to plan escapes. With the weight of Nazi discipline that was imposed upon them, escape efforts were co-ordinated and generally well planned.

A further advantage that the Germans had was that most of them had not long been in a prison camp. They were relatively fresh. Inevitably, a lengthy imprisonment saps the will of a soldier to fight, and lowers his fitness level, however brutal the camp discipline to which he is subjected. Many German prisoners in camps such as Camp 23 had only been in custody since August or September. They were front-line troops. The discipline maintained in the camps ensured that German prisoners still regarded themselves as a part of the Third Reich, and that if ordered to do so, they would fight for it in whatever way necessary.

The greatest other potential advantage for a prisoner of war was outside help, if they could get it. For a foreign prisoner, held in a land far from his home, where the language and local customs were different, breaking out from his prison camp was perhaps the easiest part of an escape. What he faced once he got out was far more difficult – a lengthy covert journey across a strange land, where a language that he could not understand was spoken, and where habits and practices might be very different to those at home. What was of the utmost value to him was the help of local sympathisers, who knew the countryside, who spoke the local language, and who had friends who would also help him. That is what the British Fascists could offer – if they were prepared to.

By October 1944, Ramsay, Greene, Leese, Beckett and Mosley were all free men, released from their periods of detention, and all the more bitter for it. Mosley may well have been a broken reed, but the others still hated what they said was a British government controlled by Jews, and wanted to hang Churchill and his Cabinet. Ramsay, Greene, Leese and Beckett were fanatics. However, they were not foolhardy. In the first part of the autumn of 1944, everyone in Britain believed that the war would soon be won, and that the German Nazis and Italian Fascists would be vanquished. Ramsay and the others had always planned for an uprising of British Fascists, but only when the Germans invaded Britain. They could only inspire their extremists, and the rabble who supported them, if there were the prospect of an imminent victory, not defeat. It was not until 16 December 1944, when the Ardennes offensive was launched, that a German victory again became a possibility, and that the British Fascists were prepared to rise up in support of it.

Prior to December 1944, there were many German attempts at escape, and Ireland was usually the target. A Special Branch security report in November 1944 told of three German prisoners who had got free from a Monmouthshire camp on 17 November, and were successful in reaching the port of Holyhead, before they were finally re-captured on 23 November.[1] It was an advantage to German and Italian escapers that Britain was now full of foreign servicemen from many Allied nations, in the same way as it helped British escapers in Germany that there was a large foreign workforce present throughout that country. Foreign accents and broken English might be acceptable if the escapers were masquerading as friendly Allied servicemen or foreign workers, and were well disguised. However, with a hostile local population, movement through the country was always difficult. These three Germans pretended to be Free French, and it was a pretty feeble pretence. Only one spoke any French, and he had a very limited vocabulary. All three carried forged papers purporting to identify them as Frenchmen, but they were poor quality forgeries. The French seal on the documents had apparently been created by 'rubbing over' a French one franc coin. When re-captured, they said that all the documents had been made within their prisoner of war camp. Their cover story was that they were French seamen, proceeding to Dublin to see the French Consul there. Their efforts did not fool those who arrested them, and it would be surprising if they fooled anybody else during their seven days of liberty.

When interrogated, the three Germans said that they had stayed in Birmingham and Liverpool on their journey to Holyhead, and claimed to have bought civilian clothing in Liverpool. The photographs that now appeared on their Identity Cards had been taken in Liverpool. They claimed that their disguises had been good enough to get them all that way and to keep them free for seven days. Could that have been true? Or had they had help from within Britain? This appears on the face of it to have been a fairly incompetent escape. How had they got so far, and been undetected for so long, without British Fascist help?

By late 1944, there was a Fascist organisation in being that was later to entitle itself the Prisoners of War Assistance Society (POWAS).[2] It was run by Fascists, and it is clear from later events that its 'Assistance' included helping escapers. M15 was slow to pick up on its activities, since it was some time before it had any sort of official existence. POWAS, as is clear from its postwar activities, was initially set up by British Fascists as a means of making contact with Nazis and Italian Fascists who were being held in Britain 'behind the wire'. Once the war had finished, and Germany had lost, such a society, concerned about the welfare of the hundreds of thousands of German and Italian prisoners of war held on British soil, was capable of earning a certain moral acceptance. The prisoners were no longer a threat, they had been defeated, and the many thousands of former enemies in the United Kingdom should be allowed a better life, and should be returned home to their families. Therefore, POWAS emerged into the light from the shadows, registered itself as a trade name in May 1946, and in due course tried to register itself as a charity.

However, in the autumn of 1944, the situation was different. German V-weapons continued to fall on London and other cities. The Germans were still the enemy, and were still taking British lives. Almost two years later, MI5 discovered a document that shows that

POWAS started its activities in 1944. It was a contact point between Nazi prisoners and British Fascists who were prepared to help them.

The official post-war letterhead of the Prisoners of War Assistance Society described it as being for 'Personal Services to Prisoners of War and their families ... Non-Political, Non-Partisan, *Amor Vincit Omnia* [Love Conquers All].' It listed a number of prominent churchmen as its supporters, together with the Duke of Bedford (the former Marquis of Tavistock). The honorary secretary was a woman called Mary B. Foss, an associate of Arnold Leese, and the treasurer was her mother, Violet Edith Foss. Violet Foss had been interned during the early years of the war as a dangerous British Fascist, and an important member of Arnold Leese's Imperial Fascist League. Another member of the Foss family, Mary's brother Alan C. Foss, had also been a member of the League. In 1946, the chairman of the society was Michele Edward Gerald Huntley, who had been convicted and imprisoned in 1941 for offences of causing disaffection amongst His Majesty's Forces – trying to persuade them to desert.

MI5 first became suspicious of the activities of POWAS in early 1946, and in due course obtained a Home Office warrant to intercept its mail and telephone calls. POWAS was found to be in contact with a man called Gittens, a lieutenant of Leese's. One of those later found to be involved in postwar Nazi prisoner escapes, Lady Clare Annesley, was a prominent supporter of POWAS. MI5 was very late in realising the danger that POWAS posed. It was probably as a result of correspondence from Mary Foss in the *Catholic Herald* in late 1945 that MI5's interest began. With telephone and mail intercepts in place, Mary Foss was found to be admitting that she and her mother were embarked on 'quite unauthorised work', and had been stockpiling comforts for the prisoners: 'We have, quite unofficially and illegally thousands of cigarettes, woollies, comforts, food, sweets etc., and have made many personal contacts.' An MI5 report comments that: 'Foss and her sympathisers had made unofficial contacts with a number of prisoner-of-war camps in this country, and were engaged in passing presents of one sort or another to the inmates.'

On 30 August 1946, an MI5 memorandum reads:

> 'There is ample evidence to show that a number of prominent
> Fascists are interested in the Society and there is reason to
> believe that Mary Foss and Michele Edward Gerald Huntley,
> Chairman of the Society, may be concerned in illegal activities
> connected with attempted escapes of prisoners of war.'

As will be made clear later, after the war hard-core British Fascists
were involved in assisting Nazi prisoners to escape to South America.

In early 1947, Violet Foss wrote (in an anonymous letter to a Frau
Helga Proilus, a German lady who had given an interview to the
Daily Herald praising life in Britain): 'There are many loyal English
homes where the Führer, whom you probably "Heiled" when it suited
you, is <u>respected</u> as one who could have saved your country from its
present plight and Europe from its future one.'[3] There were still die-
hard Nazis in Britain.

Perhaps the most important question was the availability of
weapons to the British Fascists in the autumn of 1944. It must
be remembered that back in 1940, the Imperial Fascist League of
Arnold Leese, of which Violet Foss was a prominent member, had a
number of sidearms hidden away. No doubt those were still available
to them. It should also be remembered that Mrs Ramsay, given the
opportunity, had intended to attack Brixton Prison, blowing open the
gates and releasing her husband. Clearly the Right Club had access
to weapons. Further, by December 1944, there would have been
plenty of guns 'adrift' in Great Britain – souvenirs of war, 'misplaced'
guns lost by British or Allied troops or stolen from the stores, and
guns lawfully carried by British Fascist servicemen. Where they were
needed, radio transmitters and receivers would not be too difficult to
smuggle into the camps.

The best way to judge what POWAS may have been up to in
November and December 1944 may be to look at what they were
found to be doing after the war had finished. There were still many
thousands of German and Italian prisoners of war in Britain, and
from early 1946, MI5 was gathering information on POWAS's

activities. In August 1946, Mary Foss herself went to Alton in Hampshire, and attempted to gain illicit entry to Prisoner of War Camp 294 there. Her technique was no doubt one that she had used many times before. She approached a parked, empty, Army truck, and slipped a packet of twenty cigarettes onto its floor, with a visiting card for POWAS attached to it. No doubt this was intended as a low-level bribe to the driver. As it happened, the truck was being driven by an officer, Lieutenant Victor Henry Watts, and when he returned to his vehicle he discovered the cigarettes. Undaunted, Foss then approached him, and asked him to take her into the camp, so that she could converse with prisoners there. She said POWAS had a large amount of money that was going to be spent sending parcels to prisoners. With a corruptible soldier, she might well have hoped to be smuggled into the camp in the back of the truck, and taken out again later in similar fashion. Lieutenant Watts was having none of it. He told Foss to communicate her request to the War Office, and left her on the streets of Alton.

However, although Foss failed in her attempt to corrupt Lieutenant Watts, she clearly enjoyed greater success on other occasions. On 8 November 1946, Heinz Schilde escaped from Camp 294 near Alton. He stayed free for two days, during very wet November weather, and then surrendered himself back to the camp on 10 November. He arrived back dry and clean-shaven. Somebody had clearly been looking after him. On his person was found a letter from Germany that mentioned Mary Foss. Schilde was asked if Foss had sheltered him, but denied it. Eventually, however, he admitted that he had seen her during the past three months (which must have been at an illicit meeting or meetings), but continued to deny that it was her who had sheltered him. The letter found on him had apparently originally enclosed a separate letter addressed to Mary Foss. Presumably Schilde had delivered that to her.

So, if POWAS covertly started its work in 1944, what could the British Fascists do to help the Nazi and Fascist prisoners? Firstly, they could get word into the camps that they were there, ready and able to assist a break-out. Most easily, this could be done through British

Fascists in the armed services – men of the same character as Private Schurch. This book will tell later of an arms cache said to be hidden near the prisoner of war camp in Devizes, and of agents on the outside hiding a radio transmitter nearby for the use of German prisoners. Some agents were said to be dressed in British Army uniform. All this sort of thing was well within the capabilities of the then secret POWAS organisation, and the existence of POWAS at that time was unknown to the British authorities. It was entirely 'off the radar'. If there was a successful mass break-out, and the Germans were able to secure arms, tanks and guns, and perhaps paratroop support, then with a minimum of 250,000 German prisoners in Britain, the equivalent of a German invasion would have begun, and British Fascists under Ramsay's command would have supported them.

German prisoners continued to make escapes, and it is simply not known whether they had any outside support. In November 1944, Special Branch reported that a prisoner, who had escaped from a camp in Huntingdonshire, had made a 'lone run' to a nearby airfield.[4] This prisoner was not a pilot, but had been on the ground staff of the Luftwaffe, and believed himself capable of stealing a Mosquito aircraft, and flying to Germany. He was recaptured on the airfield and returned to his prison camp. The Germans were, of course, aware of the importance of airfields, and the opportunities that they offered.

On the evening of 7 December 1944, two Germans escaped from Camp 78, at Braintree in Essex. One was caught next morning still close to the camp, but the other got all the way to Notting Hill in London, despite the fact that he was wearing patched battle dress. That could never have happened in the fraught days of 1940 or 1941, with the Home Guard and British civilians regarding all strangers with great suspicion. Was it just that, in the autumn of 1944, every-one, even MI5, believed that they could relax, and that the war was as good as over. Or had he had help?

Chapter 17

Plans for the Big Break-Out

Back in September 1944, Hitler knew that he must use every available resource to ensure the success of his Ardennes offensive. He also knew that a huge number of German troops were now being held in prisoner of war camps in Britain, and that that number would certainly increase in the time that it would take him to mount his offensive.

The plan for a big break-out in Britain has been considered by a number of authors, the first of whom was Lieutenant Colonel Scotland himself.[1] No one has, however, previously identified the threat from the British Fascists, which was necessarily a key element in Hitler's planning. What else was Germany's Fifth Column for? The British Fascists had the power to make a plan that seemed too fantastic to be true turn into reality. Some authors have relied upon the contemporary reports of MI19, but many of these clearly misread the situation, and did not appreciate the enduring potential of Germany's British Fifth Column.

The evidence, mainly collected by MI5, makes clear that the leading British Fascists were prepared to use violence to further their aim of creating a Fascist, anti-Jewish government in Britain. The evidence is that, with the possible exception of Mosley, the years of imprisonment under Regulation 18B had done nothing to dampen the ardour of the Fascist leaders; in fact the opposite was the case. The evidence also shows that the British Fascists had access to weapons and explosives, and that they were prepared to use them in support of a German invasion. They were in communication with Berlin, through Greene in particular, and judging by Greene's words to Ramsay upon Ramsay's release at the end of September 1944 – that he had been released at exactly the right moment, and that he was the natural leader everyone had been waiting for – the British Fascists knew that Hitler had something planned for Britain in November or December. Hitler was always aware of presence in the United Kingdom of British Fascists – indeed he had met a number of them before the war. Through Greene, if nobody else, Hitler knew that the views of the British Fascist leaders had not changed. As he looked for any possible way to support his Ardennes offensive, he did not overlook them. They were one of the cards that he could play in his desperate last bid for victory.

The large number of German troops in British prisoner of war camps could potentially make up a powerful army close to the seat of the British government. SS men were in control of most of the camps in Britain, imposing their will on anyone who expressed doubt as to Hitler's invincibility. Hitler was prepared to use any deception or trick to bring him victory. Whether it was his own idea to use the German troops who were in prison camps in Britain, or whether it was suggested to him by a subordinate such as Skorzeny is not clear, but it was potentially a brilliant move. Estimates of the number of German prisoners in Britain vary, but since the Normandy landing in early June 1944, hundreds of thousands of German troops had been captured. A good proportion of them were disciplined and battle-hardened, some of them Waffen-SS. They had been prisoners for a few months at most, would still be fit, and had maintained their discipline. The Nazi salute was still used in all German camps, and the Waffen-SS in each camp made sure that Nazi rule was imposed.

As with Allied prisoners of war in Germany and Italy, in Great Britain, the German prisoners found ways of communicating with Berlin. There were no doubt codes in letters, messages in parcels, and some home-built radio transmitters. British camps in Germany and Italy received messages from London (such as the disastrous 'Stay Put, we will come and get you' message from London to all prisoner of war camps in Italy before the armistice of September 1943), and the same applied to Germans in British camps. The timing of the December escapes that occurred in Britain proves that there was a high level of communication, whether through radio, written word or British Fascists.

Hitler planned that at the time that his troops launched the Ardennes offensive, catching the American troops in front of them completely off-guard, there would be a major break-out by German troops from their prison camps in Great Britain. The break-out would centre on Devizes and Sheffield. The details of the Devizes break-out plan are known. Those of the Sheffield break-out still remain a mystery. There were 7,500 prisoners, mostly Germans, in the Le Marchant camp. They would break out en masse, by force, overpowering their guards and arming themselves. They would over-whelm the two nearby American hospitals and steal their vehicles. Using the cover of the American hospital vehicles to throw everyone off-guard, they would attack an armoured vehicle park in order to seize the equipment that they needed to establish a fully operational military force, including tanks and field guns. They would also seize an airfield, so that they could send a plane back to Berlin to notify Hitler of the establishment of a German army in Britain. They would then cause as much damage and confusion as possible, rampaging as a significant armed force behind Allied lines, and destroying the 'safe haven' in which Allied troops could rest, recuperate and train. The Devizes force would advance to link up with those who had broken out from Moor Camp, Sheffield, and would be a rallying point for all other German troops who managed to break out of their camps.

The plan included the intention to thrust into Britain's capital city, London. Why London? London was the home of the British government, and the capture or killing of Churchill and his leading supporters would be a substantial prize, in the same way that evidence suggests that Hitler hoped to capture or kill Eisenhower in Paris. Churchill had personally turned Chamberlain's appeasement-orientated government into an aggressive and successful wartime one. Previous plans to assassinate Churchill in Casablanca and

Algiers had failed. The plan now, that German troops should drive into London and seize or kill Churchill and his ministers with the inside support of the British Fascists, was entirely feasible, but obviously high-risk for those involved. Although the idea of German troops 'marching' into London and seizing or killing the British government at first sounds fantastic, in reality it was not, as is explained below.

Whatever else, if the German prisoners of war got out, obtained the necessary armament, and went on the rampage in Britain, the Allies would have to withdraw a significant number of troops from the Continent to deal with the threat to their rear, whilst they were still reeling from the Ardennes offensive. Like the counter-attack on mainland Europe, it was a high-risk strategy that could bring significant rewards. This was Hitler's last throw of the dice.

As stated above, local intelligence and support is invaluable to any enemy force operating behind enemy lines. The German prisoners all over Great Britain knew very little of the country and the people outside the confines of their camps. They had some maps, made or stole weapons, and sent out some reconnaissance parties from their camps (as will be explained), but they needed outside help. As with the actions of the Resistance in Europe after D-Day, any intelligence and support that the Germans could get in Britain once they broke out of their camps would be vital. The break-outs would, if all went well, occur in various parts of the country, and then the German troops would link up with each other as soon as possible. Presuming that they had successfully commandeered transport, they would need to know which routes they could use, and which they should avoid, in order to link up with their comrades and consolidate their force.

The Germans' major advantage was the help that the British Fascists could give them. They always had been, and still were, prepared to use violence to support a German invasion or uprising. It is therefore no surprise that Hitler called on them to give what support they could. Most of those who had been detained because of their wartime Fascist activities had been released by the late autumn of 1944. Ramsay was free, Greene was free, Leese was free, Beckett was free, and so was Mosley. All five still had the remnants of their organisations available to them. Ramsay was still an MP, and still had his extensive covert network of agents. Their opponents in MI5 thought that the war was nearly over, and the Home Guard had been stood down.

Greene was in contact with Germany, as no doubt were others. However, Greene must have been thought more reliable than many – he was half German, his sister was well placed in Berlin, and if MI5 was right, he had been in the pay of the Nazis since 1936. Furthermore, he had battled away with success to overturn the Detention Order against him, and had taken a former British Home Secretary to court. He was exactly the sort of man Hitler was looking for in Britain. When Hitler conceived the idea of creating a German army within Britain is not entirely clear, but Greene seems to have known of the plan by the time that Ramsay was released from detention at the end of September 1944. As soon as he was out, Ramsay began re-establishing his contacts with the Fascist groups in Britain. He moved to live with Ben Greene in Berkhamsted, where he spent half of each week.

The proposed 'social' for ex-detainees on 16 December was obviously intended to assemble all those who could support the break-out. The date cannot have been a coincidence, and it was what Ramsay had always planned to do – to bring together all the different Fascist groups and unite them in action under a single leader. It was hoped that 16 December would be a day of high Fascist morale, as the German armies smashed through the American defences in the Ardennes. The break out from Devizes (and, one presumes, Sheffield) should occur on the night of 16/17 December 1944, so Ramsay could announce at the 'social' that the break-out was to be that same night. If all went well, break-outs from other German camps would occur simultaneously in various parts of Great Britain. Once this started, secrecy would no longer be important; all the Fascist leaders and foot soldiers could be told. That must have been the purpose of the ex-detainees meeting – to inform them, give them their orders and galvanise them into action. Why else would there have been a meeting planned of Britain's senior Fascists on 16 December?

Four long years had passed since the Fascist activities of 1939 and 1940 in Britain, and certainly some of those who had supported Hitler's Nazi government would have changed their views, particularly after the heavy German bombing and British losses on the field of battle. Also, before 16 December and the Ardennes offensive, Hitler's total defeat seemed to be the only realistic outcome of the war. The British Fascist leaders believed that the supposed threat of international Jewry, which they passionately opposed, would grow significantly if Hitler were defeated – the 'Jewish threat' could only be strengthened by the removal of the single force fighting against it. For this reason, British Fascism was alive and well in the autumn of 1944, and would endure far beyond the end of the war. The British Fascist leaders had lost none of their enthusiasm for battle and blood. Although they had always known that they would not be able to get their supporters to rise up in armed support of Hitler until there appeared to be a real chance of a Nazi victory, here at last was that chance.

If not to target Churchill, why was London an objective of the break-out? Was it fantasy to think that 'Churchill and his crowd' could be captured or assassinated? Not if Hitler had agents within the House of Commons. Driving an armoured column all the way from Devizes into London to Parliament Square, and then mounting an attack on the seat of the British government, or upon the nearby 10 Downing Street, or the Annexe or the Cabinet War Rooms, might be totally unrealistic, but for a smaller squad, travelling perhaps in American military ambulances stolen from Devizes (echoing the ruse of Skorzeny's men in the Ardennes offensive), and with a few English-speaking British Fascists aboard, such an attack might well be possible. Captain Ramsay, MP, was a dedicated Fascist who had just been imprisoned for more than four years by Churchill and his crowd, whom he wanted to face Vehmic justice. He had unrestricted access to the House of Commons. Once, early in the war, he had apparently had eleven like-minded Fascist MPs in his Right Club

– many of them still remained in the House of Commons. Ramsay would need only one or two to help him.

Winston Churchill was in London during the pre-Christmas period of 1944. He answered questions in the House of Commons on 14 and 20 December 1944, before leaving on Christmas Day to visit the recently liberated Greek capital of Athens. Others of his ministers were also there, including Anthony Eden, the Foreign Secretary. After all, it was the lead-up to Christmas, and, until the Ardennes offensive began, it was hoped that it would be the happiest Christmas of the war.

Hitler was, as we have seen, perfectly content to authorise 'dirty tricks'. His men, under Skorzeny, would wear American uniforms in the Ardennes offensive, and would drive American vehicles. Why not do the same in Britain – taking uniforms and vehicles from the US military hospitals in Devizes, and elsewhere? Hitler had himself survived a bomb plot on 20 July 1944. Would it be possible for agents to place a bomb in parliament to kill Churchill? Or make certain of his death by infiltrating Waffen-SS men into the House of Lords (where the House of Commons sat) to use guns and grenades? Any attack might be a suicide mission, but Hitler's SS were happy to lay down their lives for the Führer and the Third Reich.

Chapter 18

The Two Centres
Devizes and Sheffield

The plan for the 'big break-out' in Britain was nationwide, but one of the two intended centres was to be Camp 23, Devizes.

Camp 23, at Le Marchant Barracks, Devizes in Wiltshire, was chosen as a centre of the German break-out for a number of reasons. In some ways it was a strange choice, since it was situated only a little to the north of Salisbury Plain, in an area normally containing many Allied troops. Indeed, there were two other military barracks adjoining Le Marchant, Waller Barracks and Prince Maurice Barracks, both of which were just on the other side of the main road on which Le Marchant Barracks was situated. Wiltshire had been a military county for very many years, Devizes was a military town, and Salisbury Plain was and is a major training ground for the British Army. Le Marchant Barracks itself had been the home of the Wiltshire Regiment since 1878, when it was built. It was named after Sir John Gaspard Le Marchant, a past commanding officer of the 99th Regiment of Foot, which later became a part of the Wiltshire Regiment. The core buildings still stand on the south side of the A361 road from Devizes towards Marlborough. They have been converted in modern times into flats and houses, and the parade ground and old prisoner of war camp have been covered by housing estates. The 'keep' of the old barracks, which still stands beside the road, is an imposing building.

The prisoner of war camp had been built out of corrugated iron and concrete – it consisted of thirty 'Romney' huts built in a field about 500–600 yards square, to the east of the barracks, surrounded by two rings of barbed wire and watched over by a number of watchtowers with searchlights. The Romney huts had originally been built to accommodate the many troops gathering on the British mainland prior to D-Day. Each hut could accommodate up to 700 men in bunk beds. After the invasion of mainland Europe, the camp was left empty, and was converted to serve as a prisoner of war camp. At first it was used as a transit camp, and then in November 1944, it became a permanent prison camp.[1] The prisoners were guarded by Free Poles, who had every reason to hate the Germans who had overrun their motherland in 1939.

From Hitler's point of view, one of the advantages of Le Marchant camp was that it was very large – by December 1944, it contained 7,500 enemy troops, the majority of whom were Germans, although there were also some Italians. Another advantage was that many of the soldiers, sailors and airmen were specialists. They included Waffen-SS troops and U-boat men, many of them ardent Nazis. It was a camp under Nazi control. A third advantage was that the Germans in Camp 23 were fairly recently captured. One of the common effects of long-term imprisonment in a camp was a deterioration in morale and discipline. That had not happened yet to the men in Camp 23. They still regarded themselves as soldiers, and a rigid discipline was maintained.

Two of the prisoners, Staff Sergeant Hermann Gensler of the naval artillery, and Hermann Hildenstein, produced an illustrated commentary on camp life. It emphasises the disciplined lives they led. Hildenstein (who wrote the words in verse that accompanied the illustrations) says:

> The morning roll call now behind you,
> And the always happy marriage
> Of white bread, tea and porridge,
> Bed making is next.
> The blankets are folded up
> Neat and straight
> Then the large room is swept
> Pretty clean, as is proper,

> To show that even a glance from outside
> proves that here are soldiers housed . . .

There is pride in Hildenstein's words, and it is clear that the German prisoners in Camp 23 maintained good morale, and they still regarded themselves as soldiers of the German Reich, albeit that cruel Nazi discipline played its part. Life in the camp was hard in the British winter, with the men living in huts made of corrugated iron and concrete. It was harder still in the 'cooler', the official punishment section, comprised of British Army bell tents which allowed little comfort.

Another advantage of Camp 23 was that it had good road communications with other parts of Britain. Since it was in a military area, road links were important. There were complaints, however, that tracked vehicles (including tanks) had done a lot of damage to the local roads. A further advantage was that because the area did contain (or had contained) many military establishments, all within easy range of Devizes, it also contained arms stores and military vehicles. These, in December, were mainly denuded of troops, because so many units had been sent to mainland Europe. Also, the airfield at RAF Yatesby was only about six miles away. The significance of the arms dumps, vehicles and a nearby airfield is obvious.

The final, and the most important, advantage of Le Marchant Camp was that there were two American hospitals close by, one each in the Waller and Prince Maurice Barracks on the other side of the road. With military hospitals would come hospital vehicles, and enough of them between the two hospitals to carry a large German covert force. What better camouflage could there be than Allied ambulances for escaping German prisoners? There should also be a ready supply of US and other Allied uniforms – patients lying in bed would not be wearing their uniforms. This is was what made the Le Marchant Camp ideal as a major centre for the break-out. The hospitals were within yards of the camp, and provided a good supply base for all that was necessary for a major covert operation.

Camp 17, Lodge Moor Camp, Sheffield, the second centre for the break-out was in open country some miles to the west of Sheffield. It had once, briefly, been a racecourse in Victorian times, but had closed after a few years, probably because then it had been too remote from Sheffield and therefore was not making any money. In World War One it was used as a military training camp, and then in World War Two it was used as a prisoner of war camp, firstly for Italians, and after D-Day for Germans. As with Le Marchant Camp at Devizes, Lodge Moor Camp contained a very large number of hard-core Nazis. Nazi personnel and Vehmic courts maintained an iron discipline amongst the 10,000–12,000 inmates. The plan was apparently to tunnel out of the camp, rather than go through the wire as they did at Le Marchant, Devizes. There may have been a faint hope at Sheffield that if the Devizes break-out had succeeded, a resulting armoured German column might make sufficient speed to reach Lodge Moor Camp and come in through the front gates, overpowering any resistance, and freeing all the inmates. However, the distance was great, and it is far more likely that there was a plan in place similar to that at Devizes – for a squad to break out through a tunnel, and for that squad to kill or overpower the guards and let their comrades out.

The advantage of using Lodge Moor Camp as a centre for the break-out was that it was under hard-core Nazi control, and contained a huge number of troops. It may also be that communication with Berlin was better than at most camps. The immediate problem was transport. The guards and administrators would not have had nearly enough vehicles at the camp to transport all of the prisoners. They would, however, have had enough to carry a covert squad of Germans to another target but where that was is not known. At such a target the escapers from Lodge Moor may have hoped to seize further vehicles and armament. No one at Lodge Moor Camp talked, total secrecy was maintained, and therefore there is no record of what the plan for escape was. There must have been one – to disperse thousands of escaped prisoners from a fairly remote camp such as Lodge Moor is a major undertaking.

A report from the London District Cage written in April 1945 paints a black picture of conditions in Lodge Moor, and gives a good reason why it may have been selected by Berlin, along with Camp 23, as a centre for the big break-out.

'There is not the slightest doubt that this camp is organised fully on the most complete and thorough Nazi lines. The general idea is the usual one of an apparently outwardly cooperative Lagerführer who is 100% Nazi and rules his compound on complete Nazi lines. Beatings up are frequent, particularly in Compound 2. These are arranged by the Lagerführer on information provided by the hut leaders. The execution is carried out by a regularly organised thuggery squad of some 80 men working as a Flying Squad on direct orders from the Lagerführer, to maintain 100% Nazi political orthodoxy. This is known as the Boxing Club, and it does in effect meet once or twice a week in the compound theatre or dining room. They have gloves issued by the camp authorities and regular inter-compound matches are held. The head of the Boxing Club is an Olympic Champion (SS). This practice seems most undesirable.

The general atmosphere is 110% Nazi. They give the most definite impression of being even more fanatical National Socialists now than they were in 1939. Re-education of these people is a complete impossibility and waste of time. Complaints of food are general and frequent. The general impression is of a seething mass of discontented prisoners of war (there are some 10–12,000 in 6 compounds) and a totally inadequate and understrength British guard company of a few hundred.

Unfortunately, there are a considerable number of anti-Nazis mixed up among this crowd, only partially rejects of the Repatriation Scheme (for disabled prisoners and the like). The unavoidable conclusion is that serious trouble is to be anticipated as soon as news of Germany's final collapse comes through. The first reaction will be one of total disbelief, followed by an outburst of fanatical rage which will be directed against all individuals suspected of anti-Nazi tendencies. The result might easily be a massacre which the guard will be powerless to prevent.'[2]

It is perhaps sensible, at this moment in the narrative, to pause, and to count heads. In World War Two, a British infantry division might comprise anything between 8,000 and 20,000 men – most usually it would be between 10,000 and 15,000 men under the command of a major general. An army would consist of a minimum of 100,000 men, and a maximum of about 150,000. There were enough German prisoners of war in Britain to constitute at least two armies. The men from Devizes alone (7,500) would, if they got hold of armoured vehicles and tanks, have nearly constituted an armoured division. They would certainly have amounted to two brigades. With a trained and disciplined (which they were) force of that size, if they were able to maintain surprise, the prisoners of war could do substantial damage. The men from Sheffield, perhaps 12,000 strong had they got out en masse, would also have constituted an enormous threat.

It must be emphasised again that the situation in Britain in December 1944 was totally different to that in mainland Italy when the Allies had invaded in September 1943. There, about 85,000 Allied soldiers were in the camps and most of them had been in prison for more than a year. It was believed by the Allied authorities that the prisoners would be unfit and ill-disciplined, and that if they broke out they would simply constitute a nuisance to the advance of the Allied armies – therefore a 'stay put' order was issued. Many ex-prisoners would argue that they were still effective soldiers and that the order was completely wrong, but there is no doubt that the Allied camps did not have the iron discipline of the Vehmic Law system. A combination of fanaticism, indoctrination and fear meant that the troops in the Nazi camps remained front-line military units, only temporarily in captivity.

Chapter 19

Preparations at Devizes

The orders for the break-out went out some time in the autumn of 1944 to a number of prisoner of war camps in Britain and we have seen that Ben Greene clearly knew that something was imminent. What details Greene knew at that early stage are not on record. Greene was probably told only that there would be a major German counter-attack at some time in the autumn, and that there would be a break-out from the camps timed to coincide with it. It is extremely unlikely that Greene knew any dates or detail. It was, however, necessary to give some instruction to the British Fascists, so that their help could be used in the co-ordination of the efforts of the German escapers.

When trying to reconstruct what was planned and what actually happened, the author has looked at the known facts as recorded by the Allied authorities, and has considered these alongside the various accounts given by the participants at the time. The author believes that the significance of the British Fascists – the British Fifth Column – and the help that they could give to any break-out, is usually underestimated. Lieutenant Colonel Scotland of MI19 missed the British Fascist connection, and Scotland's written account, although persuasive in parts, appears to clash with many of the known facts. It is based on the result of interrogations at the London Cage.

It has to be borne in mind that the official reports of the Devizes plot were written very soon after 16 December 1944, because great concern was caused by the discovery of the plot, and reports had to be submitted quickly. Apart from the benefit of hindsight, and consideration of the role of the British Fascists, the murders which were to follow of suspected informants in both the Devizes and Sheffield camps can be argued to have demonstrated how deadly serious the escape plans had been.

The threat of a significant break-out was taken very seriously once it was discovered – there was a nationwide tightening of security, and the Devizes plan was considered at Cabinet level. The military were briefed, and the information that they were given is probably more factually revealing than some of the MI19 interrogations and reports. Scotland says in his book that the Devizes plan was to be a part of 'an extraordinary armed sweep through hundreds of miles of built-up England, from the West Country, through the Midlands, across Yorkshire to the East Coast'.[1] An attack on London was planned. If the big break went well, there would of course be endless possibilities – the Germans did not have to stay together as a single unit.

As has already been made clear, Camp 23 was a large one, containing up to 7,500 men by late November 1944, 6,170 of them in huts, 1,330 in tents.[2] Those in captivity there had, in the main, been captured quite recently, and for them the war was certainly not over. SS men ensured that they had control of each compound of the camp. As was common in the armed forces of Nazi Germany, the minority of hard-core Nazis controlled the majority. Many of the Germans in Camp 23 were young – the young Nazis had been indoctrinated throughout their school days with Nazi values.

Understandably, whatever the Nazis in Le Marchant Camp had been told about the British Fascist help that they might receive, they needed to do a certain amount of their own reconnaissance. A weak point had been discovered in the wire fence that surrounded the camp that could be exploited for reconnaissance purposes. On 18 November 1944, nine days before the first date set for the big break-out, five men escaped from the camp. They were Unteroffizier Joachim Engel, Obergefreiter Bruno Kloth, Obergefreiter Karl-Heinz Zasche, Obergefreiter Ernst Krebs and Obergefreiter Herbert Nierenkoter. They got out through the wire, at the weak point, in suitably murky weather. They did not even need to cut the wire, it could be held open with two sticks. They reached an airfield that must have been RAF Yatesby, which no doubt had been their assigned target, on the second night, lay up during the day, and entered the airfield on the third night to examine the planes. Having completed their mission, they gave themselves up on the third day, on the pretence that they were cold, hungry and wet, and had only had raw turnips to eat since their escape. They were returned to Le Marchant Camp, and placed in the punishment compound.

Escapes were punishable, according to the Geneva Convention, by a maximum of twenty-eight days in a punishment block or compound. However, there was a lurking fear amongst some Germans, particularly the SS, that they might receive the same punishment as the fifty British prisoners of war who were murdered by the Gestapo after what is known as the Great Escape from Sagan prisoner of war camp in German-occupied Poland. News of those murders had reached the German prisoners. Of the seventy-six prisoners of war who escaped through a tunnel at Sagan, fifty were executed once they had been recaptured. Three prisoners got to the safety of Allied or neutral territory, and the remaining twenty-three were returned to various camps.

Because of these murders, and the fear of a British reprisal, escaping by German prisoners was not just a sport anymore (if it ever had been). There had to be a serious purpose to it. It seems obvious that when Engel and his companions escaped, they would not have given up so easily had they not had instructions to do so. Nor would they have escaped without carrying rations. Food was being stockpiled by the prisoners in the Le Marchant Camp. Surprising though it may seem, the story of hunger, cold and damp that the five men gave appears to have been accepted by the camp staff without further interrogation. The five prisoners were, of course, not shot, but were sent to spend time in the punishment compound. Being in the punishment compound would have been no problem when the day of the break-out came. The whole camp was to be liberated.

On the evening following the escape of Engel and his four companions, 19 November, after darkness had fallen, two more prisoners escaped from Camp 23. They were Unterscharführer Beier, twenty-two years old, and Feldwebel Westermann, aged thirty. Beier was described by an interrogator who interviewed him much later as an 'unpleasant type of young Nazi', and Westermann as quiet and unintelligent. Beier and Westermann again remained at large for a surprisingly short time, before returning to camp, on, it seems, the night of 20/21 November 1944. They successfully broke back into the camp, but were spotted and arrested coming back in. The same comments as with Engel and his squad must be made – escaping was a potentially dangerous pastime, not to be undertaken without a purpose. Beier and Westermann were later to say that they too had been cold and hungry, and fed up with turnips! Again, the Le Marchant Camp administration accepted the explanation and simply sentenced them to time in the punishment compound.

There was a third break-out on the evening of 19 November. This, it seems, was as short as that of Beier and Westermann. Unteroffizier Rolf Herzig and Kanonier Gunter Rese escaped from Camp 23, stayed out for a night, went somewhere and saw something or someone, and then returned to surrender to the guard the following day. They also, with little more ado, were sent to the punishment compound. In summary, nine men had broken out in three batches on 18 and 19 November 1944. All had returned or given themselves up by 21 November. Why?

Two others tried to get out on the night of 20 November, the third night of escapes, but failed. They were both dedicated young SS men, Unterscharführer Joachim Goltz and Grenadier Kurt Zühlsdorf. They were hardened fighters, who had been totally indoctrinated by Adolf Hitler and his National Socialists. They were apprehended as they tried to break out, and also sent to the punishment compound.

Finally, there was a three-man party also intending to escape on 20 November, led by SS-Schütze Hermann Storch. However, Storch's escape was betrayed by an informant, apparently a Ukrainian conscript into the German Army called Petar Urlacher,[3] and he was arrested before he could leave the camp. Storch was found to be in possession of a compass, a sketch of the area which he said had been lent to him for copying, and a large kitchen knife. Storch's arrest as a result of an informant's tip off undoubtedly rattled him, as we shall see later. Storch was also sent to the punishment camp.

In the result, nine men got out, and it is clear that they did whatever was necessary, and then returned. Three men were arrested before they could escape. This rash of escaping, and the surprising return to camp of the three successful parties, was not adequately explained at the time, but the only logical answer is that the prisoners were carrying out reconnaissance, or meeting/communicating with people outside the camp. It perhaps demonstrates how lackadaisical the administration at Camp 23 had become, as a certain victory loomed just around the corner, that they accepted the return of these men to custody without any real questioning, and did not realise that the escapes and returns must indicate a larger plot. In answer to such questioning as there was, the nine prisoners gave nothing away. However, something was obviously left undone, because Goltz and Zühlsdorf attempted to escape from the camp again on 26 November, this time from the punishment compound. They did not succeed.

In subsequent thorough interrogation by members of Scotland's London Cage team, it was at one time stated that the German escapers had had meetings with 'agents' outside the wire. These, if the account was true, would have been with the British Fascists, and/or members of POWAS. However, this confession was later retracted, and therefore it was eventually dismissed as fiction by Scotland's team. It appears to this author highly likely to have been true.

It was always dangerous to escape from prison camp – an escaper might get spotted by a prison guard (Poles in this instance) and be shot whilst attempting to escape. There had to be an important purpose for any escape. Usually, it would be an attempt at freedom. Once out, for an active young soldier who had been deprived of his freedom for months, the feeling of liberation after the depression of captivity would be euphoric. It was not something to be willingly surrendered. Therefore, the only logical explanation was that the Germans who escaped had been ordered to do so, and had been ordered to return once they had completed their allotted tasks.

Colonel Scotland, who was in charge of the subsequent interrogations, said in his book that appointed men had been sent out through the wire to survey roads and the lie of the land, the position of food stores and arms stores. The doors and padlocks for such stores were examined. It seems obvious that he was right about this. Preparations were being made for the break-out – then intended for 27 November 1944. Thus, whatever reconnaissance and outside meetings were necessary, much of the work had been done a week before the break-out date. The preparations were made with Teutonic efficiency. It was necessary to identify those with the necessary expertise, and to ensure that they were briefed and ready – however, briefing could not take place too soon for security reasons. The initial stage was to find the vehicle and tank drivers, the gunners, radio operators, pilots and so forth, whose expertise could be used once the break-out happened. The break-out and take-over of the camp and its surrounds would be made by a few hundred of the Germans. Orders would be given once the camp was liberated to the thousands of other German servicemen, and they would obey them – they would have no choice because of the iron discipline that was imposed.

Hitler had always wanted the Ardennes offensive to start on 27 November 1944. If it had done, the Nazis in Camp 23 were ready to go. Like the Ardennes offensive when it was eventually launched, the break out from Devizes would have taken the British completely by surprise. The US military hospitals would have been at the mercy of the Nazis, there would doubtless have been much bloodshed, and an armed and armoured German force comprising thousands of men would have been active in the heart of Britain. If they had advanced, as intended, towards London, Churchill was at home – he spoke in the House of Commons on 28 November. If the Nazis had been supported by the likes of Ramsay and the other Fascists,

Vehmic law would have come quickly, and bodies would have been swinging from lampposts on the streets of Britain.

Then, reluctantly but driven by necessity, Hitler put off the date for the Ardennes offensive and the break-out.

Chapter 20

Two Words that Saved Churchill?

The new date for the Ardennes offensive was set for 16 December 1944. By 8 December, all was ready at Devizes, and no doubt elsewhere. Only the fine-tuning remained. There were eight days to go.

Then everything changed because of two words spoken in German.

Throughout the first half of 1944, there were many US units based in the United Kingdom, as the build-up towards the D-Day invasion mounted speed. Then, after the invasion had taken place, there were far fewer, but new units came and went. Amongst these was a US prisoners of war interrogation unit based in Devizes. Since the aim was to interrogate newly captured prisoners, in order to obtain up to date intelligence on German movements and tactics, a number of the US interrogation unit spoke fluent German. On 8 December 1944, a mere eight days before (unknown to the Allies) the Ardennes offensive was to begin, two officers from an interrogation team of XVIII Airborne Corps entered Camp 23 as a part of a familiarisation programme. They were in US uniform, but the German prisoners could not have known that they both spoke fluent German. They were Captain Frank Brandstetter and Captain Joseph Hoelzl. They were having a general look around, and at one point they entered the German sergeant major's office, where there would often be a number of prisoners gathered, involved in one sort of administration or another. As they did so, they heard a snatch of conversation in German, which was immediately cut off as they entered. There is some confusion in the evidence as to exactly what was said, but it included two words that were highly significant. They were 'arms store'.

Those two words may well have saved the lives of Winston Churchill and many of his ministers, and may even have prevented the fall of Britain to the Nazis. As a result of what they had heard, the two Americans were worried. Why were the imprisoned Germans, for whom the war was meant to be over, talking about an arms store? There was an arms store in Camp 23, but only that used by the sentries when drawing their weapons prior to going on duty. However, there were three barracks in the immediate vicinity, Le Marchant itself, Waller Barracks and Prince Maurice Barracks, as well as two military hospitals. All would have some store of weapons, even though there were few troops in the barracks.

Brandstetter and Hoelzl reported what they had heard, and the immediate conclusion drawn was that there must be an escape planned. That would make sense of the various escapes, attempted escapes and voluntary returns that had happened in November. Therefore, it was decided to interview thoroughly all those who had recently escaped, or had attempted to. Help was sent for from London, and some of Scotland's men came down from the London Cage

All of those who had escaped were interviewed. The five who had first escaped on 18 November had been led by Engel. When interviewed on 12 December (some days after the two words had been used), Joachim Engel said that they had waited a week for the weather to be right.[1] They had discovered a weak point in the fence, and had got out on the night of 18 November by holding the wire apart with two wooden sticks. According to Engel, they travelled by night, and hid during the day. The first day was spent hiding in an empty sheep pen. On the second night, they reached an airfield about eight miles from the camp. After hiding in bushes near the airfield during the second day, they attempted to steal a plane. Engel said they successfully entered two planes, but both had cold engines and would not start. Therefore they gave up. When daybreak came, because the five men were cold, wet and hungry, and they had only had turnips to eat, they decided to give themselves up, which they did in a nearby village. They were therefore returned to Camp 23, and placed in the punishment block.

Clearly Engel was lying. Engel was an experienced and battle-hardened soldier who had served on the Western and Eastern Fronts with assault-gun units, until he had been captured ten weeks before at Lille. Having broken out of the camp with a squad of four other men, and spent only two nights and a day on the outside, why did he give up so easily? He would have suffered far worse on the Eastern Front. Furthermore his interrogator describes him as highly intelligent and well-spoken.

Beier, who had escaped with Westermann, claimed that he wanted to join the US Army and fight against the Japanese, and was hoping to steal a plane from a nearby airfield, or stow away in a transport aircraft. Failing that they would stow away on board a ship bound for America. The plan was for them somehow to reach the United States of America, where Beier would then volunteer to fight. However, Beier said that they had seen a nearby airfield (presumably the same one as Engel said that he had visited), but they had only watched trainer planes landing and taking off. He said that they were cold, hungry and footsore, fed up with eating turnips, and disheartened, and so they had decided to return to camp. On the evening of 20 November, they apparently visited the greenhouse of a Devizes hatter called Pritchard, where Beier had found some detonators and fuses in a drawer when looking for food. They had left them there.

Beier's account was supported in most parts by Westermann, but again what they said was highly improbable. A fit young SS man, with an older companion whom he may well have ordered to come with him, got out of the camp and then returned after only two nights away, having, by their account, not even reached whatever airfield it was that they saw.

Goltz and Zühlsdorf said that their objective was to break into the rations store of the US General Hospital across the road at Waller Barracks.[2] This explanation was probably partly true. It would have been useful to reconnoitre the store in order to ascertain what security there was to protect it, and what quantity and type of rations it contained. Large quantities of supplies of all kinds would have been necessary for the break-out, and food, lots of it, would be very important for the thousands of Germans who hoped to escape. Goltz and Zühlsdorf could attempt to explain away their expedition on the basis that the prisoners in Camp 23 wished to supplement their own food in the camp, but in reality a vast amount of food would be required to feed their armoured column.

The author has not found any record of the reasons given by Herzig and Rese for their break-out and return.

It was Storch who cracked. A US Lieutenant Voegeli interrogated Storch, the man who had been betrayed before he could get out of Camp 23. Storch knew that he was in a weak position, because he had been informed on. What he did not know was how much the informant knew of his real activities, and how much he had told his handlers. Nor does history tell us exactly what Voegeli knew. Probably it was not very much. However, during the interrogation, Voegeli accused Storch of being the instigator of the 18/20 November escapes, and told him that he would be in real trouble if that was proved. It seems that Storch was genuinely frightened by this, and decided to try and change sides, and to become an informant himself. Storch may have expected a fate similar to that meted out to the fifty Sagan escapers. After all, if his own people did that sort of thing, why shouldn't the British and Americans?

Unfortunately, Storch proved to be a liar, changing his story a number of times over the days that followed, and clearly trying to improve his own position in the eyes of his interrogators. However, his first confession, that he was involved in a mass break-out plot, was accepted by Lieutenant Voegeli, and since he was offering to help the Americans, he was released back into the camp so that he could mix with his fellow Germans, and work as an informant, supplying further information to the Americans in the final stages of the plan. It soon became clear that Storch himself was heavily involved in the plot, and that the plot was well organised, far advanced, and on a massive scale. Storch told the Americans that the 'big break' was to take place on the night of 16/17 December, so only a week away. Of course, neither the Americans nor the British realised then that 16 December was intended to be the day of the Ardennes offensive, and certainly Storch would not have known that. That was still top secret.

Because Storch was proved to be so unreliable, everything that he said has to be examined with great care. During his interrogations, it is probable that some things slipped out that Storch had not originally intended to tell his interrogators, matters perhaps which were so important that, upon reflection, he regretted saying them. If so, he simply withdrew them on a subsequent occasion, and said that he had been lying. Storch claimed that the idea of the break-out came from Obergefrieter Herbert Wunderlich, a fellow prisoner, and that Wunderlich was the leader of the plot. Wunderlich was interrogated and also eventually confessed to a part in the plot, but, like Storch, he proved to be an enthusiastic liar, telling his interrogators one thing, and then retracting it.

Devizes was in the Salisbury Plain Military District. The District's War Diary for December 1944 sets out an ominous summary of the plot that emerged, based on what the various interrogations had revealed:

> 'On 8 December, a US Interrogation Team from XVIII Airborne Corps, working in Devizes Camp, discovered what was to be a large scale plot of the German Prisoners of War to break out. A Prisoner of War named Storch was the informer . . . in broad outline, the plot was to overpower all the guards, seize all the arms in the camp, Le Marchant Barracks, and at 141 and 228 US General Hospitals, all of which adjoin. Some 50–60 vehicles were to be obtained at the two hospitals, where also a food store was known to be located. Army personnel, including panzer elements, were to seize a large US tank depot in the vicinity, whilst German Air Force personnel proceeded in the captured lorries to a nearby training airfield. The training aircraft were to be seized and to be used in an attack on the

nearest operational airfield. The first suitable aircraft was to be flown straight to Germany, where two Airborne Divisions were waiting in Holland ready to be dropped in support of the Prisoners of War. The whole was then to develop into an attack on London.

The ringleader, Obergefreiter Wunderlich, was alleged to be in contact with two German agents in the camp in British uniform, one a Staff Sergeant and one a Corporal. Storch was a well educated and very logical man, whom interrogators suspected of being an officer in the guise of an Other Rank.

The plot was reported to Southern Command and two interrogators from MI19 were sent to the camp. By 14 December, they had convinced themselves that Storch's information was genuine, and had obtained the names of the ringleaders. It was discovered that the escape date had been advanced . . . permission was obtained to break up the whole scheme. Accordingly, the 30 ringleaders were moved to the London District Cage on the evening of 14 December.'[3]

Chapter 21

Investigation and Interrogation

The first to talk were Storch and Wunderlich. Further arrests and interrogations would follow, but it was these two who supplied the early information at Devizes after the 8 December investigation had begun.

Wunderlich said that there were at least four British outside agents helping with the plot. One was a sergeant major, described as 180–185 centimetres tall, reddish-brown hair, well built, with a scar on his chin; another was a corporal, 165 centimetres tall, light hair, short thickset build, round red face. Wunderlich said that there were two different agents who had built a wireless transmitter in a nearby wood. They were disturbed on one occasion by an armoured-car exercise, and had to depart rapidly. In total, therefore, four agents from outside the camp had helped them. Wunderlich's account has the ring of truth, and its detail is persuasive. What he said is corroborated by what is now known about the British Fascists.

Apart from any weapons that could be obtained from the camp armoury, or from Le Marchant Barracks and the American hospitals, the Fascist agents advised Wunderlich that there was an arms dump only 800–900 yards from the camp, which they could attack and take over. Transport would be obtained from the American hospital, where Wunderlich said that he had gone on working parties, as would adequate rations.

Storch said that, amongst themselves in the camp, they needed to find out how many tank drivers, how many gunlayers and so on they had available. The prisoners could apparently hear that there was a training ground for armoured vehicles not far away from the camp, perhaps no more than three kilometres away.

The plan was for the various compounds of German prisoners to supply men to form a break-out task force over 500 strong. Camp 23 was divided into a number of compounds, each separated from the others by a wire fence. A-1 compound was to provide 200 men, A-2 100 men, A-3 200 men, and from H Compound 40–50 men at most.

A map of the camp was drawn up to assist planning. When the time came, six men were to go through the wire from A3 Compound to cut the telephone lines to the various sentry boxes. At the same time, the guards were to be silently disarmed, hence, no doubt, the large kitchen knife recovered from Storch. A number of other weapons were found in the camp later which could have been used to kill or disable the guards. No shots were to be fired, because that would alert the whole district before the task force had sufficient control of the situation. The six men who had cut the telephone wires would then open the gates to the camp from the outside. The 200 men from A-3 compound would occupy the barracks and the American hospitals.

The men in Compound A-1 should start their action simultaneously and disarm their guards. Once the task force was out, and armed, Camp 23 would be completely in the hands of the Germans.

Storch told the interrogators that the target date was the night of 16/17 December 1944. He said that he had first heard of the plan from Goltz.

What Storch and Wunderlich were telling the investigators after the discovery of 8 December was cogent and coherent. They spoke of a carefully prepared plan, which had every chance of working. Wunderlich described the outside agents who were helping them in considerable detail. It all made sense. However, when further interrogated in the London Cage, after they had been transported there with the other thirty suspected plot leaders, they retracted many of the more significant things that they had said, including the involvement of British agents.

It was decided to release Storch back into the camp, so that he could mix with his fellow plotters and obtain further information. Once released, Storch carried on with the organisation of the breakout, playing a significant role in the plot whilst at the same time reporting back information on what was going on. The organisation appears to have been very thorough. In proper military style, as the day approached, Orders of the Day were issued, which later came into the hands of the investigators. An Order of the Day dated 12 December 1944, when translated, read:

Men of the Freedom Movement

The hour of our liberation has approached and it is the duty of every German to fight once more, arms in hand, against World Jewry.

I demand of every German man to fight for his fatherland without hesitation.

It is the duty of every leader of the Freedom Movement to fight as a German and not to wage the fight for liberation like a plunderer and murderer.

I call and demand of all men to stand by their colours faithfully and bravely.[1]

This Order of the Day was signed by Storch. Whoever the real leader of the plot was (and Storch had named Wunderlich), Storch obviously held a very senior position in it. Storch carried on perfecting the preparations for the break. He was playing a strange double game.

On the same day, 12 December, the plotters issued a further order, again signed by Storch. When translated it read:

Order of the Day – General Situation

Utmost secrecy in every respect.

Honourable fighting and tenacious holding on.

Everyone will be held responsible who offends against discipline and international law; severe punishment will be imposed in such cases.

Plunder, theft and similar offences will be punished by execution.

> The leaders will be responsible to put up fighting groups,
> each of the strength of a company of 150/180 men; these will
> be sub-divided into platoons and sections.

A fragment of a meeting agenda was also recovered from Storch when he was re-arrested, purporting to be for a Leaders' meeting for the following day, 13 December. It read: 'I wish to know from every leader the strength of individual arms! SS tank drivers, infantry, lorry drivers, pilots and other air force personnel.'

Thus, by the night of 13 December, virtually everything was ready for the break-out. Although Storch and Wunderlich had said that the date set was the night of 16/17 December, the US and British authorities did not trust them, and did not feel it was safe to let the situation in Devizes continue any longer. The date might be brought forward, or they might have lied about it. Colonel Scotland and the US teams had no idea that the break-out was to be synchronised with the beginning of the Ardennes offensive, and it is probable that the plotters in Camp 23 Le Marchant did not know either.

On the afternoon of 14 December, two days before the intended break-out, the Allied authorities took action. Happily, there was a hardened body of British soldiers nearby – 6th Airborne Armoured Reconnaissance Regiment was resting at Larkhill, before returning to the Western Front where they had already fought from D-Day until September 1944. They had undoubtedly encountered, and defeated, some of those Germans imprisoned in Camp 23. A significant body of men was moved to Devizes, under the command of 8th Parachute Battalion, to assist in the arrest of the ringleaders at Camp 23, and, if necessary, to prevent any riot or attempt at escape. The arrival of the paratroopers, armed and wearing uniforms familiar to, and feared by, many of the Germans, had the desired effect of quietening any possible unrest as the believed ringleaders of the plot were arrested and removed. They were the Leaders from each compound, and others who had been named by Storch and Wunderlich. The British paratroopers were fully armed, and quite prepared to use their weapons if necessary. Twenty-eight men were arrested on the afternoon of 14 December, and four more the following day, making a total of thirty-two. They were Hermann Storch and Herbert Wunderlich themselves, SS men Brüling, Goltz and Zühlsdorf, and (in the order that they are listed in the report from MI19), Engel, Beier, Westermann, Urlacher (the informant against Storch), Kaufmann, Hacker, Gebhardt, Lanckalt, Kloth, Rosterg, Reinhold, Hufnagel, Krebs, Rese, Nierenkoter, Goritz, Kleindieck, Irtenkauf, Bultmann, Baumann, Fishinger, Peetz, Stamer, Kaufmann, Schrader, Herzig and Koch.[2]

All of them were interrogated by Colonel Scotland's team. Storch and Wunderlich admitted to the plot, as they had already done when interrogated at Devizes. Goltz also admitted his involvement. A young man of nineteen, he was a friend of Wunderlich's, and Wunderlich's chief assistant in the plot. His role, he said, was to contact friends in A-1 Compound, and to select tank troops for the break-out in that compound. Goltz apparently first informed Storch of the plot. Goltz admitted to 'escaping' from the camp on two occasions in order to steal provisions from the American hospital stores and as we have seen he had been caught attempting another such raid on 26 November with Zühlsdorf. Hufnagel was the agent for H Compound, where he undertook to raise forty of fifty men for the break. Brüling was Wunderlich's representative in A-1 compound after Goltz was caught on 26 November.

Petar Urlacher was, according to MI19, the informant who had betrayed Storch's November attempt to escape. He confirmed that there was a plot for a mass escape. Clearly, he was arrested with the others to draw suspicion away from himself, and for his own protection.

Scotland's account of the Devizes conspiracy is set out in some detail in his unpublished manuscript.[3] Strangely, it varies from the official, contemporary reports in numerous ways. By 1955, Scotland was in his seventies, and his memory was clearly failing. His original manuscript is lengthy, and those parts of it which were eventually published in 1957 had been polished and made more readable by a professional author. In the book, Scotland summarises the purpose of the Devizes plot as follows: 'From Devizes they would head north. The goal was Sheffield. Here, a similar mass break from another German Prisoner of War camp would be staged, and the two escaping forces would join together as a hostile column.' Scotland therefore confirms that the other centre for the break-out was Lodge Moor Camp, Sheffield, but does not, for some reason mention the attack on London.

Scotland's methods of interrogation have already been described. In his published book, Scotland says:

> 'The ringleader (Storch) of the escape project, who had admitted to us that our story of the plot was correct, was given a firm and well-deserved thrashing by four prisoners who were permitted to question him; their violence against him was stopped before it went very far.'[4]

He makes no reference to Storch acting as an informant during the final stages of the plot itself. Scotland says far more in his manuscript, where he describes Storch's interrogation in the London Cage:

> 'Eventually, all the information pointed to Sergeant Storch being the main ringleader, the man who originated the mass-escape idea, who sent out recce parties through the wire at night, and who proposed killing the guards when the escape started. When he denied our charges, he was told that the information had been provided by his companions. He was astonished and angry, but from then on he, too, began to give us further facts which helped us to fix others principally involved.'

As already noted, the accommodation at the London Cage was a mixture of single rooms and small dormitories. With thirty-two prisoners from Devizes, it was inevitable that some of them would be put into dormitories and would have to live together for the short time that they were in the Cage. On Scotland's account in his manuscript: 'The prisoners continued fighting amongst themselves and various men were savagely beaten up. We had to stop this.' The plotters were clearly trying to find out who had been responsible for their betrayal, and using their customary Vehmic violence to do so. Scotland's solution to this problem, according to his own manuscript, was utterly disgraceful.

> 'We decided that the best way was to tell them that their own leader, Storch, had given us full details of their plan; and to let them have it out with him. We had to get him away from them after ten minutes for they beat him up severely, though many of them received some useful exchanges from Storch, a powerful man who had been a butcher by trade and was normally well able to look after himself.'

No doubt the Nazis wanted to kill Storch. Scotland had betrayed his informant, and thrown him into the hands of the hangmen. They were allowed to beat him up severely before Scotland stopped it. There were 'many' of them, and only one of Storch, whether or not he was a powerful man.

Scotland's account of the treatment of Storch is a shocking one. No doubt he would have justified his actions by saying that he himself had not laid a hand on Storch, but the betrayal of Storch was his, and he arranged for the inevitable beating. In betraying him, Scotland was potentially signing a death warrant not only for Storch, but for his wife (if he had one) and his family. If what he says about the brutality and violence between the prisoners is true, then it is understandable that Storch and Wunderlich changed their stories. There were obviously all sorts of pressures on them apart from those in the interrogation room, in particular that they should not give away the outside helpers or the real target of the break-out – Winston Churchill. Although they had been betrayed and prevented from carrying out their intended actions, there were other camps whose Nazi inmates might succeed where they had failed.

In Christmas week, the Ardennes offensive was going extremely well, V-2 rockets were still landing in Britain, and many Germans held in Britain still believed that a German victory was possible. They were not likely, therefore, to tell their American or British interrogators anything that might genuinely damage the plot or the chances of a German victory. The fanatical Nazis would not do so because of their love for the Führer, those less inclined to the Nazi faith would keep quiet through fear of retribution to their families. Things which had slipped out under pressure of interrogation would be retracted.

Most of the Devizes conspirators were sent north to Camp 21, Comrie, but Storch was held at the London Cage until 21 December, when he made a final statement saying that he had now told the truth, and would not escape or assist in any escape in the future. He also said that, in the last resort, 'I should be prepared to work against Nazi Germany.' Now that he had been exposed by Scotland as a traitor to the Nazi cause, Storch really had no choice. He could not safely return to a prisoner of war camp.

Lacking any knowledge of the Prisoner of War Assistance Society or the intentions of British Fascists such as Ramsay, Scotland and his team seem to have accepted the retractions by Storch and Wunderlich of vital parts of their confessions. The involvement of British agents in the plot, as described by Wunderlich but later retracted by him and dismissed by Scotland, fits absolutely with the known methods of the Prisoner of War Assistance Society after the war had ended. The evidence now available suggests that he was telling the truth.

The Salisbury Plain War Diary, referring to 14 December, continues:

> 'Since that date, all has been quiet and normal in the Camp, and information from the London District Cage, via Southern Command indicates that whilst there was a concerted plan of escape, the story of outside assistance from Germany and from British agents was not true. The object of the break was to cause as much trouble as possible, under cover of which it was hoped that some of the escapees might succeed in gaining neutral territory or back to Germany.'

The author suggests that the London Cage staff were wrong in their judgement. The episode of Storch's beating throws severe doubt on Scotland's judgement. The interrogators were apparently totally unaware of the activities of the likes of Ramsay, Leese, Greene, Beckett and Mary Foss's Prisoners of War Assistance Society. The subsequent conduct of some of the Devizes Nazis when they were sent to Camp 21, Comrie, shows how important to Germany's future the break-out plan had been. They were soon to murder one of their own, in the belief that he had betrayed them, though in fact they killed an innocent man. Three of the Devizes plotters, SS men Zühlsdorf, Brüling and Goltz were to hang for that murder.

Chapter 22

The Hangmen Kill
A Vehmic Court Passes Judgment

If there was any doubt as to the seriousness of the conspirators at Camp 23, Devizes, it evaporated within days because of events which occurred at the British equivalent of Colditz, Camp 21 at Comrie. Those believed to be the ringleaders from Devizes, with a few exceptions such as Storch who had already been beaten up by his comrades, were sent there because it was believed to be the securest place for them, and was many miles from Devizes. There were twenty-eight of them. However, Comrie still contained a large contingent of young fanatical Nazis. It was described later by a Lieutenant Colonel Faulk as having been a 'really Black camp'.

Having been held in the London Cage for a week during interrogation, the Devizes men arrived at Camp 21 on 22 December. The Ardennes offensive was raging, and the Germans were reportedly still enjoying great success. The Devizes Nazis were angry and frustrated. They believed that they had been betrayed by others as well as their leader Storch, and looked for someone that they could punish for this. When, at last, they arrived at Camp 21, they were again amongst their own kind, and swiftly moved to exact their revenge.

Camp 21 officially had a capacity of 4,500 prisoners and in December 1944 housed about 3,000 Germans. It had been a transit camp until the Allied successes of August and September, but now was a full-time high-security camp. The prisoners were held in four separate compounds, each divided from the next by a fence of barbed wire. The accommodation was in Nissen huts – long buildings with a concrete base and a curved corrugated-iron upper structure and roof. A Red Cross report dated 13 May described the local Scottish climate as 'extremely harsh'.[1] Compounds A and B contained the most dangerous Nazis, many of them SS men, paratroopers or U-boat crews, and here the Vehmic courts were still in control. Compounds C and D contained those regarded as less dangerous – the Greys and the Whites.

The Devizes Germans, together with the Comrie Nazis, chose as their target Feldwebel Wolfgang Rosterg, who was not in fact a Nazi any more, but had been arrested and sent to Comrie as one of the believed ringleaders of the plot. It has been suggested that Rosterg was in fact a spy for Lieutenant Colonel Scotland of the London Cage, but there is no evidence for that, and Scotland denied it. He certainly had not been the informer who gave away the plan for the big break-out. He appears to have been simply a man who once was a Nazi, but whose views had changed, and whose support for the Nazi Party had weakened.

The hours of darkness are long in Scotland in December. In the Comrie Camp, the lights in the huts were switched off at 2300, and turned on again at 0600.[2] In the dark of the night, the Vehmic court went to work. Exactly when they came for Rosterg is not clear, but it was soon after lights-out on 22 December, the day of their arrival. By dawn the next day Rosterg had been tried, convicted and executed. Afterwards, as the British authorities investigated, obtaining evidence from witnesses, all of whom were German, was extremely difficult, and it was a long time before a clear picture emerged.

On his arrival, Rosterg was billeted in Hut 4 in Compound B, and so it was there that the so-called Vehmic court gathered. One of the attractions of a Vehmic court to the Nazis was that the only qualification to be a judge was to be a 'pure-bred German'. Anyone purporting to have that basic qualification could join in the vigilante mob rule. But at night, the doors to the huts were locked by the camp guards. The guards in charge of the camp had changed on 20 December 1944, and a contingent of Polish troops now watched the prisoners of war. The Poles hated the Germans because of the brutal take-over of their country by Germany in 1939.

A witness called Grenadier Otto von Goll was living in Hut 5.[3] The huts were only a few feet apart, and the walls were made of corrugated iron, so noise carried easily from one hut to another. Goll said that shortly after lights-out he heard shouts of 'Swine' and 'Traitor' coming from Hut 4, and what he described as someone 'whining'. No doubt it was the unfortunate Rosterg appearing before the Vehmic court. Then, according to Goll, there was loud singing, a tactic often used by the Nazis to cover up the sound of whatever they were doing. It seems clear that beneath the sound of singing, Rosterg was being beaten and tortured.

Goll went to Hut 4 the next morning, as soon as he was dressed and the huts were unlocked, to see what was going on. When he entered the hut, he saw a man on his feet near one of the windows. His face was so badly swollen from the beatings that he had received during the night that it was almost unrecognisable. It was Rosterg. His face was covered in blood, and there was blood on his tunic. Around his neck was a rope noose. The other end of the rope was being held by Pallme König, a young SS man who had nothing to do with Devizes, but who was urging the men gathered around Rosterg to hit him, which a number of them did.

Another witness, Hermann Bultmann, was one of those who had been sent from Devizes via the London Cage, suspected of being involved in the break-out plot. He was a friend of Rosterg's, and had arrived at Camp 21 with Rosterg the day before.[4] Bultmann was billeted in Hut 2. Bultmann last saw Rosterg, fit and well, at about 2100 on the evening of 22 December. The next morning, immediately after reveille, Bultmann was fetched, as were others who had arrived from Devizes, and taken to Hut 4. When they entered that hut, there was already a crowd, and Bultmann saw Rosterg on his feet, in the same battered condition as Goll described, with a noose around his neck. His 'judges' had got hold of a file that Rosterg had. It contained a number of lists of prisoners of war who had been at Camp 23, and they were accusing Rosterg of compiling them to give to the British. In fact, Bultmann knew that the lists were entirely innocent. Rosterg had been a 'compound sergeant' at Devizes, and had compiled the lists for things such as delousing squads. Rosterg was a good linguist, and had also acted as an interpreter in Camp 23. However, Rosterg's 'judges' had no interest in the truth, to them the lists were further evidence that Rosterg was a traitor and a spy. Wunderlich saw his name on the lists, and repeatedly hit Rosterg in the face and body as a result. Rosterg was told to 'stand to attention' whilst he was being questioned, but it was all that he could do to stay on his feet.

Bultmann now found himself accused by some in the crowd of being a traitor as well, which he denied, claiming that he had been a member of the Hitler Youth. That apparently was enough to quieten his accusers for the time being. However, when he tried to leave the hut, Bultmann was stopped, and then eventually taken to the Compound office. The Compound Leader, a man called Pirau, was there, together with König and some others. Rosterg, badly injured, was also in the office. König ordered Rosterg to stand to attention, and when he was unable to do so in military fashion, struck him again on the head. A document was read out accusing Rosterg of having committed crimes against the Third Reich in France. It was said that he had given up German girls working as auxiliaries to the French Resistance, and had disclosed the whereabouts of petrol dumps. Rosterg had no opportunity to present any defence, and had no one appointed by the 'court' to defend him. He was already badly injured, and incapable of coherent thought.

Bultmann, still under suspicion, was taken back to Hut 2, and a little later, all those who had arrived from Devizes were summoned to return to the Compound office. Bultmann went with them. It quickly became clear that Rosterg had been sentenced to death, with, apparently, the approval of Compound Leader Pirau. Pallme König came out of the office and announced to the crowd of about fifty men who were now assembled: 'This swine is going to hang himself and if he doesn't you bloody well know what you have to do.' König then indicated Bultmann and added: 'And I want to see that this tall fellow here is a proper National Socialist and takes part in it.'

Rosterg was then pushed out of the office, screaming in pain. The rope was round his neck. Two of the Devizes plotters, Goltz and

Brüling, were at the front of the crowd, and Goltz jumped at Rosterg, and pulled him to the ground by the rope around his neck. He sat astride Rosterg, tightening the rope until Rosterg's cries stopped, whilst others kicked him, and stamped on his head and face. A number of men took hold of the rope, as well as König, and they dragged poor Rosterg by it towards the latrine block. His body was inert, the rope was around his neck, and it was taking the full weight of his body as he was dragged the distance of 40–45 yards. He was undoubtedly dead. As they reached the toilet block, a shout went up: 'There is a guard coming!' and many of the crowd dispersed. It was left to the hard-core Nazis to drag Rosterg inside, and to lift up his body so that he could be hung from one of the pipes. His body was left hanging there as his killers slipped away into the anonymity of their barrack huts. The Vehmic sentence had been carried out. Until his body was discovered by the camp authorities, the dead Rosterg would be on display in the latrines, a part of B Compound that all its inmates would visit. Any inmates who might be beginning to doubt their Nazi values would learn the dreadful penalty that they would suffer if they betrayed their comrades.

Much of Camp 21 still stands, now under the care of the Comrie Development Trust. Although Hut 4 of Compound B no longer exists, the latrine block where Rosterg's body was left can still be visited.

Fritz Hübner was a resident of Hut 1. On 22 December 1944, four new prisoners arrived in his hut. They included Zühlsdorf and Herzig from Camp 23. Early on the morning of 23 December, between 0600 and 0700, Zühlsdorf and Herzig were ordered to go to Hut 4. Hübner went with them out of curiosity, and they went into the hut. Hübner described a similar scene to the other witnesses, adding that König was holding the noose around Rosterg's neck with both hands, one close to the knot at the back of Rosterg's throat, the other holding the rope a bit further back. The rope was already tight around Rosterg's neck, and König threatened Rosterg that each time he cried out in pain, he (König) would tighten the noose. According to Hübner, the allegations put to Rosterg about betraying German women and fuel dumps to the French Resistance were based upon a piece of paper allegedly found in Rosterg's possession. However, that piece of paper had been read out in the camp before Rosterg arrived – it had already been there, and had nothing to do with Rosterg.

After further beatings with metal pokers from the stoves (there were two in each hut), Staff Sergeant Pirau was fetched, and then Rosterg was taken to the Compound office. Hübner went with a crowd of about twenty other men, and waited outside. After only five minutes, König came out and told the crowd: 'Keep quiet, he has signed a confession, and you will have him soon.' It was shortly after this that Bultmann was taken into the office. According to Hübner, after another twenty or twenty-five minutes, Rosterg was brought out of the office and handed over to the crowd to be killed. The rope was around his neck, and according to Hübner, Goltz, Herzig and Zühlsdorf dragged the body by the rope towards the latrine block. The route from the office to the latrines was crowded with prisoners and Rosterg's body was dragged through the crowd. Once in the latrine block, it apparently took four men to hoist Rosterg's body up. He was left hanging from a pipe with his toes about six inches from the ground. His attackers then dispersed, and soon after the 0830 roll call took place. After this, König came to find Hübner, and took him to Hut 4, where the attack on Rosterg had begun. König then threatened Hübner that if he talked about the killing, he himself would be killed. The story was to be that Rosterg had hanged himself – presumably, the numerous other injuries would be explained as punishment beatings for his crimes, after which Rosterg was so ashamed that he committed suicide.

After the killing, those involved boasted to their friends about it. Brüling told his friend Charles Albert Lergenmüller: 'Rosterg had betrayed the escape attempt at Devizes, that is why we killed him.'

Bultmann, the other suspected traitor, was allowed, for the time being, to return to his hut. Having seen the brutal murder of his friend, and knowing that he too was under suspicion, Bultmann surrendered himself to the protective custody of the British staff that same day. Rosterg's body was recovered from the latrine block.

Bultmann decided to tell the authorities all that he knew. Lieutenant Colonel Wilson, the Commandant, and Staff Sergeant Sulzbach, a German Jew who had fought against Britain in the First World War, and who was an interpreter for the camp, began an investigation into the murder.

In due course, five suspects were taken to the London Cage for interrogation, and eventually, in late March 1945, Bultmann, under heavy protective guard, identified a number of other men from the camp. An account of Bultmann's identification procedure by Sulzbach refers to the fury of the 1,000 inmates of Compound B when this took place. There were shouts of 'Traitor' and other threats as Bultmann was taken from hut to hut to make his identifications. Quite clearly, there had been no change in the Nazi domination of the compound.

In total twelve men were arrested and taken south to the London Cage for interrogation about the Rosterg murder. The younger prisoners in particular seemed totally unconcerned about the killing, and simply argued: 'We are Germans and the man we killed was a German. We demand to be sent back to be tried by a German court.' As a matter of law this was a bad argument – the murder had occurred on British soil and was subject to the rule of British law.

Eventually, in August 1945, eight men were put on trial for Rosterg's murder. The trial was held within the walls of the London Cage before a military court. Of the eight accused, two were acquitted; one was convicted but his sentence was commuted to imprisonment; five were convicted and sentenced to death. They were hanged together at Pentonville Prison on 6 October 1945. It was the last mass hanging in British criminal history.

Chapter 23

The Plot to Kill or Capture Eisenhower

The first evidence of the big break plot was picked up in Devizes on 8 December 1944. By the afternoon of 14 December, the Allies were sufficiently convinced of the existence of the plot to arrest all of the suspected leading conspirators at Devizes, and to raise security in all other German camps. The network of informants in the camps, carefully cultivated and built by Scotland's teams, was used to good effect. Tunnels were betrayed, searched for and found. A nationwide alert went out, and, in the belief that a break-out might take place any day thereafter, security was heightened throughout Britain, and a lot of Christmas leave, which would have left prison camp security weakened, was cancelled.

When the Ardennes offensive began, with devastating effect, two days later on the morning of 16 December 1944, concern was raised still further. Undoubtedly the increased security had a marked effect on a number of camps where otherwise there would have been a break-out.

So far as the British Fascists were concerned, news of the events of 14 December would have reached them rapidly. The action taken immediately thereafter to tighten security in all of the German camps would also have been known to them. The bubble of hope that there would finally be a German 'invasion' had burst. Ramsay, their intended leader, did not attend the 'social' on 16 December; there was nothing to announce. Although the Ardennes offensive had started by then, the prisoner break-out and Fascist revolution had not. It seems that the British Fascists simply crept back into their hiding places, and waited for another day.

Also, after the plan for the mass escape was discovered, and because of the results of the interrogations, it was believed that the German high command might send aircraft to the assistance of the escaped prisoners. At the time, escaped prisoners were regarded as primarily a police matter, and police radio messages were sent in plain language, not in code. It was known that the Germans listened to all broadcasts in Britain, and that they would be able to pick up police messages indicating the whereabouts of prisoners of war. Therefore, a decision was taken, with the agreement of the Home Office, that no police radios should be used to warn that an escape had happened, and that if descriptions of escapees needed to be circulated by radio, they could only be circulated if six or fewer prisoners had escaped. Any more, it was believed, might alert the German high command to a mass escape (presuming, of course, that the escapees had not already done so themselves), and they might supply some sort of air support.[1]

At Cabinet level, there was discussion and investigation of what had, so nearly, gone very wrong.

Unfortunately, a day or two after the plot had been foiled at Devizes, a *Daily Express* journalist called Vivien Batchelor was in the area, and picked up some information that an incident had occurred in the Le Marchant Camp. He investigated locally, and on Tuesday 18 December the *Daily Express* published his report under the headline: 'Germans plan mass escape; Camp-break bid to seize airfield and fly home from England'.[2] Although the article contained a certain amount of invention and exaggeration, it also contained something of the truth. It read:

'South-West Town, Sunday. A large number of German prisoners of war planned to escape from a camp in South-West England, seize a nearby airfield, and fly back to Germany. The plot was frustrated at the last minute. The Germans are known to have been prepared to lose half their numbers in a desperate attempt to get away by plane. Plans prepared in the most minute detail for ruthlessly killing the guards, seizing the armoury, forming up at an assembly point outside the camp and rushing the airfield, are in the hands of the authorities. The scheme was probably hatched in Germany for use by any large body of prisoners who might be housed near an airfield. Many of the men are from the Luftwaffe and U-boat crews – fanatical Nazis . . . It was the keen watch of a soldier guard which prevented the mass escape. The guard watching from a raised tower overlooking the camp first noticed groups of Nazis in furtive conversation.'

These last two sentences were, of course, not true.

The Devizes plot having been foiled on 14 December, and security having been substantially increased, Churchill and his Cabinet were hopefully safe for the time being. Not so General Eisenhower – Skorzeny's men were about to breach the American front lines and come looking for him.

Operation Greif was the name given to Otto Skorzeny's infiltration of members of his English-speaking battalion behind US lines. He successfully slipped eight of his nine jeep teams through the US lines, dressed in US uniforms and driving captured US vehicles. Their orders were to take the important bridges over the Meuse, and cause confusion wherever they could, by turning around road signs, and cutting US communication links such as telephone lines. Although they failed to take the bridges, they certainly caused confusion and alarm amongst the Americans. Rumours about their presence spread like wildfire, and soon genuine US troops were uncertain who they could trust. Checkpoints were, by necessity, set up all over the area behind the US lines, and those travelling through them were stopped and thoroughly questioned about things that any good American should know – baseball scores and the like. One effect of this was to slow down enormously the flow of traffic trying to reinforce the front line. Even General Omar Bradley was stopped and questioned.

The checkpoints did, however, lead to the capture of a number of the disguised German commandos. Often this was because suspicion was aroused by the fact that the Germans were travelling three or four to a jeep. US troops rarely or never did this; they had plenty of jeeps to go around. Only one or two men would travel in each one. Even though some of the commandos were wearing their German uniforms under their US ones, the Americans believed that they had no defence to the charge that they were spies, and they were later shot. The Germans clearly knew the fate that awaited them if they were captured, but when they were ordered to go behind enemy lines dressed up in US uniforms, like most good German soldiers, they obeyed the order.

One of the jeeps that was stopped, at a place called Awaille, contained three commandos – Günther Billing, Manfred Pernass and Wilhelm Schmidt. They were arrested at a checkpoint because they failed to supply the correct password. They had travelled thirty miles from the front line. All had false papers, and in their jeep were found £1,000 and $900 in cash (at a time when a British craftsman might earn £6 or £7 a week), together with their German paybooks, two British Sten guns, two Colt .45–inch pistols, a German sub-machine gun and six US hand grenades.

When Schmidt was later interrogated, he stated that their objective was to go to capture Eisenhower in Paris.[3] Although Skorzeny himself later denied persistently that such an order had been given, it is worth considering the circumstances in which Schmidt and his companions were caught before dismissing it. Schmidt's was not the only group to claim that they had this objective, and it fits with Hitler's general intention to assassinate Allied leaders if he had the chance. Schmidt's jeep had successfully slipped through the US lines, and then driven thirty miles to Awaille. Where were they going? They were carrying what was, for 1944, a very large sum in cash. Why? They would not need that sort of money if they were simply intended to skirmish around behind the US front line. They clearly had a secret agenda. If, as Schmidt said, they were driving to Paris, and then hoping to kill or kidnap Eisenhower, they might well need significant cash to oil the wheels of their enterprise. They might have to wait in Paris for a while before the opportunity to act against Eisenhower arose. They might have to pay off some of those who helped them. Getting out of France, with or without Eisenhower, would probably prove far more difficult than getting in, and might cost money. The weapons that they were carrying suggest that they were expecting to fight – but if the fighting was only to be as a part of the Battle of the Bulge, why carry the money?

A pointer to the truth may be that Skorzeny's original plan for Operation Greif had included the use of ten US generals' uniforms, and seventy staff officers' uniforms. If he had obtained enough of these, the commandos' chances of penetrating an Allied HQ would have been much greater.

Another of the jeeps was stopped on the edge of Liége by military police.[4] This carried four men, under the command of a Lieutenant Günther Schultz. All four men were wearing US uniforms and were found to be carrying German weapons and explosives. They had swastika brassards under their uniforms. Schultz was forthcoming when interviewed. He said that he was a member of a long-range reconnaissance team, and his secret orders were to penetrate Paris and capture General Eisenhower and other high-ranking officers. Schultz spoke of an 'Eisenhower Aktion' carried out by a special group commanded by an Oberleutnant Schmidhuber. This was a large *Aktion* group of eighty people, said Schultz. The plan was to get to Paris, where they would liaise at the Café de l'Epée or the Café de la Paix. The Germans had occupied Paris for four years, and without doubt had left behind friends and sympathisers when they had been forced to retreat a few months earlier. They may well also have left behind German covert units. These would have been available to help the *Eisenhower Aktion*.

Another interrogation report said that in order to gain access to Eisenhower's headquarters (and thereby to have access to the Supreme Commander), the 'Americans' might pretend that they had in their custody a German officer, and that they were taking him in for questioning – thus they needed access to the HQ building.

It is difficult to believe that the *Eisenhower Aktion* was anything other than the truth. The men who admitted to it were facing probable execution as spies, and were unlikely to make up a story that would worsen their position very greatly in the eyes of their captors. Skorzeny himself, after his capture and arrest, repeatedly and completely denied that there was a plot against Eisenhower, and suggested that it was only a 'latrine rumour' amongst his men. It is interesting, when assessing the truthfulness of Skorzeny's denials, to remember Colonel von der Heydte's dismissal of him as a man who 'had fantastic notions and wanted to use dirty methods – a typical evil Nazi' and who had broken orders and lied in order to grasp the credit for Mussolini's rescue. Skorzeny's captors were Americans, and it would hardly have helped him to admit that he had planned the assassination of their commanding general. Furthermore, Skorzeny was a glory-seeker with a reputation for dramatic successes. The abject failure of the *Eisenhower Aktion* would not have sat comfortably with that reputation.

The US authorities who interviewed these men, Schmidt and Schultz and their comrades, had sufficient belief in their accounts to greatly increase the security surrounding Eisenhower and their other generals. The Americans could not know how many jeep-loads of German killers had penetrated their front line and were now wandering about France looking like Americans. They had caught some, including Schmidt and Schultz. They had found large sums of money and weapons, which must have been carried with them for a purpose. What is more, the men making these confessions almost certainly knew that they were likely to be shot. Why on earth would they make their situation worse by confessing to a 'spy plot' to kill or capture Eisenhower?

It is a general rule in the courts of the United Kingdom that confessions made against the interest of the person confessing are more likely to be true than confessions in their interests. Here, to confess to being a member of a covert squad intending to kill or capture General Eisenhower was hardly going to help a prisoner – it would only make his position worse.

Any suggestion that the Germans may have left a covert 'stay behind' unit in Paris when they retreated would have been taken seriously. Such an operation was accepted military practice, and indeed the British, when awaiting an expected German invasion after Dunkirk, had prepared to do just that. Major General Sir Colin Gubbins, later the head of the British Special Operations Executive, had commanded what were known as the Auxiliary Units, a stay-behind force that was intended to 'go to ground' behind the advancing German invasion units, and later carry out acts of destruction of various kinds.[5] In the event, the Americans tightened their security around Eisenhower very considerably.

Comparing the details of the *Eisenhower Aktion* with what the US and British investigators had discovered a few days earlier in Britain, there appear to have been two parallel operations, with objectives which, if achieved, would have thrown the Allies into confusion and dismay as the Ardennes offensive continued to smash through towards Antwerp. Those interviewed may have watered down the object of the *Eisenhower Aktion* a little, by suggesting that Eisenhower was to be kidnapped rather than assassinated, but the practicalities of the situation would make that virtually impossible. How would they get Eisenhower back to Germany? Exactly the same was true for Churchill. As we will see when considering the outcome of the Ardennes offensive, the Germans were quite happy to kill their prisoners if they had no use for them. More importantly, the assassination, in wartime, of a significant enemy leader was an acceptable tactic.

A comparison of the plan for London with the plan for Paris throws up a number of very obvious parallels. In France, the plot was for the murder of Eisenhower by Germans dressed as Americans and driving American vehicles, with their disguise enabling them to get sufficiently close to their target to kill him. In England, the plot was for Germans to steal American hospital vehicles, and to go to London – the author suggests to kill Churchill. In their attack on the American hospitals in Devizes, the German prisoners could easily have seized enough uniforms to disguise themselves and/or the British Fascists. It was the logical thing to do. If Hitler's special forces could take out both Churchill and Eisenhower in December 1944, then Hitler would have believed that his chances of victory or a favourable negotiated peace would be considerably improved.

Chapter 24

Doonfoot
The Greatest Escape

Scotland was Ramsay's home country. His family home of Kelly Castle was in Angus, on the east coast. Ben Greene had moved his family to Kinross, not very far north of Ramsay. At Comrie, on the moors to the west of Perth, was Camp 21, Cultybraggan, Britain's equivalent of Colditz Castle, a high-security, vigorously Nazi camp. It held some of the most dangerous German prisoners but it was remote, and the surrounding countryside was a deterrent to escape. It was very far north of Devizes, and it was extremely unlikely that any German task force from the west of England would be able to reach it, or that the prisoners in Comrie Camp, if they did escape, could succeed in making their way south, even with help from Ramsay or Greene.

The break-out and uprising was not, however, to be confined to England and Wales, or to German prisoners. In Britain, there were also many thousands of Italian prisoners of war. As already stated, Britain's approach was to categorise Italian prisoners in the United Kingdom as 'Co-operators' or 'Non-co-operators'. The Non-co-operators were Fascists, many of them still vehemently pro-Mussolini. Camp 14, a few miles south of Ayr on the west coast, held a large number of Italian Fascists. The camp itself was just outside the small town of Doonfoot, and reasonably accessible, although still far north of Devizes and London.

Camp 14 was chosen to hold many of the most vehement Fascist Italian prisoners of war, the worst of the Non-co-operators. Escape once outside the confines of the camp was far easier it would have been at Comrie. However, it was on the wrong side of Scotland for

Ramsay or Greene. There appears to have been no local Fascist contact to help escaped prisoners when they got out and, of course, by 16 December, the major Devizes break-out had been prevented. Somehow, probably by a secret radio, the Fascists at Doonfoot had received the order to join in the big break-out – and they successfully obeyed it, escaping in substantial numbers on the night of 15/16 December. The Italians of Doonfoot carried out the biggest Axis escape in Britain of the war. Ninety-seven men got out.

It is worth pausing to consider what conditions in the camps were like. Many of them had not been built to a particularly high standard – they had often been constructed in a hurry, to meet a rush of prisoners, such as after D-Day. Those who guarded the camps were usually 'third-line' troops – the old, those only partially fit, foreigners from the Pioneer Corps and so on. Front-line troops were, of course, in the front line, or at home on well-earned leave. In contrast, the Fascists of Doonfoot were led by front-line troops, battle-hardened and fit. They were mainly young men, who had a lot of time on their hands which they wanted to fill. Their skills would be enormously varied – they were in fact a huge talent pool of fighting men, engineers, technicians of all kinds, miners, musicians and artists.

In a previous book,[1] the author studied life in a prisoner of war camp in Chieti, Italy, and was impressed by the enormous variety of activities that the prisoners arranged for themselves. Many of them had a secret purpose, connected to escape. A drawing class where the students were asked to draw yachts would be used as a means of instructing would-be escapers on the type of boat they might try to steal (the coast was nearby), and how to sail it to freedom. The digging of tunnels through which prisoners might escape was a universal pastime for prisoners of war of many nationalities. There were only four ways out of a prison camp: through the gates (by bluff and subterfuge); through the wire or wall; over the wire or wall; or under the wire or wall by means of a hidden tunnel. But for all prisoners the most difficult part of the escape was what to do once you were out. That was where the sort of outside support that Ramsay and the British Fascists offered was so vital to success.

Another important consideration for escapers would normally be the weather. If it was summer time, there would be far better cover with the foliage in full bloom. However, the days would be long, and at night, if there was a clear sky, the phase of the moon would be all important – the dark of the moon was highly preferable for escapers. In winter, the advantage would be long nights of darkness, the escaper's friend, but bad weather could pose a major problem. In the case of the 'big break', of course there was no choice. The escapes had to be timed to coincide with the start of the Ardennes offensive, and should all happen within a day or two of each other. Obviously, once the authorities realised what was happening, they would attempt to clamp down on all prisoners in all camps. That happened in all the German camps in Britain after the discovery of the Devizes plot, but it seems that the Italian camps were overlooked.

Thus, despite the bitter winter weather in Ayrshire, the escape went ahead in mid-December. The Italians at Doonfoot decided to tunnel out. Italian engineers had always been good tunnellers, and took on the task with enthusiasm. The camp contained a series of huts for the prisoners, surrounded by a wire fence topped with razor wire. As usual, there were searchlights and armed guards. As with any secret tunnel, the first task was to find a suitable starting point. The author has found no record of the starting point of the Doonfoot tunnel – it was probably in one of the barrack huts. The camp itself has long since been demolished and replaced by housing. What is known is that the tunnellers had a considerable distance to cover before they reached the boundary fence, and then dug on under the fence a good distance into the adjoining field. A report in the *Daily Express* said that the Italians dug a tunnel 'from well inside the camp to a considerable distance outside'.[2]

Tunnels, particularly long ones, posed a multitude of problems for the tunnellers. In the tunnel they needed air and light, and something to prop up the roof to prevent a collapse. Outside, there was always the problem of disposing of the soil – not so difficult in summer, but very difficult in a snowy winter such as December 1944. There would doubtless have been a large team working on the tunnel: the tunnellers themselves, the support teams, the earth disposal teams, the lookouts and so on.

Unusually, clothing did not present a very great problem for escapers in the Great Britain of 1944. The escapers were often wearing mixed uniform, since replacement uniforms were not always available in sufficient numbers through the Red Cross, and where they were not, British or US Army clothing would be supplied. The only distinctive marking would be a red circle of material sewn onto the uniform, marking them out as prisoners. It was not difficult to remove these circles before an escape. In any event, varied uniforms were commonplace on the streets of Great Britain at this time. Apart from numerous types of British and US uniforms, there were many other Allied nations who now had troops on the British mainland. Few could tell one uniform from another with any certainty. Thus escaping Germans and Italians in uniform could pretend to be Allied nationals, whilst wearing their own uniforms, presuming that any obvious German or Italian markings were removed. According to a report in the *Daily Express*, all the escapees from Doonfoot were wearing chocolate-coloured battledress.[3]

A more pressing difficulty with tunnel escapers was to keep their clothing reasonably clean. If they emerged from a long winter crawl through a muddy tunnel with their clothes caked in mud, that would doubtless give rise to suspicion in anyone they met. Thus escapers would usually wear overalls on top of their uniforms or imitation civilian clothing, which they would discard after exit from the tunnel.

In the event, during the hours of darkness on the night of 15/16 December 1944, a total of ninety-seven Fascist Italian escapers crawled through their long secret tunnel and out into the field beyond the wire. All ninety-seven prisoners got clear of the camp, and the guards did not immediately know that they had gone. Only at first light was the escape discovered, probably because the exit hole from the tunnel was spotted.

When the guards discovered the tunnel, the Camp Commandant, believed to be Major W. H. Snell, ordered a roll call to discover how many prisoners were missing. For as long as possible, the remaining inmates messed about confusing the count to buy their comrades time, but eventually Snell discovered that ninety-seven had escaped. He raised the alarm, alerting the Ayrshire police, and all Army units in the area. A massive manhunt began.

The Doonfoot escape had so far been a great success. Ninety-seven enemy soldiers were now on the loose in Great Britain. Their escape was clearly orchestrated to assist the big break at Devizes, and timed to coincide with the Ardennes offensive. Had the plan for the escape from Devizes not been discovered, and had an armed force of Germans taken to the road, complete with tanks, from that camp, then the break-out from Doonfoot, and from the other nominated camps, would have caused total chaos, whether the various bodies of enemy troops met up or not. If groups of British Fascists rose up in armed rebellion at the same time, then Hitler's plan might well have come to fruition. In the event, the vital break-out at Devizes having been prevented, the escapees from Doonfoot were left unsupported.

History does not fully record what happened. Were the escapers met by a member of the Right Club or some other Fascist group when they got clear of the tunnel? Were they given any information as to what had happened at Devizes, or at the other camps or did they already know? Did they remain together at first, as a significant force, albeit as yet unarmed? Or was the plan always to split up into small groups, go in different directions, and cause as much of a distraction and as much destruction as possible? According to the *Daily Express*, an officer of Scottish Command commented: 'There are some difficult men amongst those who escaped. If they got a chance they might attempt sabotage.' Some of the Fascist Italians were indeed highly trained, for example Lieutenant Pietro Graff of the *Folgore* Parachute Division.

For whatever reason, the Italians split into small groups, and most of them made their way south. Perhaps they simply hoped to travel south to find a way of getting to Eire, the nearest independent country, and also, like Italy, a very Catholic country, and so more likely to help.

Once their escape had been discovered, the Italians had little chance of getting away. They needed to be well clear of South Ayrshire before the alarm was raised. Once that had happened every stranger was being stopped and questioned. Three prisoners had been recaptured almost immediately and by the end of 16 December, forty-seven in all had been secured. Most of these had gone south; they were caught in the villages of Maybole and Dalrymple, and in the fishing port of Dunure, no doubt hoping to steal a boat and sail across to Ireland. Four of the Italians had gone north, reaching Newton Mearns, a southern suburb of Glasgow, a distance of thirty miles, before they were caught.

On day two, 17 December, another thirty Italians were caught, all of them tired and hungry. Twenty men remained free. The weather was brutal. By day four, 19 December, fourteen were still at large. A Cabinet Office file shows that there was a committee meeting on this day at which the Doonfoot escape was considered. A Colonel Sheppard reported that the ninety-seven prisoners had tunnelled 'for some distance under the camp barbed wire'. Bearing in mind what was now known about the Devizes plot, Colonel Sheppard commented that it was not yet known if the prisoners had any definite plan of action. He said that some of them had been found in the suburbs of Glasgow, and as the camp was situated less than ten miles from Prestwick airfield it was possible that some prisoners might have been heading there. Describing the escapers, Colonel Sheppard said: 'The inmates of the camp were all malcontents, who had been removed from labour camps, were not fit for any employment and were difficult to control, particularly by the type of guards presently available.'[4] In other words, they were dangerous. Colonel Sheppard's comment about 'the type of guards presently available' highlighted a major part of the problem. Almost all available good-quality troops were occupied with the campaign on the mainland of Europe.

On day six, 21 December, when a question about the escape was asked in the House of Commons, only eight were still free. Two of them were Pietro Graff and an unnamed sergeant major. They were found hiding in a goods wagon at the tiny station of Dalrymple, not very far from Doonfoot, on that same day. They had spent six bitterly cold, hungry days on the run. The remaining six escapees were recaptured not long afterwards.

After their recapture, little of the true reason for the escape emerged. Enormous effort over a number of weeks, or more likely months, had been put into the digging of the escape tunnel by many of the prisoners. The escape was perfectly co-ordinated with the beginning of the Ardennes offensive. That was no coincidence, since otherwise nobody would chose to escape in the most brutal of Scottish winter weather. Had they not had orders, they would have waited for better weather. One escapee apparently handed a note to a British officer listing ten grievances that prisoners had with the way the camp was being run, another wrote that the escape had been caused by the denial of a radio to the prisoners, so they could not listen to programmes from home. Neither explanation fits the facts. No doubt the orders not to disclose the real reason for the break-out if caught had been unequivocal.

Chapter 25

Teddesley Hall Camp
Penkridge, Staffordshire

The escape plans were in place all over Britain. Camp 194 was at Teddesley Hall, near Penkridge, located between Cannock and Stafford in the Midlands of England. The camp was in the grounds of a stately home which had been requisitioned initially by the Army. An escape took place there on 18/19 December. The escape was confined to the officers' compound, and thirteen officers got out by cutting their way through the wire fencing with home-made cutters. According to press reports, dense fog provided the cover that the Germans needed for their escape.[1] If the *Daily Express* is to be believed, those who escaped were Luftwaffe pilots, merchant navy officers and infantry officers from 'the Western Front'. Some were in civilian clothing, some in field grey, and some in blue Luftwaffe uniforms. The escapees made their way to a nearby river, which they crossed, making it impossible for the camp's tracker dog, which was used to search for them about an hour later when the escape was discovered, to follow their trail any further.

Once away from the camp, the Germans split up, and went in various directions. They succeeded in getting further from Teddesley Hall than most of the Italians had from Doonfoot. Heading south, two reached Walsall, and two reached Wolverhampton.

A group of four stole a car, and drove it north-east to Derby. It got them well away from the immediate search area of the camp, but they ran out of fuel in Derby – fuel was scarce and heavily rationed in Britain. The four Germans were seen by a Police Constable Richards, who noticed their German uniforms and spoke to them. They claimed to be Poles trying to get to Nottingham, to the east of Derby. PC Richards, acting with considerable good sense, told the Germans that he would show them to a place where they could get a lift to Nottingham. They went with him, and he led them straight to the local police station, and began to take them inside. Three of the Germans realised where they were and ran off, but were quickly captured. So ended the escape of those four German officers. Two others were also recaptured in Derby.

When recaptured, all the prisoners were searched, and razor-sharp knives, civilian clothing and food supplies (bully beef and bread) were found on them.

Remarkably, two Germans who went north-west got as far as Liverpool. Although there is no clear evidence of how they got there, logically it can only have been by train. Liverpool was a sea port that offered the chance of transport to Eire. The two Germans loitered too long on the quay, hoping to find a vessel that would take them to Ireland, and were spotted by a sharp-eyed police constable. PC John Roberts noticed that although both men wore civilian overcoats, their trouser legs were unusual. When he approached them and spoke to them, they replied in broken accents saying that they were Polish, that they were on leave, and that they were trying to get to Nottingham – the same 'cover story' that the four Germans whose stolen car ran out of petrol in Derby employed, and a pretty nonsensical reason for loitering on the quay at Liverpool Docks. PC Roberts pulled back the overcoat collar of one of the men and saw his German uniform with Wehrmacht badges underneath. The game was up. They too were recaptured.

Meanwhile, back at Teddesley Hall, the guards found themselves under direct threat from the remaining German officer prisoners. The mood amongst the prisoners was rowdy and aggressive. They shouted, booed and hissed at the guards, taunting them with cries of 'You'll never catch them,' and kept up a disturbance throughout the night – stamping on the floors of their huts, and beating tattoos on the wooden walls. On the following morning, once they had collected together outside for a coal detail (when the officers would shovel enough coal for their huts), they assembled into a military formation, and advanced on the gates, brandishing their shovels as potential weapons.

However, the guards did not give way. Under the command of their sergeant major, they stood firm, levelled their Sten sub-machine guns and prepared to fire. Had the Germans attacked, they would have suffered enormous casualties. The Germans broke formation and returned to work, shovelling coal. Their bluff had been called. Extra guards were posted all around the officers' compound, with bayonets fixed, or with Sten guns at the ready.

On 21 December 1944, the *Daily Express* summed the incident up in the headline: 'German prisoners try mutiny – Foiled by armed guard'.[2]

Vivien Batchelor was busy again in the *Daily Express* of 22 December 1944, writing under the headline 'Germans Escape to Plan – Given Get-Away Lessons', it reads:

'Special precautions are being taken at every German and Fascist-Italian prisoner of war camp in Britain. Since the present wave of escapes and attempted escapes – there have been four in the past week – it has been discovered that detailed escape plans are worked out, probably in Germany before the men go into action. These plans are elaborate, and vary whether a man is a soldier, sailor or airman. Certain Nazis are appointed leaders before they leave Germany. These men organise Nazi "cells" in the prison camps, and arrange the break-outs. Escape plans for airmen include the capturing of aircraft and sabotage on our airfields. German sailors are told to make for the ports and to try to seize or sabotage ships. Captured Allied planes are used to give airmen instruction on how to fly them.'[3]

The *Daily Express*'s reports were considered at Cabinet level after they had been published. A Major Carter said:

'Although the articles were not entirely accurate, there is a good deal of truth in them. It is regrettable that they should have appeared and undesirable that they should be followed up by similar articles. The War Office is considering what additional precautions could be taken to prevent these escapes, and they would probably also suggest that Press reports should be more strictly dealt with in the future.'

Nobody was happy – except no doubt Vivien Batchelor!

Chapter 26

The Battle of the Bulge

The Ardennes offensive was launched at 0530 on 16 December 1944. It began with a major artillery barrage, and total surprise was achieved. The weather conditions were suitable – heavy cloud that was predicted to last for a week – but there was also thick snow on the ground which, together with poor traffic control, slowed down the advance. The other two criteria – speed of attack and the capture of Allied fuel dumps were to prove more difficult. Fearful of the abilities of Allied intelligence, German commanders ordered complete radio silence in relation to the operation. German units assembling in the area were issued with charcoal rather than wood for their cooking fires, in order to reduce the smoke, and the chance of being spotted from the air.

The prospects of Operation Stosser, the planned parachute assault of 800 paratroopers under Oberst Friedrich von der Heydte to the rear of the US lines, were ruined by a bad parachute drop. The whole operation had been put together at only eight days' notice and von der Heydte had not been allowed to use the men of his own regiment in case the Allies got wind of it and realised that something was up. Von der Heydte led a conglomerate of paratroopers taken from various regiments, and he had no time to lick them into shape. It is suggested that the pilots who flew them to their dropping zone had no experience of dropping paratroopers, and in the event, once on the ground, von der Heydte could only gather together 300 out of his 800 men, and a small proportion of his supplies. His objective had been to drop into the High Fens area behind US lines, and to seize the Baraque Michel crossroads. With too few men and little ammunition, he had no chance of doing so. Von der Heydte converted his mission into one of reconnaissance, and then withdrew towards Germany, launching an attack on the rear of the US lines as he did so. A fraction of his men, thought to be about 100, returned successfully through the German lines. Operation Stosser appears clearly to have been a last minute add-on to Hitler's plans for the Ardennes offensive, showing perhaps how desperate he was. Some 700 out of 800 of von der Heydte's men were lost, and nothing was achieved.

On the northern shoulder, leading the attack, was Kampfgruppe *Peiper*, commanded by SS-Obersturmbannführer Joachim Peiper, which contained the cream of the Waffen-SS and Germany's newest and most powerful tank, the Tiger II. However, Kampfgruppe *Peiper* started late, and had to be rerouted because German engineers had not repaired two overpasses which had collapsed. By 17 December, they were already running the better part of a day behind schedule. At 1230 that day, Kampfgruppe *Peiper*'s advanced guard passed through the area of Malmédy. They encountered a lightly armed unit of the 285th Field Artillery Observation Battalion, US 7th Armored Division, which put up a short fight, but then surrendered in the face of overwhelming firepower. The advanced guard moved on, but when the main body of Kampfgruppe *Peiper* arrived, they murdered at least eighty-four of the US prisoners. Two other massacres took place on the same day. Clearly the SS had *carte blanche* to kill their prisoners if it was easier than passing them back behind the fighting line.

Peiper made progress throughout 17 and 18 December, but failed to capture any fuel. By the morning of 19 December, this had become a problem. He was meeting stiff resistance from the US infantry and, lacking fuel for his tanks, Peiper could not advance further. Since no relief reached him, on 23 December, he and his men abandoned their vehicles, and made their way back to the German lines on foot. They had been the élite of Hitler's attacking force.

The assault through the centre was far more successful. The Fifth Panzer Army attacked positions held by the US 28th and 106th Infantry Divisions, surrounded them, and forced them to surrender.

It was a huge reverse for the Americans, and they lost well over 7,000 men and a substantial amount of equipment. The Germans advanced on St Vith, and eventually took the town and its environs on 23 December, the morning that Rosterg was murdered, with the US troops withdrawing west of the Salm River. The German forces pressed forward, taking the town of Celles, but late on Christmas Eve, the German advance ground to a halt within sight of the Meuse River. It was this attack which brought great hope to Berlin, and received considerable publicity worldwide.

In the south, the German advance was less successful. The important town of Bastogne was fiercely defended by the Americans, and the Germans were forced to place it under siege and bypass it. By 22 December, the position of the US forces defending Bastogne seemed hopeless – they were low on ammunition, and the weather still prevented resupply by air. The Germans demanded of US Brigadier General Anthony McAuliffe, commanding US forces in Bastogne, that he surrender. McAuliffe's now famous response was to endorse the written request for his surrender with the single word: 'NUTS!' (American slang at the time for 'rubbish'). Happily for the Allies, on 23 December the weather began to clear, and it was possible to resupply McAuliffe by air over the next five days. The improved weather also gave use of their offensive airpower back to the Allies, and they began to prepare a counter-attack. By 24 December, the German offensive had effectively stalled just short of the Meuse.

General Patton's Third US Army battled to relieve Bastogne, which it finally did at 1650 on 26 December. The tide appeared to be turning in favour of the Allies. However, the Germans responded with a fresh counter-attack on New Year's Day 1945. This comprised a major air offensive against Allied airfields which, whilst it destroyed or gravely damaged some 465 Allied planes, caused the Luftwaffe irreparable losses, and a land offensive against the Seventh US Army, which had been weakened because it had sent men, equipment and supplies north to reinforce the American line in the Ardennes. Seventh Army found itself in dire trouble, and during a battle lasting over three weeks, it was forced to withdraw to defensive positions on the south bank of the Moder River. On 25 January 1945, the German offensive finally came to a close – they simply did not have the equipment, supplies and reinforcements to sustain it.

In the Ardennes area, Allied forces counter-attacked in early January, using Patton's and Montgomery's commands. The weather was snowy and bitterly cold, and it was not until 25 January that the combined US and British forces succeeded in driving the Germans back to their start point of 16 December. The Ardennes offensive, or the Battle of the Bulge as it has become popularly known, was over. Like the big break-out in Britain, it had failed.

Chapter 27

The Serchio Offensive and Operation Galia

Operation Winter Storm was, in the event, a far more modest counter-attack than the Ardennes offensive, down the Serchio Valley in Italy, towards Lucca and Livorno. German forces in Italy were short of both men and equipment, and Mussolini's *Monterosa* and *San Marco* divisions were under-strength and many of their men not yet fully trained. The Allies had total dominance of the air, and therefore any substantial build-up of troops and tanks would be observed. In the event, the Axis troops did without tank support, because it would be too obvious if they gathered a force of tanks together, but nonetheless their preparations were observed, and the Allies moved two battalions of Indian Army troops (Mahrattas and Gurkhas) into the reserve area behind the US 92nd Division which held the Serchio valley.

With the Battle of the Bulge still raging, Operation Winter Storm was finally launched at 0300 on the morning of Boxing Day, 26 December 1944, and initially met with the same level of success as the Ardennes offensive. No doubt Christmas Day had been enjoyed by many of the 92nd Division, and that may have contributed to what was a weak defence by the Allies. Over the first days of the advance, the Germans/Fascists enjoyed considerable success. Advancing on a front that was 25 kilometres wide, they attacked and took the village of Sommocolonia and the town of Barga. They reached the outskirts of Bagni di Lucca. The troops opposing them were routed with relative ease. It was their first action. The Germans/Fascists captured a considerable quantity of Allied guns and munitions, which were enormously valuable to them. However, the weather was good for flying, and the Allies struck back with heavy bombing raids, stopping the enemy advance. The German/Fascist retreat was orderly, however; they evacuated their positions rather than being forced out of them. Barga was retaken by the British Indian Army troops on 29 December, and Sommocolonia on 30 December, as the enemy forces fell back to their Gothic Line. Witnesses say that Axis troops masquerading as partisans caused much confusion amongst the Allied forces.

The Axis success had shown how fragile the Allied defence of their position on the west coast was. There was concern at Allied headquarters that the Serchio counter-attack had in fact been a reconnaissance in strength, and that a much larger break-out would follow, as was happening in the Ardennes. Before Operation Winter Storm had been turned back on 29 December, action was taken by the Allies which illustrates very well what the effect of the big break-out in the United Kingdom might have been. On 27 December 1944, in Operation Galia, a troop of thirty-three men of 2nd Special Air Service Regiment were dropped by parachute in the Rossano Valley, a high mountain valley in the north of Tuscany. Their objective was to cause damage and confusion behind enemy lines in northern Tuscany, and to provoke as large a response as possible.[1]

There is nothing that a military commander likes less than to have an enemy force to his rear, behind his own front lines. Such a force poses a threat to his communications, supply lines, military installations of all kinds, and the safety of important personnel. Britain in World War Two had long been alert to the danger of German paratroop units landing within its shores, and fully appreciated the danger that they could cause. In all occupied countries, the Special Operations Executive had long been helping to foment resistance to Nazi rule, encouraging underground fighters and inserting co-ordinators and saboteurs. Gubbins had written three pamphlets giving instructions to would-be resistance leaders on how to organise and run their bands. In Italy, the partisans were making a significant contribution to Allied victory. But there was a significant difference between resistance fighters, many of whom were civilians, and a well-trained, battle-hardened squad of soldiers.

The men of 2 SAS, under the command of Captain (later Lieutenant Colonel) Bob Walker Brown, DSO, a real fighting soldier, landed in the Rossano Valley in the afternoon of 27 December 1944. Their orders were to cause as much havoc as they could over as wide an area as possible. They stayed behind enemy lines for more than fifty days, in the most appalling winter weather, and attacked all available targets, with the intention of forcing the enemy to use a large number of their troops to try to catch and kill them.

There are various parallels that can be drawn between Operation Galia's position in Tuscany, and the situation that would have faced the Germans in the United Kingdom a few days earlier in December, had they succeeded in breaking out from their prison camps and arming themselves. When Operation Galia arrived on enemy soil, it was immediately provided with local help, which lasted throughout their time behind enemy lines. SOE partisan liaison officer and ex-prisoner of war Major Gordon Lett, DSO, and his Italian partisans and helpers were awaiting the SAS when they landed. Lett had a very detailed knowledge of the area. He could supply local guides to lead the SAS to their targets, mules to carry their heavy kit, and could identify suitable objectives. His partisans, and other partisans in the area, could support the SAS and fight alongside them when necessary. Bob Walker Brown divided his force into six 'sticks' – squads of five or six men who would operate as independent units. Thus it was possible for targets to be attacked simultaneously at up to six different points, over a wide area. Local knowledge was vital not only to get a squad to its target without detection, but perhaps more importantly, to get them away again without capture.

Operation Galia attacked north, east, south and west of their landing area. They were resupplied when necessary by air. They attacked the main roads, since most of the railways had already been put out of action by Allied bombing and the partisans. They would generally target small convoys, particularly those including staff cars. Although Walker Brown lost one of his sticks early on, when they were captured and their Italian guide was shot, he was able to mount a number of different attacks on any one day, and thereby to create the impression that his force was much larger than it was. With the Germans and Fascists now relying heavily on the roads to supply their defence of the Gothic Line, the attacks of Operation Galia began to have a considerable effect.

The tactic had the desired result. The Axis command decided that it could not follow up its Serchio Offensive with a heavier attack until it had dealt with the problems to its rear. A huge 'clean-up' operation was launched over the mountains of the Rossano area, beginning on 20 January 1945, to catch and kill the paratroopers and the partisans. Estimates vary, but probably more than 10,000 enemy troops were required to comb the area. Only 9,100 Axis troops had been used for the Serchio attack. The clean-up operation lasted until 25 January 1945, but not a single SAS man was captured or killed during it. They were fit, strong, well-led professional soldiers, with, most importantly, excellent local guides. As soon as the enemy operation ended, the SAS regrouped and went back into action, attacking many of the same main roads again. The Axis search had used a huge number of troops, had killed some partisans but no paratroopers, and had utterly failed to stop the damaging attacks to the rear. The Axis generals could not risk another counter-attack from the Gothic Line, and the idea was abandoned.

In late February, Captain Walker Brown, with his men now exhausted, decided to exfiltrate through the Gothic Line to Allied territory. This was accomplished without the loss of a man, due again to good local guides and local knowledge. Operation Galia has always been regarded as hugely successful, and a very good example of how effective small units behind enemy lines can be when they have local support.

Operation Galia had thirty-three men; three times that number escaped from Doonfoot and at Devizes there were more than 7,000 Germans under orders, and at Sheffield between 10,000 and 12,000. Many of those at both Devizes and Sheffield were very professional, and very ruthless, military men, from various branches of the German services including the Waffen-SS and the paratroop arm. Their break-out plan was entirely feasible and well planned. With the all-important help of the British Fascists, they could have caused mayhem. As Operation Galia demonstrates, if a covert military force is working with good local guides who speak the local language, then small well-armed sections can inflict wholly disproportionate damage on their enemies. As Hitler considered his plans for the Ardennes offensive, and decided on a simultaneous break-out in Britain, it is inconceivable in this historian's view that he did not also plan to use the support of the British Fascists. Hitler's tactics before and after the outbreak of the war had been to cultivate and build up Fifth Columns in all of the countries on which he had designs, and he had used his Fifth Columns to good effect in Czechoslovakia, Poland and elsewhere. William Joyce was working for the Germans in Berlin, and he knew all of the British Fascists, and there were others like him. All of the evidence points to the fact that when the time came for the big break, the British Fascists would give it vital support. Had the big break-out happened on 27 November 1944, as originally intended, it would have had a devastating effect.

Carrying out sabotage and causing disruption were the obvious activities for escaped prisoners if they remained under direct orders from Germany, which, thanks in significant part to the SS and their system of Vehmic justice, these Germans did. Trying to get home was not an option for them. The numbers involved in the plot would have been sufficient, if they were able to seize guns and armoured vehicles, to fight small battles with Allied troops. However, as with all armies, if they were unassisted, they would have had problems with resupply of fuel, munitions and food. Even if they had advanced on London at speed, without picking up support from Camp 17 at Sheffield or other camps, and had travelled overnight on 16/17 December, it is unlikely that an armed column would have been able to reach the British capital without being stopped, or slowed sufficiently to allow the Allies to gather strong enough forces to stop them. But a column of ambulances, stolen from the hospitals at

Devizes and containing crack Nazi troops, but driven by English-speaking British Fascists, could conceivably reach Parliament Square unchallenged. Once there, Jock Ramsay MP and his fellow British Fascists might well find a way of giving such a force an opportunity to assassinate Churchill and his Cabinet.

Chapter 28

The War Goes On

Camp 198, Island Farm, Bridgend

Following the failure of the break-out, the escapes went on, despite the increased awareness of the British authorities. Extra precautions were put in place. For instance, the RAF was alert to the problem that escaped German pilots might try to steal some of its aircraft. On 2 January 1945, Wing Commander Arnold told a Cabinet committee that the precaution had been taken of draining practically all the petrol from 'dispersed aircraft' parked at civilian air stations. On its own airfields, the RAF clearly presumed that the security arrangements would be sufficient. Nonetheless, on 22 January 1945, a German prisoner of war who had escaped from a camp at Crewe two days earlier, reached an RAF aerodrome at Bitteswell, Leicestershire. He succeeded in penetrating the airfield perimeter, and crept up to a Wellington bomber, which would have had the range to reach Germany.[1] The information subsequently received was that this pilot could fly solo most types of British aircraft. He was attempting to break into the aircraft when he was spotted and arrested. He had come very close to success. When searched, he was found to be wearing two pairs of underpants, with a piece of silk hidden in between. This had drawn on it a rough map of England, with large towns and roads to the east coast marked. The plan at Devizes was much more ambitious than this solo effort, but the near success of this escaped prisoner shows how feasible the Devizes plan was.

In Wales, the Island Farm Camp had originally been built to house workers at the new, vast munitions factory in Bridgend. Twenty-two huts were erected, each capable of housing 100 workers.

It was a uninspiring place, but it provided cheap and convenient accommodation for the workforce close to their place of work. It was not, therefore, designed as a prison of any sort. As the war moved forward, Island Farm was used for US troops assembling and training for D-Day. After they had moved on, the camp was used for a while as a low-security prisoner of war work camp, with a mixture of low-ranking Italian and German prisoners billeted there, who went out to work each day. However, a decision was then taken in November 1944 that Camp 198 should become a high-security German officers' camp. Some 2,000 Germans were to be held there.

In many ways, it was a curious decision, since Island Farm had never been designed to be a prison camp. Many of the accommodation huts were within twenty yards of the perimeter fence, unusually close and lending themselves to the efforts of tunnellers. The length of an escape tunnel was vitally important, since it would normally need to be shored up throughout with timber, the workers had to conceal the soil removed, and there had to be an air supply. A tunnel of twenty to thirty yards would require far less timber and would generate far less spoil than one of a hundred yards.

The camp had a perimeter some two miles long. Two large barbed-wire fences had to be built around the entire perimeter, the perimeter had to be lit, watch-towers put in place, and arrangements made so that the perimeter could be patrolled. The huge munitions factory nearby was an obvious target for saboteurs, and there were plenty of other industrial targets in the area, as well as good road and rail links. In November 1944, it was still believed that the main objective of German escaped prisoners in the UK would be sabotage, so the camp was potentially dangerously placed close to the factory.

Camp 198 became a camp under strict Nazi control. The SS officers amongst the 2,000 took charge, and as usual every hut contained an SS presence. Discipline was strong, the men marched as a unit, and the Nazi salute was always given. Probably because Camp 198 was only set up in November 1944, it does not seem to have specifically featured in the big break-out plan, despite its high Nazi content. However, the Cabinet Office files contain the suggestion that two incomplete tunnels were found there in December 1944, so some of the inmates at least may have intended to try to join the break-out plan.[2] Whether or not their tunnels would have been ready for 16 December, there is no doubt that the Nazis of Island Farm would have rapidly joined in any break-out that occurred if they were able to.

Escape activities were, however, very much a part of the life of the Camp 198 prisoners. After the December failure, two new tunnels were started, one from Hut 16 and one from Hut 9; both huts were believed to offer short and safe routes under the wire. The lighting around the perimeter was still poor, despite the attempts of the British Camp Commander, Lieutenant Colonel Edwin Darling, to improve it. Once out of the camp, escapers would still have open ground to cross before they reached the safety of the nearby woods. The digging began, its noise covered up by almost constant group singing. This choral singing would often go on all day, and much of the night. It was a source of strength for the Nazis, a demonstration of their unity. Orders were given that there should be no individual escapes. As in many of the German camps, home-made wireless receivers were built which enabled the prisoners to receive the latest broadcasts from Germany. It is not known whether they also managed to build a transmitter in the Island Farm Camp.

As always, the Nazis faced the problem of how to dispose of the soil that they were digging out of the tunnels without it becoming obvious. The Todt Organisation engineers were advising on the construction of the tunnels, and it may well have been one of them who came up with the idea of how to hide the clay soil. In Hut 9, a completely false wall was constructed in the large shower and latrine area, using scavenged bricks sealed together with dried porridge. The porridge was brought into the hut each day as a part of the breakfast served to a number of senior officers who were living in the hut. Once the false wall was constructed, the clay from the tunnels would be hidden in the space between the false wall and the real one. A conduit pipe was built out of empty tin cans, carrying air to the workface of the tunnels and solving another difficulty. Both tunnels progressed very satisfactorily until the end of January.

Then disaster struck one of them – two diligent British guards discovered the tunnel in Hut 16. The whole camp was then immediately searched, but the Hut 9 tunnel was not found. The escape rations that had been gathered, and other escape supplies, were found, however, which set back the escape team for Hut 9. Food was saved by siphoning it off from the men's daily rations. With a Nazi Vehmic system of law in force, nobody protested if their breakfast, lunch or supper was smaller than normal. After the discovery of the tunnel from Hut 16, security was tightened up, and an extra roll call instituted each day. In response, the embargo on individual escape attempts was lifted by the Nazis. The camp leaders believed that it was no longer possible to lull the British into a false sense of security, and escape attempts might distract attention from the remaining tunnel.

The night of 10/11 March 1945 was finally chosen for the break-out. The tunnel from Hut 9 was now calculated to be ten feet beyond the perimeter fence. Immediately after lights-out on that night, a squad of men went down the tunnel to prepare the exit. There was a cable running down the tunnel which, thanks to the ingenuity of the engineers, carried electricity for lighting. The men could see what they were doing, and if the lights were switched off, it meant that a guard was on patrol nearby, and work should stop. Starting at about 0300 on 11 March, the Island Farm Nazis began to make their escape. The tunnel functioned for about two hours. All those involved in the organisation that had built it passed through, after which the tunnel was there for all to use, and the escapes continued. Finally, one of the Germans, Lieutenant Heinz Tonnsmann, was spotted – he had made the mistake of carrying a white kit bag. Tonnsmann got out of the tunnel, and began to make his way across the open ground to the cover of the woods. He made it half-way before a challenge rang out, followed by a shot that hit him in the shoulder. The game was up. A number of other Germans were caught still out in the open, and surrendered. It is probably this fact that subsequently caused a variety of different estimates to be given as to the number of escapers. Author Peter Phillips says that fourteen men were recaptured in the open ground outside the perimeter fence.[3] The Cabinet Office files record that the number of escapes from Bridgend was seventy, but that only fifty-six had got away.[4] Peter Phillips is right therefore to say fourteen were recaptured immediately.

In the House of Commons, a question was asked about the escape on 15 March 1945. The figures given in the response vary from those in the Cabinet Office report. Mr A. Henderson replied for the government saying:

> 'An escape by 67 German prisoners of war took place at 0400 hours on 11 March from a camp in South Wales. Forty-eight of them have now been recaptured. The escape was effected by means of a tunnel twenty yards long, the entrance to which was in a corner of a living hut, an eighteen-inch square of four-inch concrete having been carefully cut out and carefully camouflaged.'

The alarm was raised immediately. So late in the war, it seems that the men from Island Farm had no plans to seize weapons, commit sabotage or march on London, they simply wished to get away. The Cabinet Office report states that the men had escaped in batches of ten or twelve, splitting into pairs once they were out, and moving off in different directions. For all of them, the escape was short-lived. Only eight of the fifty-six succeeded in putting any distance between themselves and Island Farm, two were recaptured at Eastleigh, Southampton; two at the Severn Tunnel Junction and four at Castle Bromwich, Warwickshire. All had been re-captured by 17 March. There is no suggestion of outside help by Fascist sympathisers. All those recaptured were found to have plenty of food rations, maps and home-made compasses. None of them put up any resistance to arrest.

The Island Farm escape was a major achievement. Had it happened in December 1944, the fifty-six Nazis from Island Farm would likely have played their part in the big break-out. The tunnel was built with such sound engineering techniques that it still survives to this day. In the summer of 2017, two archaeologists, Jamie Pringle of Keele

University and Peter Doyle of the London South Bank University conducted a scientific investigation at Island Farm, and discovered that the tunnel was still 'remarkably intact'. They found that sawn-off bed legs and other materials from the prisoners' huts were still supporting the tunnel walls and roof. They found that the tunnel ran out from Hut 9 at a relatively shallow depth of 1.5 metres, and made a most remarkable video recording of the journey down the tunnel.

So, in summary, the Island Farm escape was a 'what might have been'. If it had occurred in December, the fifty-six men who got out might well have been able to take action against the camp guards and liberate the camp – but in March the war really was nearly over, and the German counter-attack of the Battle of the Bulge had been defeated.

Chapter 29

The Hangmen Kill Again

Murder at Sheffield

Camp 17, Lodge Moor, Sheffield, was still run along strictly Nazi lines. It stood some miles outside Sheffield, surrounded by inhospitable Yorkshire moorland. Following D-Day, it was used for the increasing number of German prisoners arriving in Britain. The huts were long and narrow, holding two lines of double bunks, with an alleyway running between them down the centre. The huts stood close together, about five yards apart, and there were pathways in front of the huts about six yards wide. The Nazi inmates managed to dominate the camp population in the same way as at Devizes, Comrie and Island Farm.

The objective, back in December 1944, had been to have a joining of forces between the Nazis of Camp 23 and Camp 17. Lodge Moor, like Devizes, contained many hard-line Nazis. No escape or break-out took place there on 16 or 17 December, however, despite the plans of the inmates. The authorities at the camp had, of course, been warned in advance, and security was tightened. The camp was thoroughly searched, and an escape tunnel was found. Presumably the plan had been to get men out of camp so that they could take control of the gates from the outside. Whatever the plan may have been, it was frustrated by the discovery of the Devizes plot, which led to tight security over the Christmas period.

However, according to research recently done at Sheffield University, on 20 December a group of Germans did manage to escape. Just how they did it is not clear, but they were not at large for long, and were caught in Darlington after twenty-four hours of freedom.

It was thought by the Nazis that the finding of the tunnel was the result of an informant and Lodge Moor did hold some anti-Nazis. The Nazis in Lodge Moor believed that they had been betrayed, but they had no idea who the informant might be. Once the dust had settled, they got back to work, and dug another tunnel. There was no question of them giving up. When this tunnel too was discovered on 24 March, the Nazis became convinced that they had again been betrayed. They were right – information about the tunnel had been given to the British authorities by two men, Obergefreiter Neuschild and Obergefreiter Diesner,[1] who were moved from the camp on 23 March. Diesner had previously been beaten up as an anti-Nazi.

Desperate for revenge, and utterly frustrated, the Nazi mob looked for someone to blame for the discovery of the tunnel, and their suspicions fell on two more of their fellow prisoners – Otto Huth and Gerhard Rettig.[2] These two men were either 'Whites' or 'Greys' who had, for some reason, ended up in a 'Black' camp. They lived in the same hut, A6 in Compound 1, for fourteen days before the tunnel was discovered, and already they had been vilified for not being Nazi enough – they were accused of being traitors and were told that they would face punishment beatings. As a result of the threats, within three days of their arrival in Camp 17, Rettig and Huth applied to the Intelligence staff to be removed from Compound 1. Rettig wrote out an application for himself and Huth. This was a standard procedure in prisoner of war camps throughout Britain – prisoners who felt themselves in danger could apply to be transferred to another compound or another camp. The risk, however, was that this would be reported back to Germany by the Nazis, and that their families would then be in danger. However, it was now very close to the end of the war, and probably Rettig and Huth thought that the risk to their families was slight. They may even have been in Allied-occupied territory by this time. Rettig handed in the application to the British camp administration, but as the days passed, nothing happened.

The tunnel was discovered at 0800 on 24 March 1945 during a search. Suspicion immediately fell on Huth and Rettig. They were threatened again with a beating. Both men were now in considerable fear, and in the afternoon, at 1600, Rettig and Huth again applied to leave the compound, by means of a note that Rettig passed through the wire to a camp guard. This time, with tension high following the discovery of the tunnel, the camp authorities took the request seriously, and granted it almost immediately. An hour or so later, not long before the evening roll call, Huth and Rettig were informed by the Lagerführer, Feldwebel Jedamski, a fervent Nazi, that they were to pack their things, and to report to the camp exit after roll call, which was at 1730. This was an enormous relief for both men – they should be clear of the camp, and safe, before dark. It was usually under cover of darkness that the Vehmic court acted. Tragically for Rettig and Huth, the attempt to move them came too late. Feldwebel Jedamski passed on the information that they were being moved to the Vehmic 'police'. In effect, Jedamski signed their death warrant.

Rettig and Huth attended roll call at 1730, and then returned to their hut to pack up their things. Rettig, responding to a call of nature, left the hut to go to the latrine block. As he went out through the barrack door, however, he found that there was a crowd of Nazis waiting for him, led by two called Kühne and Schmittendorf. The hangmen had gathered to execute the sentence of the Vehmic court. They attacked Rettig, punching him, and forcing him to run back into his hut, where his friend Huth might be able to help him. The hangmen followed, bursting into the hut and continuing to beat Rettig about the head and body. At some stage he was also beaten to the genitals. The focus of the attack at this stage was clearly Rettig, not Huth. Rettig had written the final request for a transfer, and he had emerged first from the hut to be confronted by the mob. As is the character of a feral attack, once his assailants had drawn his blood, they were determined to carry the assault on him through to its fatal conclusion. However, once the Nazi hangmen had entered the hut, Huth too came under attack. Huth briefly tried to help his friend, but was beaten half conscious. A man called Frenzel led the attack on Huth, calling to other Nazis: 'That is also one of those pigs!' as he went for Huth. Huth was knocked to the floor, but then left for the time being, as Rettig was dragged and pushed out of the hut door into the compound outside, where more Nazis waited. Frenzel and his companions clearly wanted to witness the murder of Rettig. There were now about a hundred men in the mob attacking Rettig.

Huth remained lying injured on the floor of Hut A6. No doubt the hangmen would come back for him once they had completed the public killing of Rettig. However, Huth's Hut Leader 'asked' Huth to get out of the hut, and Huth staggered to his feet, picked up his few belongings, and went outside. Luckily for him, the mob was still busy beating Rettig to death. Believing that there was nothing he could do to help Rettig now, Huth tried to creep away. He was spotted by more of the mob, but ran with all his remaining strength for the camp exit, reaching just in time, despite a pack of Nazis baying for blood at his heels. They had hands on him as he finally reached safety, but the guards gave Huth the protection that he needed, and brought him out of the compound to safety. Huth could hardly see – both his eyes were closed from the blows that he had received. He was taken to the medical centre, and the alarm was raised.

Poor Rettig had no chance of escape. Once outside Hut A6, Rettig was continually beaten by the men who had dragged him there. The mob that surrounded Rettig grew fast. Possibly, the Vehmic court had met some time that afternoon after the information had been received that Rettig and Huth were imminently to be transferred, and a death sentence had been passed, but such kangaroo vigilante courts had no real rules or format, and in reality this was feral mob rule. The crowd that surrounded Rettig were baying for his blood. Estimates suggest there were as many as 500 Germans. Amongst the ringleaders were Schmittendorf and Kühne, both young but extremely violent men. Ignoring Rettig's cries that he was innocent, the mob murdered Rettig in a similar fashion to Rosterg at Comrie, beating him to death.

A number of witnesses were eventually prepared to come forward and support the prosecution of some of the leading hangmen for murder. A witness called Van Balkom saw Rettig stagger from his hut after the attack inside it, pouring with blood, and protesting his innocence. He did not get far before being knocked to the ground and surrounded. Horst Hennemann, another one of those who was prepared to give evidence in the eventual prosecution, climbed up onto a pile of coke in order to see what was happening to the unfortunate Rettig, surrounded as he was by the hostile crowd of his fellow Germans. Hennemann saw Schmittendorf and Kühne standing in front of Rettig who was sitting on the ground, obviously already badly hurt. He put up no resistance as Schmittendorf and Kühne repeatedly beat him around the head with their fists until he fell to the ground. Schmittendorf kicked his prone body three times in the face. Others beat him too. Rettig was groggy, obviously badly injured, and could only raise one arm in a feeble attempt to protect his head. An examination of his remains after his death showed broken ribs and injuries to his genitals in addition to the inevitable injuries to his head. A witness called Wilhelm Shulz heard the crowd shouting: 'Kill him, kill him, beat him to death! Hang him!' At one point Rettig called out 'Comrades, help me!' to the crowd, but nobody did. The only response that Hennemann heard was a shout of 'You blackguard, you should not call for help.' Somebody threw some water over Rettig to bring him back to consciousness – he sank back almost prone on the ground, and Schmittendorf hit him again as he lay there.

Battered and bruised though Rettig was, and although according to the post mortem he was already dying from a haemorrhage to the brain, Rettig instinctively made one final great effort to survive. All of a sudden, he hauled himself to his feet and ran off, taking his assailants by surprise. His desperate attempt to escape his awful fate did not last long. Pursued by a crowd of forty or fifty Nazis still baying for his blood, he tripped over a length of wire and came crashing to the ground again. The witness Hennemann had lost sight of Rettig before he fell, but he heard shouts of 'The Tommies are coming,' and the crowd began to disperse quickly. Huth had reached the safety of the guards' compound, and the alarm had been raised. Hennemann went into his hut and, looking out of the window, he saw Rettig on the ground, motionless. Hennemann did absolutely nothing to help Rettig, but carried on with his task, which was to stoke the boiler.

Help arrived, but it was too late. It saved Rettig from being strung up, but he was already dying. Medical orderlies (referred to by the German prisoners later as 'Red Cross') came into the compound, together with some of the guards, and placed Rettig onto a stretcher. He was carried away, and was given such medical help as was possible. His injuries were too severe to be treated in the camp's medical unit, and so Rettig was taken by ambulance to the nearest hospital. He was pronounced dead on arrival.

Later that evening, Schmittendorf, the leader of the hangmen, basked in the adulation of some of his colleagues. He was seen by a witness called Norbert Schulze about two hours after the killing in a group of twenty fellow prisoners. Schulze heard someone say to Schmittendorf that it was good work that Rettig had been beaten to death. Schmittendorf replied with satisfaction that the *Rollkommando* had functioned very well. Somebody in the crowd said that the man should have been hanged (which was the Vehmic ritual), and Schmittendorf agreed, but said that the Red Cross got in the way, and that without them, they would have done better. He was repeatedly congratulated by his fellows. Another of the ringleaders, Kühne, later told the witness Hennemann that Rettig had betrayed the tunnel, and he also admitted to hitting Rettig. A sailor called Kurt Isbaner, who had been ordered join the planned escape because he was a sailor, was told about the murder of Rettig that: 'Such people had to be killed. He had committed treason against them and against Germany.' Isbaner is an example of how the German escape teams would always include men with different types of expertise – a sailor could assist with stealing and operating a boat. In Hut A2, where the tunnel had been dug, seven of the eight men responsible for it boasted that they personally had hit Rettig, beating him and kicking him in the genitals.

A post-mortem examination of Rettig's body found that death was due to an intra-cranial haemorrhage that was a result of multiple injuries inflicted upon the head.

Schmittendorf, Kühne and their fellow hangmen showed only satisfaction and no remorse at the barbaric killing of Rettig. In truth they had killed an innocent man. Rettig, although an anti-Nazi, was not the informant. Nor was Huth. As already stated, the records show that two other prisoners named Neuschild and Diesner had supplied the information on 23 March 1945, leading to the discovery of the tunnel at 0800 on 24 March.

It was extremely difficult for the British to gather evidence about what had happened. The rule of fear still dominated the camp. Only after Allied victory, when Germany was no longer in the hands of the Nazis, and therefore the prisoners did not have to fear for their families, were German witnesses prepared to support any prosecution for Rettig's murder. Huth attended identification parades, and was able to identify two men – Kühne, who had been prominent in the assault of Rettig, and Frenzel, who had attacked Huth.

A number of Germans were charged with the murder of Rettig, but because of evidential difficulties, only two were convicted of the killing: Emil Schmittendorf and Armin Kühne. The information available to the investigators was that Schmittendorf had been amongst the team working on the tunnel. On the evidence he was clearly the ringleader of the mob, with Kühne as his enthusiastic apprentice.

Armin Kühne did his best to avoid conviction, writing to a number of potential witnesses, suggesting a story that they could tell to help him get an acquittal. Emil Schmittendorf did the same. They were not prepared to say: 'Yes, we did it, it was a matter of Vehmic law and we are good Nazis.' They tried to wriggle out of it. The various letters were intercepted, and their attempts to win acquittals proved futile.

After a military court heard their cases, both men were sentenced to death and were eventually hanged at Pentonville Prison – symbolic justice for those who had pretended to act under the jurisdiction of a Vehmic court.

Armin Kühne wrote to his family during his trial, indicating that his fate would be decided on 7 August 1945. He showed no remorse, saying:

'I have risked my life for my fatherland, have given blood for my comrades and have remained a German, and will remain one to the end. One thing I know, it is only because I am a Nazi and non-Nazis accuse me.'

Two comments must be made. Firstly, it was the likes of Schmittendorf, Kühne, and their fellow Nazis in Lodge Moor, whom Hitler had wanted to arm and turn on Churchill in London. They were utterly ruthless, utterly brutal men.

Secondly, the murder of Rettig took place on 24 March 1945, at a time when Germany was imminently facing total defeat and yet these men were prepared to murder a fellow German upon absolutely no evidence. And, as the reader will see, with men like Leese and many of his fellow British Fascists at liberty, the loss of the war, and even the revelations of the Holocaust that followed it, did nothing to dissuade fanatical Nazis from their beliefs, which the British Fascists shared.

Chapter 30

The Escape Line to Brazil

Ramsay and Leese remained in touch throughout 1945, both before and after the war had come to an end. Once Ramsay ceased to be an MP in the election of June 1945, MI5 was able to apply for a Home Office warrant to intercept his communications. An MI5 report in July states that Ramsay's anti-Semitism had strengthened even further, and that he included the British government in his definition of Jewry. He spoke still of turning to violence to achieve his ends.

After his release at the end of September 1944, Ramsay had spent quite a lot of time trying to have the remaining detainees liberated, but soon found he could do nothing about them.

By Christmas 1944, MI5 observed that he seemed to be losing interest in his fellow ex-detainees. After the failure of the big break-out, no doubt he was despondent. MI5 noted that he was involved in an affair with his secretary, Ruth Erskine, and was also having affairs with other women. He remained vehemently opposed to the British government, and was preparing, they believed, as a final resort, to adopt violent methods, and was 'thinking of a revolution'.

Despite the failure of the 16 December coup, and the Allied victory in Europe, the British Fascists did not give up hope. In particular, Arnold Leese continued to work fanatically to help surviving Nazis. He had remained in touch with the remnants of his Imperial Fascist League and, even after Allied victory, controlled and ran a Fascist network in Britain. Fascism, as Leese knew well, was world-wide.

As a result of his Fascist and anti-Jewish publications over the years, Leese was in contact with many active Fascists overseas.

Even when the war had been won, and the details of the mass slaughter of Jews in the Holocaust had become known, the likes of Ramsay and Leese remained convinced Nazis and anti-Semites. On 17 April 1946, Ramsay held a meeting with Gilbert, Gordon-Canning and others. He was totally undeterred by the defeat of Hitler and German National Socialism the previous year. MI5 had a spy present, who reported that:

> 'Ramsay says that as a responsible politician he takes the view that the only possible way of dealing with the Jewish problem is to concentrate on awakening the public by "any and every means and trick" to the menace of Jewry, and to encourage a state of mind where the public would forget sentimentality and appreciate that extermination by lethal and humane means is the only solution. He is not in favour of torture or cruelty, but he thinks that the Nazis were fully justified in their methods. He thinks that the subject of kosher slaughter is one good method of attack, as the British public are more easily roused by cruelty to animals than by Jewish cruelty to millions of human beings. Gilbert agrees with this view and says he will do his bit.'

In April 1946 therefore, the British Fascists were not trying to deny that the Holocaust had taken place, they were approving of it!

The report goes on:

> 'Ramsay speaks very warmly of National Socialist Germany and it is evident that he is really a Nazi himself. He expresses the belief that Nazism will have to be "taken back to Germany" as there will be no chance of revival during military occupation. The only way of doing this, in Ramsay's view, is to fight for National Socialism until victory is secured. The Nazis still in Germany must not be allowed to lose hope. This was one purpose which Gordon-Canning had in mind when he made

his high bid for the bust of the Fuehrer [Gordon-Canning had recently paid £15,000 for a bust of Hitler]. Ramsay thinks the easiest course is to stimulate anti-Semitism and then "grow National Socialism in fertile ground". According to Ramsay, the Jewish terrorists in Palestine are doing their best to help this cause.'

The report finishes with the comment: 'Ramsay appears to have implicit faith in the sound judgement of Oliver Gilbert.'[1]

After the capitulation of Germany and Fascist Italy in early May 1945, thousands of enemy prisoners still had to be kept in custody. Many were brought to Britain, and held in camps. The Allies wanted to be sure that war would not break out again in Europe, and that German and Italian war criminals were in due course brought to justice. Many of the senior German officers who were brought to Britain were held in the Island Farm camp near Bridgend, from which the major break-out had occurred in March 1945. Many hardened Nazis did not change their views of the world, despite attempts to re-educate them into democratic thinking by the British authorities. History acknowledges that many ex-Nazis successfully made their way to South America.

Leese's network had survived the defeat of the Nazis and Italian Fascists. Two things should now be remembered – that Leese himself had successfully gone 'on the run' for a number of months in 1940, before the police were able to catch him and enforce the detention order; and that when his house was searched Leese had been in possession of an identity card in someone else's name.

Here, Ben Greene re-enters the picture. Greene had known Leese in Brixton Prison, and, as previously stated, was the 'contacts man'. He and his family knew Brazil extremely well. It is difficult to believe that he was not involved in supplying Leese with the necessary contacts in Brazil.

Whatever his involvement in the events of December–March 1944/5 may have been, it is clear that Leese had set up an escape route for Nazi prisoners of war by 1946, and that it was operating successfully. His Imperial Fascist League was now using the name of the British People's Party (BPP), Greene and Beckett's Fascist party, and Leese wanted to divorce its public image from the old League. However, Leese's network had been penetrated by an MI5 agent, and regular reports were passed back to MI5 on his activities.[2] One of Leese's main assistants in the period up to his detention in 1940 was a man called Gittens, and Gittens helped him again now. Gittens arranged the establishment of 'transit points' or 'safe houses' in the East End of London, where escaped Nazi prisoners could receive shelter, and be supplied with civilian clothes. Amongst Gittens's assistants in the East End were a father and son, Alfred and Alfred John McCarthy. The McCarthys were printers, and had printed a number of anti-Jewish publications. Thus, when the question of false documents for the Nazi fugitives arose, the McCarthys were well placed to help. All these men were previous members of the Imperial Fascist League.

Two Dutch Nazis, Meijer and Tiecken, who had joined German forces after the invasion of Holland, and who were said to be war criminals, escaped from the Kempton Park prison camp on the night of 12/13 June 1946.[3] They cut their way through the barbed wire fence that surrounded the camp, and started walking. They were in battledress, but had removed their prisoner of war patches, and wore American raincoats over their uniforms. They had a home-made suitcase, and enough food for a day.

Meijer and Tiecken had been given an address to go to if they were successful in their escape. This was the address of a man called Ray Alford, at 62 Ufton Road, Shoreditch, London; Alford was another former member of the Imperial Fascist League. Meijer and Tiecken walked for about fifteen miles until they reached Marble Arch in the West End of London, and then caught a bus. They eventually reached the address that they had been given, and Alford and his father welcomed them in, gave them shelter, and a set of civilian clothing each. Alford allowed them to live at his house for an extended period, but they had to stay inside as much as possible. The two fugitives spent their time studying Spanish and improving their English. They hoped to make their way eventually to Spain and then South America.

It is clear that Meijer and Tiecken were not the first to pass down this escape line. On about 20 July Meijer went to the Argentinian Embassy, and arranged an interview for the following day with the Ambassador, Felippe Espil. In order to secure the interview, Meijer presented a visiting card with Ray Alford's name and address. In fact Meijer had an interview not with the Ambassador but with the First Counsellor, who declined to help when told that Meijer was an escaped Nazi prisoner of war, since if news that Argentina was helping Nazis got out, it would do his country harm. Further, Meijer had no travel papers. The First Counsellor was not discourteous, however, and he and Meijer parted with expressions of mutual esteem. The First Counsellor promised not to report Meijer's visit to the British authorities.

The two Dutch Nazis remained at Alford's house until 12 September 1946, when the police visited the house at around midnight, looking for Ray Alford in connection with another matter. Whilst his father answered the door, Alford led the two Nazis to the McCarthys' house at 57 Fellows Road, Shoreditch. The McCarthys took them in, and they did not see Alford again.

Meijer and Tiecken had stayed with Alford for three months. They had been fed and cared for at a time when there was still strict food rationing. The operation was expensive, since their food must have been purchased on the black market, and there can be no doubt that Leese and his Imperial Fascist League (or the BPP) financed it.

Meijer and Tiecken stayed with the McCarthys until 10 October, when they were told that they had to move on. They were sent on to Worthing, via Victoria Station. McCarthy paid for their 3rd class rail tickets. They took a bus from Worthing Station to 107 Littlehampton Road. There they were taken in by a Mr and Mrs Edmunds and their four children. The Edmunds owned a poultry farm on the other side of Worthing. As before, the ex-prisoners told their hosts that they were German escaped prisoners (not confessing to their Dutch nationality). They slept in the loft of the house, and only went out on one occasion, when they went to Brighton to have photographs taken for false passports.

A report from a covert source referred to only as AB21, received by MI5 in August, stated that, according to Gittens, their escape route only handled 'so-called war criminals', whose bona fides they would check out from a source in America, to make sure that they were not being tricked by a British agent. They refused to help ordinary prisoners of war, because they did not wish to risk their network for unimportant individuals. Gittens emphasised that they were not in the business of helping Germans to get back to Germany, but to get away from it to South America. They hoped to reach a peak smuggling period at the end of the year.

The intelligence reports supplied very valuable information on what Leese's organisation was up to. One of Gittens's assistants, a man called Beck, was grumbling that the Spanish 'exit point' was a little clumsy, and that escapees wanted to know in advance which country they were being sent to – Argentina or Brazil. Gittens himself was worried when one of the men Leese's organisation had smuggled out was picked up on a vessel bound for Lisbon, and that 'if he talked, it would blow the whole outfit sky-high'.

Supplies of worn men's clothing were urgently being sought by the organisation for the escapees to wear. The clothing should not be new, or too ragged, but consistent with regular use.

On 30 September, a report based on information from AB21 reads:

'Arnold Leese is reported to have said that he wanted two passports for two escaped German Prisoners of War, both of whom were on the "Wanted List for War Criminals". These men could not contemplate a return to Germany as they felt certain they would be apprehended by the military authorities and put on trial, with the prospect of either a death sentence or a minimum punishment of eighteen years' imprisonment. The two men are understood to have been at large for some time, in fact from before Leese asked Mrs Lehmkuhl (a Fascist friend of his) to make enquiries at the Argentine Embassy, and during this period they have been hidden by Imperial Fascist League sympathisers. They are both desperate and fanatical Nazis, and their primary aim is to get themselves beyond British–Yiddish vengeance, with the intention of linking up with other Nazi elements either in Spain or South America. They speak fairly good English, and want to get to Ireland as a first step. Leese is reported to have said that one was of medium height, the other very tall, at least 6' 2", both blonde, aged 26 and 30. Leese said that if it were not for the fact that both these men had so much to fear from Jewish vengeance he would not attempt to hurry matters, as the "escape route" was yet in its infancy and it was a matter of extreme difficulty to get the hunted out of England. He remarked that he had bigger schemes in mind but that his hand was being forced.

It is understood that Leese contemplates at a later stage using England as a halfway house to pass on Nazi escapees from Europe to Spain and South America, and he has enquired whether Marie Connolly and Donal Hurley in Dublin could be worked into this scheme. Leese mentioned it was essential to his schemes to have reliable contacts in Eire and perhaps to have a reliable courier as well. It is intended that if, by bad luck, the Nazis concerned are caught they will on no account disclose the source of their passports, and they will pose as disgruntled prisoners of war anxious to rejoin their families ... Leese is alleged to have said that it was of paramount importance that these men were saved to join the Nazi nucleus or nuclei which he knew to be forming, but which he had not yet been able to contact.'

Leese was said to have expressed doubts later as to how reliable his Irish contacts were, but it was suggested to him in response that the Dublin group would never be guilty of a leakage as the people concerned were 'too mixed up with Nazis already'.

A report, again from source AB21, received on 4 October 1946, confirmed once more that Leese was working to effect the escape of

Meijer and Tiecken.[5] He described one of them (presumably Meijer) as speaking perfect English, and being capable of passing as a Scot or a Northerner. He mentioned that his organisation was in touch with a forger who could produce fake passport photographs. The plan was to send the two Nazis to Eire by daytime ferry, choosing a busy day in the hope that their passports would not be examined too thoroughly. For future escapers, Leese said he hoped to use the Cornish port of Falmouth, once he had found out what Spanish shipping called there. Leese was aware of MI5 surveillance, and of the possibility of arrest by Special Branch. He tried to keep the existence of the escape organisation totally secret. Communications with his agents were kept to a minimum, and were in code. The escaped prisoners were instructed on the accounts they should give if caught in possession of false passports, and Leese warned those he worked with of the methods of interrogation likely to be used by Special Branch.

By the end of October, MI5 knew where the two ex-prisoners were being hidden, but they wanted to make sure that when they arrested Meijer and Tiecken, they had the evidence to arrest the senior members of the organisation, Leese and Gittens, as well as the minnows. Leese's correspondence with Gittens was intercepted, and their code was not difficult to crack. Leese referred to the two Nazis as 'your cousins', and the passports as 'the illustrations and index cards'. Source AB21 continued to supply important information. Gittens was apparently in charge of obtaining the false passports, but failed because they were far too expensive (on the black market), and it was far too risky to try to obtain genuine ones. He was reported as saying that they could send the Nazis to Eire using only forged identity cards, and that when they reached Spain they could obtain 'false papers'.

It is clear also that Leese was well aware that MI5 was still watching him. AB21, whom Leese clearly trusted, reported that he worried about the danger of his visitors being followed. He emphasised that his people had taken every precaution that they could think of, and that the activities had been restricted to a completely trustworthy circle. Communications were kept to a minimum, usually sent by messengers, and a simple but satisfactory code had been evolved. He said that where his 'friends' were concerned he kept 'tight as a clam'. He suspected that his mail was being watched (which, of course, it was), and that a percentage of his visitors were MI5 agents. Leese commented that that was what he had to expect for fighting the Jews. He boasted of having open contact with Nazi sympathisers in twenty-four countries, but that the escape organisation was totally secret.

While Leese and a number of others were watched by MI5, and information was gathered, the escaped Nazis remained in hiding at the Edmunds' house. One day in November, Mrs Edmunds gave Tiecken and Meijer £10 in cash, a large sum of money in 1946, saying that it had come from someone else (it had in fact come from Lady Clare Annesley of the Prisoner of War Assistance Society). The false passports they were hoping for did not arrive, and eventually, acting on information, police raided the Edmunds' home on the morning of Sunday 15 December 1946. Both men were found in the loft and were arrested, together with Mr and Mrs Edmunds. The two Nazis had stayed with the Edmunds for two months. Leese clearly organised the funding for their stay.

Meijer and Tiecken were taken to the London Cage and interrogated. The report of Meijer's interrogation comments:

> 'Meijer is a most unpleasant type of person who, as a Dutch citizen joined the Landsturm Nederland, a sub-formation of the Waffen-SS, and who, in spite of many months of captivity, seems not to have lost any of the more undesirable characteristics of the fanatic SS type.'[6]

In other words, he was still a dangerous Nazi. Meijer at thirty years of age, was older than Tiecken, and was described as very much the dominant personality of the two. He had been captured in September 1944.

On 24 December Leese's MI5 file noted that Leese had applied for a new passport. The file comments that:

'The Home Office will certainly want to be consulted about Leese's application for a passport . . . Since his release from detention, he has worked indefatigably at the dissemination of anti-Jewish propaganda and the organisation of subversive Fascist activity. He is in touch with a considerable number of like-minded people, and probably looks forward to the promotion of a kind of national-socialist "International" on the pattern of the Communist organisation . . . We know from a secret source that this is a "fishing" application.'[7]

In due course, Leese and six others were brought to trial before the Recorder of London and a jury at the Old Bailey, on 27–31 March 1947.[8] When arraigned, Leese, Edmunds and Gittens pleaded not guilty. Their co-defendants, Emmanuel and Ray Alford and Alfred and Alfred John McCarthy pleaded guilty. Meijer and Tiecken had both turned King's Evidence, and gave evidence for the prosecution. Leese was charged with a conspiracy to harbour escaped prisoners of war and to give prisoners of war assistance to prevent their apprehension; with personally harbouring Meijer and Tiecken between 13 and 15 June 1946; with harbouring them jointly with the Alfords from 15 June to 7 September 1946, with harbouring them jointly with Alfred John McCarthy and Frederick Tom Edmunds between 15 October and 15 December 1946; and with giving Meijer money to help his escape. Leese, Edmunds and Gittens were all convicted. Each of the seven defendants was sentenced to a very modest twelve months' imprisonment, on the basis that the war was over, but that if it had not been, they would have received far longer sentences.

Author's Note and Acknowledgements

Researching and writing this book has taken me into a world of unbelievable bigotry, fanaticism, feral violence and racial prejudice. I have dedicated the book to my two youngest granddaughters, Zoe and Maggie, in the hope that the world that they grow up in will be able to rid itself of such extremism. Perhaps that is a vain hope.

I would like to thank all those who have helped me with my research for this book. First on the list must come Jack Birrell and other representatives of the Comrie Development Trust for their help and kindness on my visit to Camp 21. Much of Camp 21, Cultybraggan, Comrie is still intact; it is fascinating, and is very well worth a visit. I pay tribute to the excellent work that the Trust has done and continues to do.

I also send my thanks to the staff of the Devizes Museum, of the Wiltshire Heritage Centre, and of the National Archives, Kew, for their help with my researches.

Of course my thanks go to my friend and publisher Michael Leventhal – long may our lunches continue – and to his team at Greenhill Books.

Last, and without doubt most importantly, my thanks, together with my love, go to my wife Gilly, for her patience and understanding during the writing of this book – and in particular for her endurance on our trip north to visit Comrie on a very cold wintry day in February.

Appendix

German and British Ranks

Comparative ranks in the German forces and the British Army. In some cases there were no exact equivalents.

German Army	Waffen-SS	British Army
Grenadier/Fusilier etc.	SS-Mann	Private
Gefreiter	SS-Sturmmann	–
Obergefreiter	SS-Rottenführer	Lance corporal
Unteroffizier	SS-Unterscharführer	Corporal
Unterfeldwebel	SS-Scharführer	Sergeant
Feldwebel	SS-Oberscharführer	Staff sergeant
Stabsfeldwebel	SS Sturmscharführer	Sergeant major
Leutnant	SS-Untersturmführer	2nd Lieutenant
Oberleutnant	SS-Obersturmführer	Lieutenant
Hauptmann	SS-Hauptsturmführer	Captain
Major	SS-Sturmbannführer	Major
Oberstleutnant	SS-Obersturmbannführer	Lieutenant Colonel
Oberst	SS-Standartenführer	Colonel
–	SS-Oberführer	–
Generalmajor	SS-Brigadeführer	Brigadier
Generalleutnant	SS-Gruppenführer	Major General
General der Infanterie*	SS-Obergruppenführer	Lieutenant General
Generaloberst	SS-Oberstgruppenführer	General
Generalfeldmarschall	–	Field Marshal

* or 'der Artillerie', 'der Panzertruppe', etc.

Notes

Introduction: **Vehmic Justice**

1. WO 208/4140.
2. See Vincent S. Green, *Extreme Justice*, and Wilma Parnell, *The Killing of Corporal Kunze*.
3. See Jane Eppinga, *Death at Papago Park Prisoner of War Camp*, and Richard Whittingham, *Martial Justice, the Last Mass Execution in the United States*.
4. Quoted on www.uboatarchive.net.
5. This quotation is said to have been published in *'Abolish' Death Penalty News* on 1 March 1998. The original source is unknown.
6. WO 208/3530.
7. WO 208/3653.
8. WO 208/3654.
9. WO 208/3654.
10. WO 208/3635.

Chapter 1: **The Big Break-Out**

1. The author is grateful for the research done by Antony Beevor in *Ardennes 1944*, and to Peter Caddick-Adams, *Snow and Steel*.
2. Beevor, pp. 37–8.
3. WO 208/4140.
4. Beevor, p. 92.
5. WO 208/3619.
6. Beevor, pp. 91–4.
7. WO 208/3619.
8. Kesselring, *The Memoirs of Field Marshal Kesselring*.

Chapter 2: **Target Churchill**

1. Tom Hickman, *Churchill's Bodyguard*.
2. Hickman, *Churchill's Bodyguard*, p. 102.

Chapter 3: **Britain Sleeps**

1. WO 166/14443.
2. KV 2/679.
3. Wiltshire History Centre, FS/505/58.

Chapter 4: **The Enemy Within**

1. See Quentin Falk, *The Musical Milkman Murder*, Appendix 1.
2. R. J. B.Bosworth, *Mussolini's Italy*, p. 95.
3. WO 208/3650.

Chapter 5: **Maxwell Knight**

1. Henry Hemming, *M: Maxwell Knight, MI5's Great Spymaster*, Preface.
2. KV 2/841.
3. KV 2/841.
4. KV 2/3800.
5. KV 2/3800.

Chapter 6: **Captain Archibald Maule Ramsay**

1. KV 2/677.
2. *Daily Herald*, in KV 2/678.
3. KV 2/677.
4. KV 2/678.
5. KV 2/1343.
6. KV 2/678.
7. HO 45/24895.
8. KV 2/841.
9. KV 2/678.
10. Joan Miller, *One Girl's War*.
11. KV 2/678.
12. KV 2/678.
13. KV 2/679.
14. KV 2/679.

Chapter 7: **John Beckett**

1. KV 2/1508.
2. Francis Beckett, *The Rebel Who Lost His Cause*, p. 164.
3. KV 2/1508.
4. Beckett, p. 167.
5. Beckett, p. 183.
6. KV 2/1508.

Chapter 8: **Ben Greene**

1. KV 2/489.

2. KV 2/492.
3. KV 2/491.
4. KV 2/492.
5. KV 2/492.
6. KV 2/679.

Chapter 9: **Arnold Spencer Leese**

1. CRIM 1/864.
2. KV 2/1365.
3. KV 2/1365.
4. KV 2/1365.
5. KV 2/3874.

Chapter 10: **Sir Oswald Mosley**

1. HO 45/24895.
2. HO 45/24895 & KV 2/884.
3. KV 2/887.
4. KV 2/887.

Chapter 11: **Yet More British Fascists**

1. KV 2/834.
2. KV 2/877 & 878.
3. KV 2/878.
4. HO 45/23775.
5. KV 2/1344.
6. KV 2/1344.
7. KV 2/1344.

Chapter 12: **Theodore Schurch**

1. KV 2/76.
2. Archive of the Gordon Lett Foundation, Somerset; Brian Lett, *Gordon Lett, Amico dell'Italia.*

Chapter 13: **Italian Prisoners of War**

1. MH 55/1884.
2. MH 55/1884.
3. MH 55/1884.
4. MH 55/1884.
5. FO 939/357.
6. WO 106/4082.
7. FO 939/357.

Chapter 14: **Colonel Scotland and the London Cage**

1. FO 939/420.
2. Lt Col A. P. Scotland, *The London Cage*.
3. WO 208/5381.

Chapter 15: **Camp 21 at Comrie**

1. FO 939/420.
2. WO 208/3530.
3. WO 208/3530.

Chapter 16: **Escapers and Accomplices**

1. CAB 114/23.
2. KV 5/64.
3. KV 5/64.
4. CAB 114/23.

Chapter 17: **Plans for the Big Break-Out**

1. Scotland, *The London Cage*.

Chapter 18: **The Two Centres**

1. 'A Prisoner of War in Devizes' (pamphlet), Wiltshire Heritage Museum, p. 17.
2. WO 208/3654.

Chapter 19: **Preparations at Devizes**

1. Scotland, *The London Cage*, pp. 60–1.
2. WO 166/14443.
3. Roderick de Normann, *For Führer and Fatherland*, p. 81.

Chapter 20: **Two Words that Saved Churchill?**

1. WO 208/3651.
2. *For Führer and Fatherland*, pp. 82–3.
3. WO 166/14443.

Chapter 21: **Investigation and Interrogation**

1. WO 208/3651.
2. WO 208/3651.
3. WO 208/5381.
4. Scotland, *The London Cage*, p. 61.

Chapter 22: **The Hangmen Kill**

1. Red Cross report, from the Comrie Development Trust Archives.
2. According to Scotland, see WO 208/5381.

3. WO 208/4633.
4. Archives of the Comrie Camp Trust.

Chapter 23: **The Plot to Kill or Capture Eisenhower**

1. CAB 114/23.
2. CAB 114/23.
3. Peter Caddick-Adams, *Snow and Steel.*
4. NARA RG 407 ML 2279; Antony Beevor, *Ardennes 1944*, p. 174.
5. Brian Lett, *SOE's Mastermind.*

Chapter 24: **Doonfoot**

1. Brian Lett, *An Extraordinary Italian Imprisonment.*
2. CAB 114/23.
3. CAB 114/23.
4. CAB 114/23.

Chapter 25: **Teddesley Hall Camp**

1. CAB 114/23.
2. CAB 114/23.
3. CAB 114/23.

Chapter 27: **The Serchio Offensive and Operation Galia**

1. Brian Lett, *SAS in Tuscany.*

Chapter 28: **The War Goes On**

1. CAB 114/23
2. CAB 114/23
3. Peter Phillips, *The German Great Escape*, p. 135.
4. CAB 114/23.

Chapter 29: **The Hangmen Kill Again**

1. WO 208/3654.
2. WO 208/4634.

Chapter 30: **The Escape Line to Brazil**

1. KV 2/1343.
2. KV 3/60.
3. KV 3/60.
4. KV 2/1366.
5. KV 2/1366.
6. KV 3/60.
7. KV 2/1367.
8. KV 3/38.

Bibliography

I have tried wherever possible to rely on original archive material, and to cite the references in the text of this book. However, I am indebted to many authors for the excellent work that they have done. The relevant bibliography is set out below.

Andrew, Christopher: *The Defence of the Realm*, Penguin Books, 2009
Beckett, Francis: *The Rebel who lost his Cause*, London House, 1999
Beevor, Antony: *Ardennes 1944*, Viking, 2015
Bosworth, R. J. B.: *Mussolini's Italy*, Penguin Books, 2006
Caddick-Adams, Peter: *Snow and Steel*, Oxford University Press, 2015
Campbell, Valerie: *Camp 21, Comrie*, Whittles Publishing, 2017
De Normann, Roderick: *For Führer and Fatherland*, Wrens Park Publishing, 1998
Eppinga, Jane: *Death at Papago Park Prisoner of War Camp*, History Press (US), 2017
Falk, Quentin: *The Musical Milkman Murder*, John Blake Publishing, 2012
Foley, Charles: *Commando Extraordinary*, Longmans, 1954
Goodrick-Clarke, Nicholas: *The Occult Roots of Nazism*, New York University Press, 1985
Green, Vincent S.: *Extreme Justice*, Pocket Books, 1995
Hemming, Henry: *Maxwell Knight, MI5's Greatest Spymaster*, Penguin Random House, 2017
Hickman, Tom: *Churchill's Bodyguard*, Headline Books, 2005
Jackson, Sophie: *Churchill's Unexpected Guests*, History Press, 2010
Kesselring, Albert: *The Memoirs of Field Marshal Kesselring*, Greenhill Books, 2007
Lett, Brian: *An Extraordinary Italian Imprisonment*, Pen & Sword, 2014
——: *SAS in Tuscany, 1943–5*, Pen & Sword, 2011
——: *SOE's Mastermind, An Authorized Biography of Major General Sir Colin Gubbins*, Pen & Sword, 2016
——: *Gordon Lett – Amico d'Italia* [in Italian], ISRA, 2018
Miller, Joan: *One Girl's War*, Brandon, 1986

Parnell, Wilma: *The Killing of Corporal Kunze*, Lyle Stuart, 1981
Phillips, Peter: *The German Great Escape*, Poetry Wales Press, 2005
Scotland, A. P.: *The London Cage*, Evans Brothers, 1957
Tate, Tim: *Hitler's British Traitors*, Icon Books, 2018
Whiting, Charles: *The March on London*, Leo Cooper, 1992
Whittingham, Richard: *Martial Justice*, Henry Regnery /Blue Jacket Books, 1971

Index